THE MILITANT DISSENTERS

Other books by Stanton A. Coblentz

From Arrow to Atom Bomb
The Long Road to Humanity
Demons, Witch Doctors and Modern Man
Villains and Vigilantes
Ten Crises in Civilization
Marching Men
The Paradox of Man's Greatness
Avarice: A History
The Power Trap

THE MILITANT DISSENTERS

Stanton A. Coblentz

South Brunswick and New York:
A. S. Barnes and Company
London: Thomas Yoseloff Ltd

A. S. Barnes and Co., Inc.
Cranbury, New Jersey 08512

Thomas Yoseloff Ltd
108 New Bond Street
London W1Y OQX, England

ISBN 0-498-07709-8
Printed in the United States of America

Contents

Introduction

Dissenting students occupy the Administration Building of a great university, smash windows, destroy records, and drive out the President and other officials. . . . Dissenting students, on strike for "non-negotiable" demands, form picket lines and attack men and women seeking to reach the classrooms. . . . Black insurgents set fire to stores and houses, overturn cars, and maul passing motorists in a spasm of fury wherein both blacks and whites are injured, numbers are killed, and large amounts of property are stolen or destroyed. . . . Antiwar demonstrators march in "Moratorium" parades, refuse to serve in Vietnam, burn draft cards, try to halt troop trains or shipments of napalm. . . . Demonstrators gather in would-be peaceful marches that lead to police clubs pounding on heads and bodies, the unleashing of dogs or assault by fire-hoses, the spraying of mace, or the scattering of tear gas over a wide populated area. . . . The proceedings of a national political convention are interrupted by an outbreak approaching guerrilla warfare between demonstrators and police, while innocent bystanders are struck down. . . . Organizations of minority groups, departing from the nonviolence of Thoreau, Gandhi, and Martin Luther King, Jr., are formed with militancy as their watchword. . . . Meanwhile the eruptions are not confined to the United States; critical disturbances are reported in France, Italy, Germany, Japan, Communist China, Mexico, Panama, Ireland, and other areas.

Few would deny that these revolts, taken as a whole, represent one of the significant developments of our times. Yet rebellions, mutinies, and insurrections of various kinds have been prominent in the history of most lands, second only to warfare, and in some cases second not even to warfare, which they often accompany, follow, or incite. In our own country the record has been long and varied: apart from the uprisings that led to war, one recalls the labor disturbances of 50 to 100 years ago, sometimes amounting to armed hostilities, as in the Homestead steel strike of 1892; the militancy of the I. W. W. (Industrial Workers of the World), an organization composed mainly of migratory laborers, formed in 1905 and favoring the violent overthrow of capitalism; the outbursts against the Negroes, which, even in the North before the Civil War, caused the demolition of schools and printing presses, lynchings, and deaths; the anti-Chinese pogroms in California in the decades following the Gold Rush; the bloody encounters of black and white in Chicago, Washington, and other American cities in 1919 and before; the activities of terrorist organizations such as the Ku Klux Klan and the Knights of the White Camelia; the repressions of the Vigilance Committees, which, originating in San Francisco in 1851 and 1856, fought violence with violence and spread with little restraint to much of the West; and the organized forays against the Indians and by the Indians, resulting in the obliteration of whole tribes.

Even if some of the outbreaks seem to have only a superficial resemblance to current episodes, the likenesses in many are clear and meaningful. I am convinced that these uprisings, and others throughout the world have much to tell us today. An understanding of them, an insight into their causes, motivations, and history, may enable us to look upon present confusions with fresh vision—the more so because we can examine them in a dispassionate mood not always possible in regard to next-door occurrences. Obviously, it would be impossible for any of us now to work up much personal heat as to the differences of Roundheads and Cavaliers in 17th-century England, or as to the motivations of those hardy marauders, the Beggars of the Sea, in 16th-century Netherlands. But, precisely because we can look without personal involvement upon Roundheads, Cavaliers, Beggars of the Sea, and other rebellious and counter-rebellious groups, we can view them with a penetration, a just and discriminating judgment that would be difficult in the case of demonstrators who set our own porches on fire or threaten the education of our own children or the security of our own lives.

I do not imply, of course, that the study of current groups and disturbances is not essential, and I do not overlook them in these pages. But I submit that for a well-rounded and objective appraisal of present upheavals, we must call upon the rich experience of the past, in the effort to clear away our bewilderment and bring light to our tormented times.

And yet, as far as I am aware, no organized or wide-reaching survey has been made of the militant dissenters of yesterday in the attempt to understand their successors of today. And that is why it occurred to me to write this book, which covers some of the more noteworthy struggles of insurgent groups to solve the problems of society or of social factions. The material, to be sure, is abundant enough to fill an encyclopedia, and therefore I have had to confine myself to a selection of the outstanding cases. But it is not necessary to sample all the streams of the world to learn the taste of river water; the illustrations I have chosen are, I feel, varied enough and characteristic enough to speak for the entire field. Naturally, I hope that they will not only prove interesting in themselves but will offer new insights into the troubled world of the mid-20th and late 20th-century.

THE MILITANT DISSENTERS

1. Bursting Boilers of Ancient Rome

i. Peaceful Dissenters and Bludgeon Wielders

The year was 137 B.C. The man was a 26-year-old Roman, of gentle bearing and refined manners, on his way to Spain to assume his duties as quaestor. The region was Etruria, whose fertile fields the young man was viewing with shocked eyes. Everywhere the small farmers had forsaken their holdings, leaving the ruins of their houses to weeds and the wild beasts; everywhere the land-owning capitalist dominated, the slave drivers swung their lashes over cringing barbarian backs. Ruminating on the depopulation of the land, the observer reached a conclusion which he would express in an eloquent speech: the beasts of the fields and the birds of the air had their dens or nests, but the free man of Italy had not a roof to shield his head. In this thought there lay the seeds of revolution. And the revolution was to be begun by the young man, Tiberius Sempronius Gracchus.

Unlike many reformers, he was an offshoot of the privileged classes—a grandson of the renowned Scipio Africanus, who had overcome Hannibal at the battle of Zama. His father, also named Tiberius Sempronius, had held high offices, including those of censor, consul, general, and governor of the Spanish province of Ebro; his mother, Cornelia, Scipio's daughter, was one of Rome's most distinguished women, a person of high intelligence and noble character. The young Tiberius had been reared with every advantage of his age; he had been trained in the Greek language, literature, history, and philosophy, and had been inspired by the example of Athenian achievement and Athenian democracy. Under his brother-in-law, the younger Scipio Africanus, he had fought with distinction at Carthage; in Spain his diplomacy had saved a Roman army of 20,000 men. Had you been one of his circle, you would have laughed to scorn the idea that such a man could become a revolutionary. What personal complaint had he? He need only repeat the conservative pattern of his fathers, and honors, high offices, and wealth would lie before him. As it happened, however, he was not content to repeat the pattern of his fathers. He knew that the times called for change, and in his eagerness to hasten and direct events he had no regard for the safe traditional course.

This was not only because he was driven by youth's usual impatience. As we look back, we can see that the Roman state tottered in a dream world of false security, paying the heavy, unforeseen price of a long series of successful wars with Carthage and in Macedonia, Asia Minor, and Spain. The victories had cursed the victor; the inflow of spoils, slaves, and luxuries had subverted the ancient social order, torn down the old economic adjustments, and brought debilitation and demoralization.

Politically, the state was stagnating and decaying. A group of patrician families had parcelled out the coveted positions of consul and censor among themselves, giving Rome a do-nothing government of nonentities. Not that no efforts at reform had been made; but little had been accomplished by the measure that gave Roman citizens the ballot in popular assemblies, and permitted them to vote for the popular tribunals; the masses had been inflated with an ostentatious self-importance, and power had been put into the mouths of the shouting riffraff of the streets.

At the same time, the problems of the state were mounting. Rome's Italian allies, scorned and disgruntled, were demanding broader rights, and this was leading toward the revolt of the important city of Fragellae in 125 B.C. and the bloody Social War of 91-89 B.C. Meanwhile the plight of the small farmer continued to deteriorate; more and more countrymen flocked to the cities, more and more shackled and branded slaves replaced them, and slave revolts threatened increasingly. Yet how restrict the slave system and put the Roman farmer back on the land?

Tiberius Gracchus thought that he knew the answer: it lay in the vast public domain which Rome had acquired in her wars. Large land holdings might be split and made available in inalienable parcels to Roman citizens, while a regulatory commission administered the law. With this end in view, Gracchus moved into immediate action after taking office as tribune of the people in 134 B.C. Unfortunately, there were disadvantages in his plan;

some possessors, whom we would call "squatters," were excluded from territory which they cherished as their own, and on which they had perhaps spent much money and labor. Also, the members of the Senate, who belonged to the landholding class, were by nature against the idea.

It was their opposition that brought the 29-year-old statesman to a decision that harbored the germs of violent dissent. He would bypass the Senate! Like a modern lawyer, however, he looked for a precedent; and he found it in the example of Flaminius, who, a century before, had pushed a land bill in defiance of the Senate. But resistance came from an unexpected direction: Marcus Octavius, a fellow tribune whom Gracchus had considered his friend, interposed his veto.

On legal grounds, this should have ended the case; a tribune's veto was absolute. But Tiberius, going beyond legal means, exchanged constitutionality for revolution. Probably he and his followers did not put matters to themselves in quite this way, yet how else can we interpret his actions? Having suspended the business of the state, having closed the courts and the treasury, having offered his law for a second time, having encountered a second veto from Octavius, and having entered into futile discussions with the Senate, he was at an impasse. Seeing no recourse now except in an appeal to the rabble, he went before the assembly with the statement—quite unauthorized by law— that either he or Octavius must surrender his tribuneship, and that the people must decide between them. In this he took no chances; there was no question what verdict the mob, composed of every floating element—farmers, slaves, aliens, and citizens in a riotous mixture—would shout to the man who had catered to its wishes. Gracchus's proposal, of course, passed by a large majority. And now he took the violence-torn road of no-return. At his bidding, Octavius was pulled down from the bench by the lictors; then, while the mob cheered, the farm law was passed and the first commissioners were nominated: Tiberius, his father-in-law Claudius Appius, and his 20-year-old brother Gaius.

Thus he aroused questions that remain to this day. While a strong case can be made for the reforms he introduced, the results were tainted by his methods, which had in them something of the presumptuousness of the usurper, something of demagoguery and rabble-rousing, and led to results disastrous for Gracchus and costly in many ways for Rome. The element of force had been injected into his dissent, as had the substitution of force for law; and force would flourish and spread to his opponents, and would be expanded frightfully in the culminating episode of his own life.

For the first time in Roman history the person of a tribune, previously inviolable, had been attacked. And one result was that the young rebel, himself a tribune, became vulnerable as never before; his action lent color to the unjustified charge that he planned to take the scepter as king. Nevertheless, since there were nine other tribunes, any one of whom might have interposed a veto, how could Tiberius have passed his law by any course except the one actually followed?

Thenceforward he was a man besieged. Having invoked violence, he had to live by violence or the threat of violence. So hostile was the Senatorial sentiment that he felt it necessary to be accompanied by three or four thousand supporters whenever he appeared in the Forum. But even this protection would not suffice. To carry on his work—indeed, to preserve his life—he must continue to have the shield of the office of tribune. Therefore he had to cater to the masses in all possible ways. Thus he further outraged the Senate by proposing that a windfall recently acquired by Rome—a bequest of the land and treasure of the king of Pergamus—be used for the benefit of the new settlers. He is said to have also prepared other laws for the people's good, though the details have been lost. But of one proposal we are sure: that he be reelected tribune.

This proposal was the more daring since it was considered illegal for a tribune to succeed himself after his one-year term. But Gracchus remained undaunted by legal formalities. When the election was held at the regular time, he was a candidate, but the first results were indecisive, leading to a day's postponement. Meanwhile, fury was flaming ever higher. Charging once more that Tiberius sought not a tribuneship but a throne, his enemies urged the consul Scaevola to order him executed as a traitor; and when this appeal was rejected, the anti-Gracchans took the law into their own hands. Led by the brutal Publius Scipio Nasica, on the second day of the election the aristocratic rabble broke up the benches of the Forum, wielded the wooden legs as clubs, attacked the Gracchans in a frenzy, battered the reforming tribune to death along with 300 of his followers, and threw his body into the Tiber.

Thus was shed the first blood ever spilled in civic strife in the Roman Republic. Thus, in the bitter words of the younger

Gracchus, "the worst of men murdered the best." Thus the use of armed force to achieve political ends became a part of the life of the Republic. And thus the way was pointed to the gangster politicians of the next century—men such as Clodius and Milo, who carried on their rabble-rousing with bands of slaves and street ruffians, instigated riots and fights with stones and clubs, spattered the city with blood, and made it all but suicidal for any important politician to appear in public without a bodyguard.

Certainly, no one would maintain that such a rule by thuggery occurred only because of the precedent of violence provided by Tiberius Gracchus and his enemies. But this did furnish the entering wedge for the disintegration that, within a century, would lead to the overthrow of the Republic.

If Tiberius was an extraordinary figure, his younger brother Gaius was still more remarkable. Born in 153 B.C. and not yet 21 when his adored kinsman was bludgeoned in that wild outbreak in the Forum, he would nurse through all his remaining years a deep sense of injustice and a smoldering desire for revenge. Yet he was much more than a passionate and vindictive man—he shines as one of the most brilliant statesmen that Rome ever produced. In 124 B.C., returning after three years as quaestor in Sardinia, he successfully offered himself for election as tribune, and set out to carry on his brother's interrupted work, to further the rights of the people, and to undermine the power of the Senate.

In his two short years of office, after introducing what was in effect a one-man government, he pushed forward an astonishing number of reforms, including the extension of his brother's public land system, the planned emigration of Romans to form colonies, and the distribution of grain to the masses at much reduced prices (thereby initiating the system that would degenerate into the infamous dole to the idle rabble). We need not go into the details, though we cannot help wondering what the results would have been if this young man, who had made himself virtually an uncrowned king by his 30th birthday, had been granted a normal length of years. But powerful forces were determined to cut him down. And those forces found their opportunity when he committed the tactical error of absenting himself for 10 weeks to superintend the establishment of his cherished African colony of Junonia, on the site of destroyed Carthage.

A demagogue named Drusus placed himself in opposition, playing upon the covetousness of the crowd with fantastic promises, which made them desert Gracchus in favor of their self-proclaimed new friend. The result was that Gaius, running for election as tribune for the third time, was defeated.

Having driven their redoubtable opponent into a corner, the Senate set about to destroy him and his work. Less than a month after he left office, they prepared to revoke the law permitting the founding of Junonia, and their attack drew the ex-tribune and some followers to the Capitol to defend his favorite measure. The atmosphere was tense; Gaius well knew the danger, and he did his best to control the hot temper of his supporters. Unfortunately, he could not hold their violence in leash. Quintus Antullius, an attendant at the sacrifice being offered on the steps of the Capitoline temple, snapped an insolent order at one of the Gracchans, and instantly was felled by the insulted man's sword.

Amid the ensuing commotion, Gaius did his best to disclaim responsibility for the murder. But in his excitement he unwittingly infringed an ancient law that made it a capital offense to interrupt a tribune who was addressing the people. Magnifying this picayune breach into a major offense, the consul Lucius Opimius and his colleagues represented the brawl as an insurrection to overthrow the Republic.

Next morning Rome took on the aspect of a city facing an attacking army. Mercenary Cretan archers filled the Capitol; every senator went armed and fortified by two armed slaves. Yet Gracchus, dissuaded by his lieutenant Marcus Flaccus from obeying a summons of the Senate to come before it and explain his violation of the rights of a tribune, declined to go armed. Consequently, in the strife that followed, after Opimius had ordered an attack on the Aventine and offered their weight in gold for the heads of Gracchus and Flaccus, the Senate's great enemy was helpless. Taking flight, Gaius tripped, sprained an ankle, and, unable to escape, met his end beneath the sword of a faithful slave who also slew himself. Then, while a headhunter named Lucius Septumuleius was being awarded the stipulated fee, crowds of partisans were executed in prison—estimates of their numbers have been as high as 3000. The spirit that raged abroad is indicated by the slaying of the 18-year-old son of Flaccus, a widely esteemed youth who had had no share in the uprising.

And so, in that tragic January of 121 B.C., one of Rome's outstanding leaders fell in a political riot. Whatever may have been said of Gaius—and opposition to him might have been justified on several grounds—it would surely have been possible to meet him peacefully and legally. He was already out of office; he was unarmed—why should he have been slain? But hatred and passion took command; and hatred and passion, in their usual way, painted a false picture of the intended victim; invented an evil legend, a demon image. The basic situation was in no way altered by the fact that the members of the mob, as in the slaying of Tiberius Gracchus, were aristocrats; the same savage emotions prevailed as in proletarian outbursts, and the same evil results followed. Rome had taken a decisive step toward the anarchy that would increasingly curse the Republic until, 92 years later, after dictatorship, civil war, assassination, rule by triumvirate, and bloody proscriptions, the grandnephew of Julius Caesar would become the first Roman Emperor and restore order by means of an authoritarian rule.

ii. Slaves Versus Masters

We moderns, bedeviled with problems of black and white whose origins we can trace to the African slave traffic of four centuries and more, may not always remember that slavery in other lands and eras has likewise resulted in long-range unrest and revolt. In ancient Rome, for example, the challenges were severe and perennial. Like all other ancient countries, and like the prewar American South, Rome built her economy on slave labor. But this in turn was based on war, and it is therefore not surprising that the situation became acute after the series of large-scale wars that began with the three Carthaginian conflicts. These contests, including the fighting in Spain, the Near East, and elsewhere, brought Rome not only rich treasure in metal, gems, and fine cloths, but booty in one of its grimmest and most dangerous forms—that of two-legged captives, who would become abundant enough to be a cheap and disposable commodity; their discard, when they became too old and worn to be profitable, was advised by that practical old realist, Cato the Elder.

How the slaves themselves felt can only be judged by their actions, since they were not able to record their side of the case. It has, however, been well said that the slaves caused Rome to dwell for centuries on the lid of a slumbering volcano. The slave system, the reliance on the large ranches which specialized in the grape and the olive while neglecting the traditional cultivation of grain, was at the root of that decay of Italian agriculture whose beginnings had been noted by Tiberius Gracchus—a decay which sent the impoverished farmers flocking to lead disgruntled if not parasitic lives in the cities. Pictures have come down to us of branded slaves laboring by day with shackles on their legs and sleeping at night in dank dungeons or *ergastula*—and this is evidence for the view of the historian Mommsen that the sum of all the Negro suffering in America, great as it was, was "but a drop" compared with the afflictions of the Roman slaves.

Even at the time of the Gracchi, when the agricultural slave system had not yet made deep inroads in Italy, it required no soothsayer to read the omens; the tendency was already manifest, and the slave revolts were eloquent. What shall we say, for example, of the fact that, in the single year 133 B.C., the Romans executed 150 slaves in the capital and 4450 elsewhere? What too of the slave revolts in the market at Delos and in the silver mines of Attica? What of Sicily, where, in the latter part of the second century B.C., two great and menacing slave revolts erupted?

Here the situation was particularly bad. The evidence suggests that the slave-owners, in their blindness, arrogance, and greed, did about all they could to build up the forces that would break out against them in fire and blood. The slaves were mistreated vilely; there is a story that one master, being shown by his human chattels that their clothes were worn out, contemptuously asked whether the travelers along the roads wore nothing. Hard as this may be to believe, it accords with what we know of the mood of the times. Certainly, some of the slaves did become brigands; and this was encouraged, it was said, by the refusal of the big proprietors to feed them. And since brigands are not only reckless but armed men, here was a force that might turn against the lords themselves. The surprising fact is not that the Sicilian slave insurrections occurred; the surprising fact is that the slave-owners seemed not to anticipate the furies they themselves were whipping up.

In the pages of the ancient historian Diodorus of Agrium, we read how the captives, having been marched in droves from the markets, swarmed through the island in their overdriven multitudes. As a source of social disruption, they could have been exceeded by nothing short of an invading army. They murdered travelers along the roads; they began attacking the smaller farms, robbing and slaying, and making it dangerous not only to travel at night but to live in the country at all in the ancestral way. With their huge shepherds' crooks, their clubs and spears, their boarskin or wolfskin robes, and their retinue of large and powerful dogs, they must have made a formidable appearance. Why then did the authorities not act to rid the land of this pestilence?

The fact was that they dared not move. Intimidated by the power of the great landowners who claimed the brigands as their property, the governors sat by speechless and with limp hands; most of the proprietors were Roman citizens of the class of *equites* or knights, who would preside at the prosecution of provincial governors when the latter's term of office was over.

With such preliminaries, it could be only a matter of time before the armed, hardened, grossly misused daredevils struck out at their abusers.

An important incentive to the rebellion was the notorious Damophilius of Enna, whose cruel treatment of his slaves contrasted with the gaudiness of his display in his purple mansion or as he drove through his immense range-lands in a four-wheeled carriage, with thoroughbred horses, weapon-bearing slaves, and bevies of hangers-on. It was he, we are told, who directed his dependents to highway robbery when they needed clothes. As arrogant as he was rich, he seemed unable to understand that his brutalities and those of his wife Megallis were driving his underlings to revolt and murder.

The revolt, as it happened, was being secretly encouraged by the Syrian slave of another master, the self-styled seer and prophet Eunus, who took advantage of the superstitions of the masses to pose as a reader of the future with the claim that a goddess of his people had appeared to him in a dream and promised that he would become king. Revealing that fate had designated their town of Enna as the center of the uprising and preordained their success, he goaded the hesitant slaves, who released some of their comrades from chains, and collected a force of about 400 from a nearby ranch.

These desperate men, led by Eunus late one night, fell upon the town. Their war-cries ringing out, they burst into the houses, committed every crime from massacre to rape, and slew Damophilius, while Megallis was tortured and dispatched by her maids. Yet the rebels could also be moved by humane emotions; they did not molest the young daughter of Damophilius, who had always gone out of her way to treat them kindly.

Now Eunus achieved the fulfillment of his alleged dream and set himself up as king (a bronze coin, struck at Enna, still survives, in which he characterizes himself as King Antiochus). At the same time, he acquired councilors, a queen, and other appurtenances of royalty, including an army of more than 6000 men, who, equipped with every available weapon, from farm implements to kitchen spits, constituted a force formidable enough to defeat several successive Roman armies.

Thus began the first of the two great Sicilian slave revolts, which involved the eventual mustering by Eunus of an army of 70,000, and was accompanied by revolts elsewhere, in Attica, Delos, and even Italy.

Only after about two years (in 132 B.C.) was the rebellion suppressed, and 28 years later (104-99 B.C.) it was followed by another immense insurrection. The threat of these outbreaks reached even Rome, whose grain was increasingly coming from Sicily, and whose foundations and power were being challenged by men made desperate by piled-up, long-smoldering wrongs.

In the first century B.C., the war of slave against master was extended to Italy proper in another highly menacing eruption, precipitated by a Thracian named Spartacus, who was being trained in a gladiatorial school. If the gods, smiling in irony, had searched for the most fitting leader of a slave revolt, they could hardly have made a more sardonic choice. For the gladiatorial trainee was a victim whom the Romans themselves, for their own brutal amusement, were schooling in an academy of bloodshed. That such a man would turn against his masters at any opportunity should have been foreseen, and apparently was foreseen, though the Romans seem to have thought that their various precautions—such as confining the gladiators, and associating men speaking different languages as a safeguard against conspiracy—would suffice to hold the danger in leash.

The outbreak began in 73 B.C., when 200 gladiators attempted to escape from the prison-school at Capua where slaves were being prepared for the savage sports of the arena. Seventy-eight of these hardened men, who had nothing to lose, managed to break away, and chose three leaders, headed by Spartacus, described by Plutarch as a member of the nomad tribes, "and a man not only of high spirit and valiant, but in understanding also, and in gentleness, superior to his condition."[1]

Joined by shepherds and herdsmen, they soon made an imposing force, almost impossible to rout in the wild region around

Vesuvius, while they fed themselves by raiding the towns. Having escaped from the Roman praetor Clodius, who bore down upon them with 3000 men, they defeated the lesser leader Furius and 2000 Romans and narrowly missed capturing the general Cossinus, whose baggage Spartacus seized and whom he pursued, storming the Roman camp and slaying the commander. After various other successes, the slave-captain moved toward the Alps, and wisely decided to seek safety beyond the mountain barricade and permit his forces to disperse to their homes in Thrace and Gaul.

But his men, with the splash of blood on their hands and the salt of victory on their lips, were not satisfied as quickly. Spartacus was to learn, as many have learned before him and since, that an insurrection is more easily started than ended. Made proud, foolish, and covetous by victory, the followers of Spartacus insisted upon staying in Italy, whose rich towns and provinces beckoned with tempting loot. All the while the slave-army was swelling, although the reports of its eventual size—40,000, 70,000, even 120,000—must be regarded with scepticism. In any case, the rebel army became large enough to send shock waves through Rome, particularly when it defeated the forces opposing it under the Roman consul Lentulus, and captured all the enemy's equipment. Now the situation was seen as serious enough to justify the appointment of one of Rome's leading men to command in the war.

Crassus, the new general, did not make an auspicious beginning. Two of his legions, under a lieutenant who disobeyed orders not to enter into battle, were cut to pieces by Spartacus, and many of the men saved their lives only by flight. The gravity of the Roman predicament was suggested when Crassus resorted to the dire penalty of decimation: taking the 500 legionnaires said to have been the first to flee, he divided them into 50 groups of 10; one man from each group was selected by lot to be slain before the assembled army. There is no reason to suppose that Crassus would have resorted to this dreadful punishment, which was growing obsolete, had Spartacus not driven him into a corner.

The Spartacan army was not the only peril to Rome. Still more serious was the danger that the rebellion would spread; that slaves throughout Italy, perhaps throughout the Roman world, would be fired by the example of the Thracian gladiator and take arms against their masters. Since slave labor was at the roots of the Republic, the state might conceivably fall, amid scenes of riot, destruction, and massacre unparalleled in the country's history. Some such picture, when the Romans at last awakened from their complacency, must have flashed through the minds of many who, attended by swarms of slaves, had been living in a fool's paradise of luxury and ease.

The salvation of Rome, it would appear, was the disorganized nature of the rebel fighters, who quarreled among themselves, often disobeyed commands, and followed no clear plan except perhaps in grasping booty. That such a force could not in the end defeat the Roman Empire, if the Empire held together, would seem as clearly foreordained as anything in man's confused affairs can be; but it was by no means foreordained that the Empire would hold together, or that the precedent of Spartacus would not incite other insurrections that would batter down the Roman power. Hence the citizens could sigh with relief when, after the revolt had raged on for two years, Crassus won a victory in Apulia, Spartacus was slain, and the tatters of his army escaped to the north, where they were overcome by Pompey, whom they met on his way back from Spain. Six thousand captives from the army of Spartacus, nailed to crosses and left to die in slow torment along the Appian Way, showed how deeply and vengefully Rome had taken the uprising to heart.

iii.   The Troubled Middle East

On the streets or at a market or festival in any town of ancient Judea, a dagger might lash out and an unwarned victim might sink moaning in his blood, while his slayer slipped off undetected. This tragedy was enacted not once but many times during the years when the Judeans were governed by the Roman procurators, whose reign was ended by the great rebellion of 66–70 A.D. The killings were not unplanned; they were the work of a terrorist organization, the Sicarii (which has been freely translated as "Assassins"), an extremist offshoot of a larger fanatical group, the Zealots. The Sicarii, when their mania found expression in calculated crime, were in many ways like the terrorists of a later Middle East, even though they did not enjoy the benefits of guns and bombs. They too cared nothing about means in their quest of ends; they too did not hesitate to strike down the innocent—no suspected Roman sympathizer could be sure when a murderous blade would dart out at him as he took his way amid the peaceful-seeming crowd.

This situation, while not by itself the cause of the rebellion, was symptomatic of the passions and the violence that had troubled the region for centuries and led toward the rebellion. There are, it seems, certain areas that remain foci of unrest throughout the millennia: one such is a famous hill-city by the Tiber, and another is a thin patch of land along the eastern Mediterranean seacoast, a scrap of territory that has incited furies of contention as far back as we have any record. The source of the outbreak against Rome can be traced at least to the time of the revolt of the Maccabees, who in 168 B.C. arose in arms following the flouting of their religious traditions by the Selucid (Syrian) King Antiochus IV, and his attempted Hellenization of the people. Here we can see some of the motivations that would move the descendants of the Maccabees more than 200 years later in their strokes against Rome: the same resentment of foreign rule, the same fervor of religious orthodoxy, the same readiness to spill blood.

Although the Maccabees prevailed in what has long been remembered as a brave and brilliant exploit, the sequel was less glorious than one would like to believe. Violence, as usual, reproduced itself; the successors of Mattathias, the priest who started the rebellion by slaying an idolatrous Jew, pursued the path followed by more than one later people: having won their freedom, they proceeded to tear down the freedom of others. Under John Hyrcanus, a grandson of Mattathias, the Jewish state subjugated the surrounding peoples, including the Samaritans, whose temple Hyrcanus destroyed, and likewise the Edomites, who were given the choice of banishment or acceptance of the Jewish faith. It was the expression of an attitude that would recur throughout history, from the conquering Arabs to the Christians of the fourth century and the Puritans of New England: you may believe as you wish, if only you believe as we do.

But not all Judeans favored the aggressive policies of their rulers. Dissidents arose, led by the influential Pharisees; and a long period of turmoil ensued, involving, among other evils, nearly six years of civil war, which, as in most such cases, turned out to be an affliction for both factions alike; inevitably, the feuding threw the doors open for Rome. When the renowned Pompey was invited by the embattled parties to settle their dispute, it was as if two rabbits had called upon the wolf to be their arbiter. After various intrigues and much desperate fighting, the legions of Pompey did what any astute onlooker might have expected; they took Jerusalem, to which they had exactly as much right as to most territories conquered by the Romans—which is to say, none at all.

Thus, undermined by internal dissension, Jewish independence ended, while Rome and Judea piled up a new heritage of tumult. In the disturbed years that followed, the greed and arrogance of the conqueror again played their part, particularly under Crassus, who, having become proconsul of Syria, looted the Temple and incited an uprising that closed with the sale of thousands of Jews into slavery. But the Romans seemed unaware of the storms they were provoking—unaware that the vessels of bitterness of an abused people were being filled to overflow.

There were two main fountains of Jewish resentment. One was the perennial source of complaint of those exploited by an imperial power: the people were misgoverned, trampled upon, and unmercifully overtaxed. And the second was unique with Judea; it was connected with religion—the zealous, rigid orthodoxy that clung not only to beliefs but to the letter of ritual and observance. Other peoples too had been fond of their ceremonials and devoted to their gods, but most had consented to exchange them for the Roman equivalents, or to add the Roman cults and practices to their own rather than challenge the awesome power of the empire. The Jews, however, were different, and the Romans, while making various concessions, seem never to have understood the heroic faith that would so often batter its head against stone walls; in the Judeans' last-ditch defense of the Law, the conquerors must have seen no more than fanaticism. Hence they made provocative moves that a better understanding might have avoided.

Religion, in many of the demonstrations, was like a red-hot prod. Consider the protest to Pontius Pilate against the transport of the images of Caesar to Jerusalem—a move which, in Roman eyes, must have appeared harmless, but, to the Jews, seemed a profanation, an insult to their God. According to the contemporary historian Josephus, a throng of Jews rushed to the procurator's home, which they surrounded for days, throwing themselves prone in protest, while receiving no satisfaction. Later, when the wily Pilate had taken his seat in the Great Stadium and summoned the crowd under pretense of giving them an answer, the resisters found themselves staring at cold metal; the swords of the soldiers hemmed them in on all sides. But if Pilate had thought, as undoubtedly he did, that this would cow the protesters into submission, he had miscalculated the power of an embattled creed; far from yielding, the Jews dropped to the ground, swearing that they would die rather than transgress their laws. What, then, could Pilate do? He was in a precarious pass; had he not given way, the whole inflammable nation might have flared up like oil. And this episode was important not only in itself but as a warning of the spirit that would lead through militant dissent to revolution.

Such a spirit was evident also in a subsequent demonstration which blazed up at Caesarea, where a synagogue abutted on a piece of land belonging to a Greek. This the Jews repeatedly sought to buy; they offered, says Josephus, many times its value, but were goaded past the explosion point when the Greek started to build a factory up to his boundary-line, denying a sufficient passageway to the synagogue. Here we have, perhaps, no more than a rancorous property dispute of neighbors, though a dispute exacerbated by religion and possibly by prejudice; we should not be surprised at the resulting riot by some of the younger hotheads, who were suppressed by Florus, the last of the procurators. Nor need we wonder that further violence followed when Florus, having accepted a bribe, neglected to carry out his side of the deal, and imprisoned 13 prominent citizens, who had complained to him of his breach of faith and his abuse of their coreligionists.

Then, as if he had not already done enough to fan the fires, Florus committed another provocative act. A prey to the blindness that so often accompanies greed, he withdrew a large sum from the Temple treasury on the pretext that it was required by the Emperor. And thus he assaulted the religious sensibilities of his subjects at the same time as he raided their property. This, as he should have foreseen but perhaps did not, provoked riots; the people rushed in a mass to the Temple, calling upon the Emperor to free them from the misgovernment of his appointee, whom they abused in scurrilous language. Possibly, however, their rawest denunciations were less wounding than the satire of certain demonstrators, who passed through the crowd with a hat, begging small coins for the impoverished procurator.

Still graver incidents followed as Florus, plunging from bad to worse, gave further impetus to the furies of revolution by a massacre of men, women, and children. Josephus, no doubt with some exaggeration, puts the number slain at 3000; he also tells us that Florus committed the unheard-of act of scourging and crucifying citizens of the equestrian rank—Jews who had the status of Romans. Inevitably, fresh cries of rage broke out against Florus; and inevitably, also, he did his best to muffle them. To berate the governor was now a highly dangerous occupation, as was evident when a crowd engaging in this pursuit was attacked by Roman soldiers; some were clubbed, others were trampled by the cavalry, and still others died amid the crush of their comrades.

But this deadly encounter, far from putting an end to the demonstrations, strengthened their psychological roots, and induced further rioting, in which Florus was hard pressed; when the governor led his men out of the palace in the effort to reach the safety of a fortress, the crowd blocked their way, and missiles rained down upon them from the rooftops. Unable to hack a path through the narrow streets, the Romans were forced back to their camp.

It is barely possible that, even at this late hour, restraint and discernment could have averted catastrophe. Neither, however, could be expected from a corrupt administration walled off from the people, nor from an imperial government separated from the province by hundreds of miles of ocean, and preoccupied with other concerns. Yet something can be said for the Romans. Most of the procurators did try to avoid irritating the sensitive feelings of the people, and consequently prevented the legions from bringing the images of the Emperor into Jerusalem; moreover, they left the Jewish Sanhedrin in control of religious and local matters. But procurators like Florus, the ex-slave Felix, and the notorious Pontius Pilate, were self-serving men tragically unsuited to the human and diplomatic responsibilities of their post.

Their truculence was the more unfortunate since a conciliatory policy was hardly likely on the Judean side, considering the religious temper of the country, the hawkish fervor of the Zealots, and the Sicarii's murderous slashes in the dark. No people, certainly, could have been expected to remain smiling and dovelike in the face of taxes which, for the governor's private advantage, were squeezing down with a more and more unbearable weight. But one doubts if taxation by itself, though so often an incentive to insurrection, would have sufficed to produce the rising storm; what prevailed was fanaticism; rabid prophets ranged the country foretelling the end of the world and the coming of the Messiah. Beside these terrifying or glorious events, of what importance was this earthly life? Let it be risked! Let it be thrown away, and so serve the resplendence of heaven! Such was the mood of martyrdom that increasingly swept over many. To cool this hysterical ardor, wise and temperate leadership was a first essential—the very sort of leadership that did not exist.

Not all the Judeans, however, were firebrands; there were moderate elements who favored reconciliation. But hissing steam promotes more action than lukewarm water; as so often in a great crisis, it was the incendiaries who prevailed. Under their leader Eleazar, who aimed to cast off the Roman power entirely, the Zealot extremists carried the day. A move unimportant in itself, and yet as symbolic as Caesar's celebrated crossing of the Rubicon, proclaimed the rupture between Rome and her colony. At Eleazar's urging, the priests declined to make further pagan gifts or offerings—which meant that they no longer made a daily sacrifice to the Emperor. Here was an affront to the ruling power, an act of virtual lèse majesté, which, to take a modern comparison, was in a class with flag trampling by rebellious Americans. Consequently, the move was strongly opposed by priests and scholars of the old school, who, however, were unable to induce the insurgent Temple officials to reverse themselves. Thus the decision of a minority of militants threw the doors open to revolution.

In the emergency, the procurator was of no help; ignoring the appeals of the peace groups to send more soldiers to Jerusalem to avert an outbreak, he sat weakly by while the Judean King Agrippa Herod II dispatched a force of cavalry to protect the city. And this led to an armed clash. For a whole week the bitter contest was stalemated; then, on a festal day, the pleas of the Zealots enlisted the crowds flocking into the city, whose aid, added to that of the cutthroats of the Sicarii, enabled the rebels to capture the Upper City amid scenes of fury in which the line between insurrection and war was hard to define. Roman sympathizers were slain; the houses of the King, the priest Ananias, and the princess Berenice were burned; Roman guards were overcome and hacked down; Herod's palace, defended by the remaining Roman troops, was besieged; and eventually all who did not flee were massacred. In a short while, the Zealots were masters of the city.

Here, then, was the beginning of a revolution which would last four years, which would scorch the land and streak it with blood, which would provoke gory reprisals followed by even gorier reprisals, which for a time would repel mighty Rome and give the country to the insurgents, but which would end in 70 A.D. after one of the most excruciating sieges in history closed in massacre, havoc, and enslavement. On both sides, the uprising represented a tragedy of miscalculation. Rome, surely, did not foresee that her power would be strained by a small provincial people, or that she would have to send one of her ablest generals, Vespasian, and later Vespasian's son Titus, to put down the revolt. Had Rome had foreglimmers of all this, she might have made more of an effort to understand the Judeans and govern them judiciously. And the rebels, given a similar prevision, might have taken second thought before leaping into a holocaust that would destroy thousands of lives, burn down the Temple, and leave the land in ruins. But even if some omniscient power had illuminated the path ahead, would the Zealots have pulled back? One may doubt it. To the fanatic, there is no truth except in his own frenzy.

In any case, the rebellion accomplished nothing except to spill blood and treasure and tighten the Roman claws about Judea. Its terrible futility, and the fact that neither side had learned its lesson, was shown by another great outbreak 45 years after the capture of Jerusalem by Titus. In 115 A.D. peoples throughout the Mediterranean world, taking advantage of the absence of the Emperor Trajan in Parthia, struck out at the Roman power, and in this the Jews joined other nationalities. Nevertheless, peace would have been possible after the accession of Hadrian in 117, had not this emperor, otherwise one of the best of the Roman rulers, committed a psychological blunder of the first magnitude. In his ignorance of the strength of Jewish religious and nationalistic fervor, he evaded what had been taken for his binding promise, and planned to rebuild Jerusalem as the Roman city of Aelia Capitolina. The result, after some years, was a major outburst led by the aged Rabbi Akiba and the fiery, almost legendary young warrior Bar Kokba, who promised to free the land from the abasement of nearly half a century. As in the earlier rebellion, the Romans at first were defeated, but their might was too vast for any small country; finally the rebels were overcome, their surviving leaders were executed, the site of Jerusalem was occupied by a city in which no Jew was permitted, and the remnants of the Judean population, after war's decimation, destruction, and enslavement, were dispersed in all directions; never again until the mid-20th century would they claim a land of their own.

In this revolution also the results were unforeseen; the Romans evidently did not anticipate anything even approaching the actual resistance, while the Jewish leaders apparently thought that they were on the road to liberation. Here again, as in the earlier eruption, the psychological spurs were all-important— the incentive of religion, the devotion to old laws and traditions, which even the wisest of the Romans seem to have been unable to understand. Hence the sharpest, most dangerous sort of friction arose, a friction evident in many of the world's worst insurrections—the grinding clash of two opposing outlooks, two widely divergent moods, two emotional approaches, two sets of beliefs.

2. Wat Tyler Challenges the King

i. The Revolt of the Peasants

Clad in the thigh-length jackets and short skirts of the year 1381, the peasants press forward tumultuously to follow the bidding of their leader Wat Tyler, and march in two long columns from Kent and Essex. Many are armed, though only rudely, some with sticks and cudgels, some with hatchets or knives, some with ancient bows deeply browned by time and equipped with no more than one arrow each. Perhaps one in a thousand shines in defensive armor; the odor of cowdung or of the sheepfold clings to many of them. Yet they push on with lusty shouts and glittering eyes, and are not altogether without discipline.

As they approach the Thames bridges that separate them from London, a trail of violence stretches behind them. Castles and houses have been sacked; judicial and financial records have been burned; landlords and nobles have fled into the fields and woods; officials and their lawyers and retainers have been executed without benefit of trial. Meanwhile reinforcements for the rebels have poured in from the countryside; control of the roads to London has been seized, and terror has deepened among the well-to-do as the two hosts have converged and the air has been filled increasingly with the smoke of burning records and the din of angry thousands pounding and pummeling at the doors of great houses. Their ears, at the same time, ring with shouts of sympathy from villagers, peasants, journeymen, artisans, and laborers.

True, the gates of London have been ordered closed against them—and how can they exist without the supplies of the city's storehouses and markets? But agitators have infiltrated into the capital, where they find many collaborators; through the treachery of some of these, a drawbridge is let down for the marchers to pass. Almost simultaneously, a second column similarly obtains passage over another bridge. Thus the weapon-wielding swarms of rustics take the heart and most populous city of England, whose King is threatened as never before in all her history.

ii. War, Taxation, and Oppression

Before we note the further course of the rebellion, let us glance back to see what lay behind it.

Had it sprung from unbearable complaints? Actually, the condition of the English peasant had been slowly improving, and was rather favorable compared with what a traveler might have seen in most Continental areas, such as northern France, whose peasants in 1358 had broken out in the bloodthirsty, fruitless insurrection known as the *Jacquerie*.

Nevertheless, the lot of the English farm worker, half-serf and half-free as he was likely to be in 1381, would appear bitter by modern standards. He was still clamped down by feudal obligations; his master had the right to specified services and payments, and, in the case of a dispute, might sit as judge in his own court. If a serf sent his son to school (which, you may be sure, did not often happen), he had to pay a heavy fee; if he wished to marry, he likewise had to pay; and when he died, the lord might claim his best possession, while the second best fell to the parish priest. Thus the widow and the orphan were robbed by the great and strong. Beyond this, the peasants not only could not leave the land of their lord without permission but had to grind their corn at his mill, bake their bread in his oven, brew their ale at his brewery, and be charged for the privileges. They had to endure the raids of his pigeons and rabbits upon their crops; they could not marry their children without his approval; and they had to work without compensation under the command of his bailiff during a definite number of days of field service.

Yet the eventual revolt sprang not so much from the feudal system itself as from the changes that were beginning to combat feudalism. During the hundreds of years when the peasants had been tied to the soil, paying tribute of services and goods and living in rude huts in which their lot was little better than that of the farm animals, there had been no Wat Tyler to seize arms and lead them out of servitude. Why, then, the sudden outburst in 1381?

The answer is that the eruption was the product of a society riven by change. Men were tempted to revolt because the feudal way of life had begun to disintegrate, because the taste of freedom had already come to some, and because new vistas were beckoning to the common man, tantalizing him with hopes of a better existence. Two gigantic forces had injected themselves, one not of man's conscious making, the other created by the human will and human action.

The first of these great forces fell like a cataclysm upon much of Europe, Asia, and Africa. In the years between 1347 and 1350, the Black Death (now believed to have been the bubonic plague) ravaged land after land and took millions of lives; the toll in England, according to some estimates, was nearly nine-tenths of the population, though 50 percent would seem nearer to the truth. The effect of such a catastrophe upon a nation's labor force can be imagined. The workers, being so much less numerous than of old, were more in demand, and could obtain higher wages and better conditions of employment; some of them struck out for themselves, deserted the feudal lords who still tried to enforce the old restrictions, and offered their services as free men to employers in distant parts. This was important in two respects: it raised the numbers of free workers while reducing the lists of serfs, and it infused in the working classes a new independence of spirit, a realization that their own efforts might win redress for their grievances.

The second gigantic force of change involved the powerful lever of warfare—the Hundred Years' War, by which the kings of England had long been impoverishing their country in the quest of a fabulous enrichment in France, but in which there was nothing for the common man except onerous new taxes. Hence, while the masters displayed their splendor and the commoners were beaten and condemned like dogs and had to pay the costs of the stolen opulence, the natural result was rising popular irritation, envy, and anger.

The feelings of the populace have been preserved for us by the 14th-century chronicler Froissart, who puts these words into the mouth of John Ball, a wandering priest who became involved in the revolt of Wat Tyler:

My good friends, matters cannot go well in England until all things be held in common; when there shall be neither vassals nor lords; when the lords shall be no more masters than ourselves. . . . For what reason do they thus hold us in bondage? Are we not all descended from the same parents, Adam and Eve? And what can they show, or what reason can they give, why they should be more masters than ourselves? They are clothed in velvet and rich stuffs, ornamented with ermine and other furs, and we are forced to wear poor clothing. They have wines, spices, and fine bread, while we have only rye and the refuse of the straw; and when we drink, it must be water. They have handsome seats and manors, while we must brave the wind and the rain in our labors in the fields; and it is by our labors that they have wherewith to support their pomp. . . .[1]

Here, to be sure, is the perennial cry of the underprivileged. Here, in a not wholly unjustified resentment, was one of the whips that stirred up popular passions and brought crowds of followers clamoring at the heels of Wat Tyler.

Not all the incentives of the rebels, however, were of so general a nature. To provide the spark that set off the revolution, there were more specific outrages, born of the war and war-bred needs and the desire of the rulers to pile the burden on those who profited least from the strife. As so often when fuel is provided for a revolution, the authorities acted in ignorance of the popular mood and the gathering combustibles. And as in the Netherlands two centuries later, the conflagration was touched off by an unjust and onerous tax.

To Parliament and the King, the action of late 1380 may have seemed unavoidable. Like more than one other country indulging in reckless adventures overseas, England had tied herself into something of a knot: the King, heavily in debt, was about to lose his pledged jewels, and was unable to pay the wages of his garrisons on the French coast, whose men seemed ready to desert. Money, obviously, had to be raised—but how? How except from the people? The Speaker of the Commons did, indeed, protest that the masses "were very poor and of feeble estate to bear the burdens." But finally it was agreed that, if the clergy would raise a third of the required sum, the rest might be obtained by a poll tax upon every person above the age of 15. This decision was reached regardless of the fact that a poll tax, since it bears down harder on the cottager in his mud hovel than on the duke in his castle, is one of the unsoundest as well as one of the most unpopular forms of collection ever devised.

In England, in 1380 and 1381, the situation was unusually

difficult and dangerous. If you had been a peasant or hand-worker at the time of Wat Tyler's revolt, you would probably have viewed taxation as brigandage. You would have seen your hard-earned pittance taken from you for the benefit of your "betters," without any visible advantage to you or your family, and the injustice would seem the greater since you and your fellow workers were unrepresented in the tax-levying bodies. Not only that, but if you were old enough to look back a few years, you would remember that the authorities had several times before tried to loot you (or so you would have thought) by other unjust exactions. Back in 1371, your oppressors had decided upon a tax at a standard rate on all the parishes in the country—which, in the nature of things, would be hardest on the poorer parishes. This had been bad enough; but worse, much worse, had been the poll tax of 1377. For the privilege of existing, every adult who was not a beggar was to be taxed fourpence, a considerable sum in those days—which, of course, was all very well for the nobles and rich landowners, whose payment was slight in proportion to their income.

But if you had grumbled at this demand, you would have cried out in still deeper dismay when the rulers, during the financial crisis of 1380, reimposed the tax of 1377 at three times the former rate, or about the amount to be earned by a week's labor. This would have been oppressive had it applied only once to each family, but if you were a householder, who had to care not only for your wife and little ones but for an aged and helpless father and mother and perhaps some elderly aunts and sick and widowed older sisters, the burden might be too heavy for your shoulders.

Hence you would feel justified in using any possible wile to evade the tax collector; indeed, you would have to use every wile if you were not to be stripped bare. Little wonder, then, that when the King's taxmen made the rounds early in 1381, the returns were much less than the estimates; it was as if the population in the various districts, in the few years since 1377, had dwindled by from 20 to 50 percent. Concealment and falsification, if not bribery of the King's agents, might well have been suspected. And so it came about that, on March 16, the Government condemned the tax gatherers for culpable negligence and favoritism, and sent out a new round of collectors to rake in the large amount still believed due.

But this hardly improved matters. This might appear to you

as an effort to wrest from you an entirely new tax. Also, you might believe the rumors that the collectors had robbed you for their own gain, and that the King saw none of your hard-earned money.

As a result, your anger and your hatred of the officials might be heated to the boiling point. Now the targets of your fury might be not only tax collectors but other agents of the Government, including lawyers, jurymen, and the chancellor and treasurer; you might be ready to strike in defense of your rights the moment you had a captain to lead you, and comrades to march at your side. This was the situation that made possible the uprising under Wat Tyler.

iii. From Riot to Revolution

Almost as remarkable as the revolt itself was the blindness of the authorities, who sat by in lordly complacency, not realizing how soon the skies above them might collapse.

The fact seems to be that the rich, nursing their own grievances, had unconsciously been doing almost everything possible to sharpen the antagonism of the masses. In a complaint such as this from the upper classes, we gain a somewhat clearer idea of the background:

> The world goeth from bad to worse when shepherd and cowherd demand more for their labor than the master-baliff was wont to take in days gone by. Laborers of old were not wont to eat of wheaten bread; their meat was of beans or coarser corn, and their drink of water alone. Cheese and milk were a feast to them; their dress was of hodden gray; then was the world ordered aright for folk of this sort. Ha! age of ours, whither turnest thou. For the poor and small folk, who should cleave to their labor, demand to be better fed than their masters.[2]

The masters did more than complain; they took action not only through the taxes but by various ordinances. There was, for example, the order of the Royal Council, which in 1349 decreed that all able-bodied persons under 60, if lacking means of support, must either go to jail or serve anyone who required their work. Then there was the act of 1360, which provided for the forcible return and the branding on the brow, at the justices' discretion, of peasants who left their land before expiration of their term of labor or tenancy. There was also the law of Parliament which, in 1351, attempted to hold wages down to the level of five years before.

These laws were greeted by riots and strikes in the towns and by flights of the serfs, who took to the woods and formed bands designated by the authorities as "outlaws"—desperate men who might be shot down like vermin. Meanwhile the growing spirit of resistance was exemplified by the unions of laborers crying out against wage-fixing in the towns; in the villages and fields, at the same time, farmers were combatting the old feudal privileges of the duke and baron. And in the towns the hostility was fed by churchly restrictions and by the bias and economic resentment against foreigners, and was powerfully fanned by roving preachers like John Ball.

But the King and his councilors seemed placidly unaware of all this. They appeared not to realize how many ready-made rebels there were in the outlaws of the forest, including fugitives from the harsh laws of the times and tough old veterans of the French wars. And they seemed oblivious of the possibility that the training in arms received by the men of the parishes might turn out to be a weapon against the rulers.

This training went back more than 100 years, during which the kings of England had called for the defenses of the very classes who now stood out against the Crown. On various occasions during his long reign (1327-77), Edward III let it be known that he needed levies from town and country to meet his enemies. And since the man of means might buy a substitute, the poor people supplied the bulk of the troops, which had been mustered from time to time in their towns and hamlets. Here, then, was material ready-made for a rebel army, with a rude organization to distinguish its members from the uncontrollable rabbles of many popular uprisings. It is ironic that the upper classes, in their contempt for the man of common blood and at the very time when the armed forces in France and Brittany had largely stripped the land of defenders, seem not to have realized how they had smoothed the path for resistance.

But the Government was more than blind; it was asleep when, disconcertingly as an earthquake in a previously shock-free region, the convulsion rocked the land. It was the fishermen and fowlers of the Thames estuary who struck the first blow, though if they had not acted, undoubtedly some other disgruntled group would have arisen. At the marshland village of Fobbing in Essex on May 30, 1381, the new poll tax commissioner Thomas Brampton was met with abusive language and a defiant refusal to pay. And when the dissidents' arrest had been ordered, about 100 peasants threw themselves on the tax agents, beat them with sticks, and stoned them out of town.

This was to put a torch to well-oiled faggots. Immediately the country was aroused. The villagers of Fobbing and of nearby Corrington rode through the land, calling their neighbors to arms. And then, on June 2, the Government met the crisis with another ill-advised move, and dispatched the Chief Justice of the Common Pleas, Sir Robert Belknap, to put down the trouble-makers and swing the leaders from gibbets. Unfortunately, Belknap and the other officials had little idea of the popular mood. It was as if a shepherd, setting out to recover some lost sheep, had been suddenly encircled by wolves—the entire countryside had been inflamed.

Far from executing the summary justice he had intended, the judge found himself in the middle of an angry mob that swung pitchforks and cudgels, threatened him with arrows, seized and burned his papers, slew three clerks and three local jurors, forced Belknap down upon his knees, and made him promise to hold no more sessions. As he made his escape, doubtless feeling lucky to be still alive, he could see the demonstrators triumphantly marching about, bearing the heads of the slain men upon poles.

Here, then, was more than a riot; here was incipient revolution. And now the flames, feeding upon long-accumulated fuel, were springing up throughout southeast England. During the following days, as a fiery message was carried from parish to parish, the eruption came to resemble a wind-blown conflagration. Government agents were attacked; houses were ransacked, and official documents were thrown out or burned; a few men, including Flemish merchants, were killed, though not as many as one might have expected; Rochester Castle in Kent surrendered to the mob, and a prisoner was set free; the richer citizens of Maidstone were plundered, and one of them was killed. At the same time, the rebellion was given a head by the selection of a leader, Wat Tyler, who leaped into prominence out of anonymity; nothing is known for sure of his past, although the speed with which he established control lends credibility to reports that he was a veteran of the French wars if not an old leader of highwaymen.

Immediately upon assuming command, the new captain proclaimed his aims: no allegiance except to King Richard and the "true commons" (that is to say, the common people); no king named John (which excluded the hated Duke of Lancaster); and no tax except the "fifteenths" known to their fathers. For these ends, all the people should be ready to march, in order to cast out the traitors and the corrupt lawyers and court officials around the King.

While the astonished Government looked on, perhaps as badly stunned as if the workhorses of the fields had found voices and marched in companies to demand their rights, the onsurging throngs freed the prisoners from their jails, including the mob-rousing preacher John Ball. Then, as the enthusiasm of the villagers and the poorer townsmen reached new heights and the richer townsmen saved themselves by fleeing to the woods, the rebel thousands reached Canterbury, where they broke into houses, sacked them, beheaded three alleged traitors, forced their way into a cathedral, interrupted the mass, and clamored for the election of a new archbishop. Meanwhile looting and rioting were occurring at villages a considerable distance away.

Now the revolt proceeded at an even more dangerous pace. The main host, having returned to Maidstone, plunged into new riots and was joined by packs of fresh recruits; they then began moving on London, while another swarm, under a Thomas Farringdon, was advancing upon the city from a different direction. That the rebels were not wholly without restraint was shown when, chancing upon the King's mother, the Princess of Wales, on her way to London, they let her go with no worse infliction than some insults and jests.

Yet even before they had won access to the bridges and began to pour into the city, the capital had reason to tremble, and the King had cause to fear for his government and his life.

iv.   The Ordeal of Richard II

The sovereign at this time was Richard II, a boy only a few months past his 14th birthday. But surely few experienced monarchs have been saddled with a heavier weight than was suddenly thrust upon this youth.

Even before the rebels had burst into the city, the King had confronted them. Leaving the Tower on the royal barge along with some of his lords and councilors, he saw a motley, unorganized crowd gathered on a sloping bank of the Thames, brandishing weapons, waving the cross of St. George and dozens of pennons, and wildly cheering, shrieking, and howling. Of necessity, Richard kept well away from this rabble; he merely called out to them, demanding what they wanted; and they yelled back that he must disembark. "Treason! Treason!" they shouted when they saw the bargemen pushing away. Had any of them unbent their longbows, the throne of England might that day have become vacant.

Yet, as the hours went by, Richard had increasing cause for concern. Swelled by poor urban workers and professional criminals, the multitudes were swarming across the two bridges into the city, where, after diverting themselves by eating and drinking, they rushed in a Vandal mood to the magnificent mansion of John of Gaunt. There they indulged in frenzies of destruction; they hacked elegant furniture to bits; they smashed jewelry, and tore up tapestries, carpets, and fine linens; they set fire to the palatial establishment, even though, to avoid imputation of sordid motives, they lynched a man caught stealing a silver goblet. Next, in swift succession, they put the torch to various other houses and some shops; slew seven Flemings who had sought refuge in a priory just outside the city; and destroyed the Fleet and Newgate prisons. And finally they encamped for the night in the open spaces around the Tower of London, besieging the King and his Council like members of a hostile army, while a score or more of fires could be seen crimsoning various sections of the city.

How was the Government to meet the crisis? It was nearly two weeks since the first outbreak, and it is indicative of the confusion of the King's ministers that nothing at all had been done to prepare the city. Having rejected as too dangerous Mayor Walworth's plan to sally forth and attack the rebels with the 700 available archers and men-at-arms, the King and his advisers resolved upon a course hardly less hazardous. Richard was to offer to confer with the insurgents next morning among the fields of Mile End, thus putting himself, literally, in the enemy's hands. The young monarch, as he made the risky decision, may have gambled upon two factors: the reverence which the masses, despite all their rebelliousness, still felt for royalty; and the adoration of Richard as the son of the hero, the Black Prince. Yet these were frail shields against the fury of mob emotions. The triggerlike sensitiveness of the situation was shown when, as Richard rode forth with his retinue in the midst of excited country folk, his bridle was grabbed by the leader of the Essex marchers, Thomas Farringdon, who demanded vengeance upon the treasurer Prior Hales, and threatened to take the law into his own hands. Intimidated by the mob, the King's two half-brothers galloped off into the open fields, and deserted him.

But for Richard there was no such way out. His one possible escape, when he sat facing the enemy at Mile End, was through the soft byways of promise-making; he would agree to just about everything, including abolition of serfdom and free pardon and protection for all the rebels. In the ears of the simple peasants, his words had a pleasant ring; thousands of them went home, doubtless reassured to see 30 clerks drawing up charters of amnesty. But the leaders were less easily appeased; their answer was to hasten back to the Tower and cross the bridge, which was still open, while the unresisting guards stood by. Once inside, they handled the King's mother so roughly that she fainted; and they seized the Archbishop of Canterbury and the treasurer, dragged them out into the courtyard, and executed them—a particularly uncalled-for crime, so far as we can judge, since the Archbishop, as one commentator puts it, "seems to have been an honest, pious, and charitable man."[3]

Meanwhile the rioters were pillaging, setting fires, committing extortion and blackmail, and murdering many persons in the city, including, it is said, more than 150 Flemish merchants. Debtors slew their creditors, apprentices killed their masters, and scheming men turned the mob against their personal enemies. Elsewhere in England at the same time the heads of the great and proud, such as John Cavendish, chief justice of the King's Bench, were being carried on pikes by the storming rabble. Far through the countryside, even to distant counties, the revolutionary contagion was spreading; the rebels all but had command of the country; any puff of wind might have toppled the monarchy.

So it must have seemed even to Richard, when in a desperate last effort he proposed another meeting with the enemy—at the cattle market of Smithfield just north of the city. His awareness of the peril is suggested by the fact that, before going forth to the crucial rendezvous, he confessed and received absolution, and prayed before a supposedly fortune-giving golden image of the Virgin. Not content with such protective measures, however, the King and his 200 attendants took the more solid precaution of wearing armor under their gowns. Having been joined by

Mayor Walworth and a few others, their small contingent was faced by the thousands of the enemy army, drawn up before them as if for battle.

Wat Tyler, as one might have expected, was now strutting in the lordliness of power. With the whole of England apparently beneath his thumb, he had sworn to go wherever he wished at the head of 20,000 men, and to take the heads of all who opposed him; within a few days, his law would be the law of the land. And so, as the mounted and dagger-bearing insurgent approached Richard, his attitude did not suggest that of a subject toward his sovereign. Taking the young monarch by the hand, which he shook rudely, he said, "Brother, be of good comfort and joyful, for you shall have within the next fortnight forty thousand more of the Commons than you now have and we shall be good companions."[4]

Tyler then made his demands: no law except that of Winchester, no outlawry, no lordship except the King's, distribution of surplus Church goods and lands among the laity, reduction of the English bishoprics to one, and the end of serfdom and manorial dues. To this the King replied that everything would be granted that could be granted legally, the Crown being reserved to himself.

Even if this answer was equivocal, the revolution appeared to be on the brink of success. And then, in an unforeseen flash, the situation was reversed. Restraint not being one of Tyler's conspicuous virtues, he replied angrily to a yeoman who rose and called him the greatest thief in all Kent; like a czar, he ordered the man's head cut off. Amid the ensuing commotion, Mayor Walworth came forth to protest; Tyler drove his dagger at the Mayor's stomach (not harming him because of his hidden armor); the Mayor struck back with his cutlass, wounding Wat on the head and neck; one of the King's yeomen ran his sword several times through the rebel leader; and the latter spurred his horse, rode forward with a cry of "Treason!" and, after about 80 paces, fell dying to the ground.

v. The Rebellion Ends

It is easy to imagine a number of possible sequels to the mortal wounding of Wat Tyler. Some other leader might have stepped into his place and continued the rebellion much as before. Or the mob, infuriated, might have broken out into bloody frenzies, seized the King and his companions, and torn them limb from limb. Or, again, the masses might have scattered in confusion and ended the revolt. Actually, the third possibility came nearest to occurring, though for a time the second was threatened. The decisive factor, if we can believe the reports, was the courage of the young king.

In the terrible instant after Tyler had fallen, Richard saw the shafts of doom staring him in the face—hundreds of longbows, the world's most formidable weapons, were pointed toward him from the muttering masses in the square opposite. Already the shafts were bent for action; in a few seconds, at any hairtrigger impulse, volleys of the dread bolts might come whizzing toward him. Faced with this peril, what could he do? Not to act at all, or to make the slightest misstroke, might immediately be fatal.

On an impulse, Richard did probably the only thing that could have saved him. He pressed his horse forward toward the armed hundreds, any one of whom might have felled him with a single well-aimed shaft. "Sirs," his voice rang out, "would you shoot your King? I am your captain. . . . Let him who loves me follow me into the fields."

Evidently the reverence for the sovereign, inbred for many generations, remained powerful. Not one bowman let loose an arrow. As the King wheeled his horse northward, the embattled subjects followed as meekly as sheep.

Even now the shopkeepers and well-to-do citizens, alarmed at the threat to their homes and security, were rallying to join the Government with their arms. In an army of about 7000, they were mustered to pursue their still-endangered monarch as he made his way amid the peasant swarms into the cornfields. Finally a group of armored mercenaries, reinforced by thousands of volunteers and the garrison from the Tower, outflanked the rebels while Richard still sat on his horse, uninjured and conferring with the crowds.

A hot and doubtless wearying day was over. Bewildered and dispirited by the loss of their leader, the mobs were willing to accept the fair-sounding promises of the King; for all practical purposes, the rebellion was ended. Nevertheless, the ruler's conciliatory phrases had been mere gusts of air. He had not intended compliance; his actual attitude, and the contempt he felt for the struggling masses to whom he spoke so gently when he was in their power, is revealed by his own words. "Villeins ye be, and villeins ye shall remain," he told a deputation of peasants when, a week after his escape, they visited him with a request that he make good his pledges. The promises, he advised them, had been exacted by force, hence he was not bound by them. More than that, let any man continue in armed rebellion, and he would suffer dire penalties.

Thus matters returned to about where they had been before the revolt. Hundreds were arrested and tried; about 150, including John Ball and most of the other surviving leaders, were accused of treason and put to death—a toll which, while considerable, was much less than has followed in the wake of many insurrections.

And what had been gained by the peasants and the poor of the towns? The masters had not learned their lesson, nor were they willing to make concessions to the masses who, so shortly before, had terrorized them; some of the ruling class were even inclined to draw the yoke more tightly than ever.

Sixty-nine years later, in 1450, the failure of the rebellion was underscored by a rather similar uprising under the Kentishman Jack Cade, who likewise marched upon London seeking the redress of grievances, won a battle on London Bridge, executed the former treasurer Lord Say, and forced the King's retreat from London, though he too in the end was captured and slain.

But while the hand of violence did not achieve its aims, nonviolent processes would eventually give the workers most of what they had demanded. Serfdom, dealt heavy blows by the flight of workers to the city, would disappear; the rights of free men would be recognized more and more, until at last there was no one in England who was not held to have been born free. And so, where revolution had failed, the long, quiet workings of time and social evolution would vindicate the followers of Wat Tyler.

3. Singeing the Spanish Beard

i. The Image Smashers

Through the twilit spaces beneath the 500-foot elevation of the Church of Our Lady at Antwerp, the unkempt and ragged intruders crowded noisily. They did not stare in awe at the magnificently painted windows, nor at the massive columns from which, as from gigantic tree-trunks, images of birds and animals, flowers and fruit hung in fantastic designs. Clamoring like an invading army, some of the men pounded the statues with sledgehammers. Others drew forth ropes or pulleys or struck with axes or bludgeons at the ornaments and furniture of bronze, marble, and brilliantly painted wood. Some of the invaders drove daggers at an image of the Virgin, stripped off its resplendent garments, and beat it to fragments. The altar, with the figure of the crucified Christ, was demolished; the paintings, the gorgeous stained glass, were shattered. Meanwhile a group of women of the street, bearing waxen tapers from the altars, provided a flickering illumination for the whole macabre spectacle.

Having completed the devastation, the marauders started out into the streets with torches flaring, while fierce cries burst from them, "Long live the Beggars!" (the popular name for the rebellious bands). All night the fury raged; and when morning dawned in that frenetic August of 1566, every image and every Catholic symbol had been pummelled to bits. Thirty churches in all were sacked; monasteries were invaded and their libraries burned; and other buildings in the city and its environs were attacked during the next two days. At the same time, throughout the Netherlands, a similar storm was roaring; in Flanders alone, it is said, 400 churches were desecrated.

Nevertheless, the assaults did not have the bloodthirsty quality

46

of many riots. No man or woman was molested, though monks and nuns did rush shrieking through the streets; no property was borne off by the destroyers, who went so far as to hang one of their number for some minor thefts.

What, then, lay behind the raids? Examined closely, they prove to have been more than flares of religious fanaticism. They were tokens of the rising spirit of freedom, a protest of the common people of the Netherlands against the power of Spain—that despotic power which, carrying a crucifix in its left hand and an executioner's sword in its right, had been inflicting unbearable persecution upon the Low Countries. To the Protestant masses, the Church was the symbol of that persecution, as it was in fact often its direct agent. Admittedly, it was irrational, wildly irrational, to vent mob fury on paintings, images, architecture, and other products of the artist's hand; the psychology of the masses suggests that of the child who, unable to hit his enemy directly, angrily kicks the enemy's cat. Yet any psychologist will tell you that, in pouring out their hatred and vindictiveness on inanimate objects, the rabble found escape gaps for passions that might otherwise have lashed out at human victims.

The importance of the raids, however, was not confined to the purgative they provided for dangerous emotions, nor to the damage they inflicted on the art of the Netherlands. Rather, the assaults on the images stand out as episodes in the continuing struggle between two grotesquely unequal adversaries—on the one hand, the greatest empire on earth, the possessor of the world's most redoubtable army, and the lord of realms that reached halfway around the earth from Peru to the Philippines; on the other hand, 18 provinces lacking political cohesion and containing altogether but three million people. Once more David was facing Goliath. But his victory was not to be so easy as in the Biblical story. The issues were old and deep, and can be traced in part to distant sources, of which we must have some idea if we are to understand why the images were smashed, and why the episode led toward a far more serious confrontation.

ii. Freedom Versus Tyranny

For several centuries the history of the Netherlands had expressed the conflict between freedom and tyranny, with the latter usually dominant. Freedom in that era, as in most periods, was a rather scarce phenomenon, combatted by the Church with its dictatorial commands, by the lord of the manor driving his hounds and horses through the rustic's fields and whipping or imprisoning the protesting rustic, and by the kings and dukes with their arrogance and display and their bands of mercenary troops. It is less astonishing that freedom was suppressed by such enemies than that its voice was heard at all. But the spirit of freedom, though hemmed in by chains and swords, did persist, as in the England of Wat Tyler; and this was the decisive fact behind the series of bombshells that blew up in the face of the Spain of Philip II.

As far back as 1217, the people of the Netherlands had been granted certain charters—not the right of self-government, but the right to live under law, a distinct advance in those autocratic days. In the 14th and 15th centuries, when the chief towns of Holland sent their deputies regularly to the estates of the provinces, a limited form of representative government was acquired —representative, at least, of the noble and well-to-do elements. Even these limited liberties, however, began to be suppressed in the 15th century, when the dukes of Burgundy clamped down control through the strange processes of feudal inheritance and feudal rule. In 1437 Philip the Good, whose beneficence is about as easy to detect as that of a black-widow spider, assumed control of the land, and promptly rescinded various rights and privileges which he had sworn to uphold. He was followed in power by his son Charles the Bold, who aimed toward despotism but had not succeeded in slaying the love of liberty by the time of his early death in 1477, before his 44th birthday.

Under Charles's daughter, Mary of Burgundy, a girl not yet 20 years of age, freedom was resurrected as from its grave. Delegates from the various provinces, meeting at Ghent, spoke out against the "enormous taxation" and the "ruinous wars" waged by Duke Charles, asked restoration of their provincial and municipal charters, and compelled the Duchess Mary, in February 1477, to grant the "Groot Prvilege" or "Great Privilege," sometimes called the Magna Charta of Holland, which restablished the Supreme Court of the province (converted by Charles into a personal tool), and guaranteed various civil rights, such as that the cities and provinces of the Netherlands might hold diets whenever they wished, and that no new taxes might be imposed without their consent.

The seriousness with which the Netherlands viewed these provisions is suggested by an incident involving two traitors, Imbrecourt and Hugonet. In collusion with the Duchess, they had negotiated clandestinely with King Louis XI of France, who had been regarding the provinces with hawk's eyes. For reasons of policy, Louis betrayed the betrayers, and as a result they were seized by the burghers of Ghent, summarily tried, and executed regardless of the Duchess's tearful pleas.

Here, then, one can see premonitions of that rebellious spirit which, a century later, would take fire in the far greater eruption against Spain.

And how did Spain come into the picture? Enthroned far to the south, with different traditions and language, and people of another ancestry and alien bents of mind, how could the lords of the Iberian Peninsula lay just or logical claim to the Netherlands? But when have nations ever confined themselves to just or logical claims? Spanish sovereignty over the Dutch provinces was in no way more fantastic than Spanish domination of Mexico or Florida, or French or English outposts in India, or Dutch colonies in Java or Sumatra, or French or German or British strongholds in Africa or China, or any one of a thousand other extensions of power from the time of Assyria's Ashur-bani-apal to that of Mao Tse-tung.

Actually, Spanish mastery of the Netherlands was acknowledged in accordance with principles regarded as proper and just in the 15th and 16th centuries and even later. That great countries might be inherited, without regard to the people or their wishes, was taken for granted by the international codes of the times. Thus millions of human beings might involuntarily come under command of a foreign sovereign, who might punish them for any lack of obedience; and this curious situation was accepted not only by the masters for whose benefit the system had been devised, but by the populace that served as pawns and victims.

Consequently, when the Duchess Mary married the Archduke Maximilian of Austria and he took over her possessions, the Netherlands went to him as part of his nuptial property, along with the people of the Netherlands and all their wealth and rights. Later, after Mary had been killed by a fall from a horse, after Maximilian had become Emperor, and after their son Philip the Handsome had espoused the daughter of Ferdinand and Isabella, the Netherlands became tied to Spain by the marriage, without seeking or being able to prevent the unnatural union. It was the son of Philip who, six years old when his father died in 1506, was to rule much of Europe as the Emperor Charles V, and by crush-

ing the remaining liberties of the Netherlands, was to fan the
furies that led to revolution.

iii. Charles V Chastises the Netherlands

The city of Ghent, one of the largest and most prosperous
centers in the Netherlands, enjoyed in the early 16th century a
liberty unusual for the times. But liberty (that is to say, in
others) was abhorrent to the Emperor Charles and to the tradition in which he had been reared. It should not surprise us that,
when he was but 15, he took at least theoretical action against
the city by a document known as the "calf-skin," threatening to
punish all persons who held that he had sworn to uphold the
rights claimed by the people.

This was one cause of complaint against the ruler; a more
active incitement was the tax of 400,000 florins which he sought
to exact from Flanders. In this matter Ghent stood out against
her sister states of the Netherlands, which had agreed to pay 1,-
200,000 florins; her hard-working, practical burghers had no appetite for defraying the costs of a dynastic war of their sovereign—
a war not of their making, and meaning little more to them than
if it had been waged among the craters of the moon. It was natural that some of them, having obtained possession of the hated
"calf-skin," should treat it as the embodiment of their wrongs,
tearing it to bits, and trooping along the streets with fragments
of it stuck in their caps like trophies of battle. And if this action
was provocative, the wooing of the support of King Francis I of
France was even more so; it may well have seemed treasonable to
Charles when his fellow monarch, in an evident effort to ingrati-
ate himself, informed him of the attempted negotiations. Now,
Charles decided, it was time to punish the fractious city.

On February 14, 1540, the imperial armies reached Ghent in
such numbers that it took them more than six hours to enter the
city. The Emperor, surrounded by richly gold-decked and be-
gemmed lords and by cardinals, bishops, and archbishops, had a
bodyguard of 10,000 heavily armed archers, lancers, halberdmen,
and musketeers. For a month of dreadful suspense he seemed
content to awe the people with the spectacle of his might; then,
on March 17, he took action, and beheaded 19 alleged leaders of
the opposition. Six weeks later, on April 29, he read a judgment against the city itself: all its laws and privileges were to be

cancelled; its property, revenues, and stores of arms would be confiscated; and it had to make immediate payment of the disputed 400,000 florins along with an additional 150,000, and 6000 a year in perpetuity.

All this must have seemed terrible enough to the afflicted people, but possibly a deeper, more enduring grievance was one imposed for the ends of sadism and raw revenge. Thirty leading burghers designated by the Emperor, and also the great dean and second dean of the weavers and 50 members of the guilds, had to participate in a ceremony apparently as bitter to them as death itself. Bare-headed, with halters on their necks, they had to appear on a specified day before the Emperor, crying out that they regretted their disloyalty and treason, promising never to repeat the offense, and submissively begging forgiveness in the name of Christ. To make sure that there would be no interference, the streets were packed with armed footmen and cavalrymen when the senators in black robes and other deputies in linen shirts were trailing forth to the place of judgment, some of them weeping in their anger and humiliation. Calmly above them the Emperor was perched, crown on head and scepter in hand; around him sat the Queen Regent and the resplendently dressed princes of church and state; beneath him, lines of men with bows and halberds stood guard. Having listened to the prearranged confessions and pleas for mercy, the sovereign acted out the farce of considering the petition and extending his benign forgiveness.

The chief significance of the incident, however, was not what it seemed to be. It did, indeed, signalize the end of the liberties of the Netherlands for many years; and it did illustrate the overwhelming armed might, the arrogance, the cruel conceit of a great hereditary lord. But at the same time it provoked invisible counter-currents, which would grow in the dark recesses of men's minds, and after many years would join other gradually growing currents to produce a grumbling and a muttering and then a roar of revolt.

But before that revolt became reality, the people of the Netherlands were to suffer provocations beside which the inflictions at Ghent seem pale and slight.

iv. The Religious Whip Cracks Down

Many of the incitements were connected with religion, then

regarded not only as the legitimate concern of the state but sometimes as almost its chief concern. In the Netherlands, as in much of Europe, the lives of the believers had been stormy, involving much strife and oppression and a large number of dissident sects, whose members, being heretics, were condemned by the orthodox as criminals meriting the most painful death. And as the orthodox included the members of the house of the Emperor Charles, the divergent beliefs of the Netherlands were especial sources of conflict.

The situation was complicated by events in Germany. In 1525 the close of the Peasants' Revolt sent the defeated Anabaptists in considerable numbers to seek refuge in the Dutch provinces—and Anabaptists were anathema to the conservative. For they were religious extremists, some of whom led lives that on ethical grounds might be regarded as exemplary, though others gave cause for complaint by their fanatical practices and views, including murders, plunderings, and plural marriages; one notorious incident occurred in Amsterdam on a February night of 1535, when seven men and five women rushed naked through the streets with hysterical cries about the wrath of God. But quite apart from the insane demonstrations of a small minority, Anabaptism was a creed or series of creeds that questioned the efficacy of infant baptism and emphasized the will and faith of the individual. This, to the old-line believers, was almost like denying God and Christ.

Hence the Anabaptists were regarded as something below men, and indeed below the beasts. A suggestion of the savagery of the popular attitude has been preserved in a painting by Tileman van Braght (dating from 1685), in which two Anabaptists are shown tied to stakes, their faces blackened, their clothes almost burned away as the flames mount about them, while the executioner stands by with a two-pronged stick, a priest looks on, crucifix in hand, and a crowd has gathered as at a circus performance.

Since Anabaptists were loathed by the masses somewhat as Communists are loathed today in capitalistic countries, a ruler like the Emperor Charles could expect wide support in persecuting members of the sect infiltrating into his domains. It was not always possible, however, for the sovereign to draw fine lines as to who was and who was not an Anabaptist, nor would such lines have always seemed important, since all dissenters from prescribed belief were held to deserve the most drastic punishment. Consequently, all that the coming of the Anabaptists did was accentuate a strong preexisting tendency; no specific sect was the target of Charles, so much as the Reformation itself.

As early as 1521, the ruler's attitude was shown in an edict describing Martin Luther as "not a man, but a devil under the form of a man . . . all his disciples and converts are to be punished with death and forfeiture of all their goods." And this intention was actually carried into effect, as in the case of the two monks burned at Brussels in 1523, shortly after the introduction of the papal inquisition.

But this was a mere beginning. Charles, unfortunately, had not learned that the new creed throve upon persecution; he continued to regard oppression and suppression as synonymous. It is a measure of the fanaticism of the man, and of his blind confusion of values, that in 1523 another decree made it a capital offense to discuss matters of faith or read the scriptures even in the seclusion of one's own home; in enforcement of these enactments, the fires were kept merrily burning while screaming wretches roasted to death.

Yet all this was even before the invasion of the Anabaptists. In the following years, thousands would be liquidated, Anabaptists along with many of their opponents, in keeping with the humane view of the Emperor's sister Queen Dowager Mary of Hungary: "All heretics . . . should be persecuted with such severity as that error might be, at once, extinguished, care being taken only that the provinces were not entirely depopulated." Charles himself seems to have had a somewhat similar idea when in 1535 one of his edicts sentenced all heretics to death: the unrepentant were to be burned, while repentant men might enjoy the mercy of being beheaded, and their repentant spouses and sisters were to be buried alive. For the remaining 20 years of Charles's reign, the order was enforced.

Yet the Emperor's religious fervor did yield at times to pragmatic considerations. When he needed the aid of powerful Protestant princes or found that his restrictions interfered with foreign trade, he was willing to tolerate a little heresy. And in the Religious Peace of Augsburg in 1555 he came to a shaky understanding with the Protestants. Partly because of such concessions, and partly because many of his subjects approved of the persecutions and others had been awed into submissive respect for the asserted rights of sovereigns, even his severest repressions did not provoke the counter-action one might expect.

Besides, having been born at Ghent, Charles was regarded by the Netherlanders as one of them; there could even be sentimental exchanges between them, as when, in handing over the sovereignty of the provinces to his son Philip at Brussels in October 1555, he said to the aristocrats of the Order of the Golden Fleece, "Gentlemen, you must not be astonished if, old and feeble as I am in all my members, and also from the love I bear you, I shed some tears."

Nevertheless, the hatred, terror, and repression which he had planted in the Netherlands were certain to produce a bitter harvest. And that harvest would be reaped after the accession of Philip II of Spain, one of the most earnest and pitiable of rulers, and one of the great fanatics of modern times.

v. Hymn-Singers and the Inquisition

In the crucial year 1566, the demonstrators, Protestants all of them, numbered in the thousands, and their hymn-singing multitudes marched in the fields near the cities of the Netherlands, since they had been forbidden to meet in the churches. Brandishing pitchforks, pikes, sticks, swords, and arquebuses, they looked more like armed guerrillas than like worshippers at prayer meetings. Barricades of planks, branches of trees, and overturned wagons ringed them around; scouts ranged on their flanks to warn of approaching danger; hawkers passed among them selling the hymnbooks whose very possession was a capital offense. So enthusiastic were the people that sometimes, as at Haarlem, they would even climb moats and walls to reach the forbidden gatherings. Not merely one or two cities, but many were involved, and everywhere the crowds were thick—near Antwerp alone, it has been estimated, 15,000 persons were illegally assembled.

Meanwhile the regent Margaret of Parma, half-sister of the King, had issued proclamation after proclamation against the assemblages, and had announced a reward of thousands of crowns for the capture of a preacher, dead or alive. In the eyes of the authorities, what was happening was more than religious dissent —it was rebellion.

Such was the situation after Philip had ruled for a decade in the Netherlands. Another phase of the uprising, also in 1566, was represented by the smashing of the church images, which we have noted. And yet another phase involved the rise of outlaw bands known by picturesque names such as Wild Beggars and Beggars of the Sea. These "Beggars" had originated in a move of the aristocrats, who had presented the Regent with a petition demanding cancellation of the laws against heresy—a challenge that brought Margaret of Parma close to tears. "What," asked one of her advisers, "afraid of these beggars?" Laughingly the rebels accepted the designation; in pursuance of the joke, they provided themselves with plain leather wallets, carried wooden bowls such as beggars hung about their necks, and exchanged their gold lace and velvet for coarse gray-brown doublets.

To the Spaniards they were far from a joke. The Wild Beggars, or Beggars of the Forest, were little more than brigands, whose atrocities, illustrating the sad old law that terror begets terror, rivalled those of the Spaniards themselves. Even more redoubtable were the Beggars of the Sea, who protected the coastal cities of the north while preying upon Spanish commerce, waylaying convoys, and threatening to open the dikes against the enemy.

Thus dissent expanded into guerrilla warfare, itself but a portent of the greater conflict to come. What were the forces that, within 10 years of Philip's accession, had brought the Netherlands to such a perilous brink?

To a large extent, as we have seen, the situation had been inherited by Philip; the demons of fear, resentment, and hatred, created by the suppressions under the Emperor Charles V, could not easily be exorcised. Philip, however, had not moved to exorcise them; he seemed to go out of his way to spread and intensify them. One of his early official moves was to announce the renewal of his father's edicts against the dissenting sects, and the enforcement of the extreme penalties—the beheadings, the burnings, the burials alive. This barbarous decree, which was to be proclaimed once every six months in every town and village in the Netherlands, threatened death to all who succored suspected heretics, along with all who had more than once been "greatly suspected" even though nothing had been proved.

Since the orders were not only announced but enforced, the result was a guaranteed reign of terror. Although the Spanish Inquisition, with its sinister weavings and its horrors of human sacrifice in the name of Christian piety, had been imported into the Netherlands in 1521 when Charles V had appointed an Inquisitor-General, it had remained for Philip to bring the engines of persecution into full operation. The nature of their action, under a monster of sadism such as the inquisitor Peter Titelmann, was illustrated by the experience of the tapestry-weaver Thomas Calberg, who was burned alive for the crime of copying hymns from a book. Typical also was the case of Robert Ogier, who was arrested along with his wife and two sons for not going to mass and for conducting private worship at home; as the penalty for these enormities, he and his entire family were sentenced to the flames.

vi. The Duke of Alva and William the Silent

After the image-smashing, Philip II followed the old historic precedent of answering outrages with greater outrages. Having removed Margaret of Parma as regent and cancelled certain widely hailed concessions which she had made, he appointed in her place the Duke of Alva, who was to win an unenviable name for his strategy of terror against the helpless. Alva was an able military commander, and in effect he was to lead an armed invasion of the Netherlands. "Shall I not crush these men of butter?" he asked, as he marched into the country with an army of 10,000 hardened veterans.

His methods, however, were not exclusively military. One of his chief instruments was the "Council of Troubles" or "Council of Blood," which could sentence any person in the Netherlands to death for such an offense as tolerating public preaching, neglecting to protest against image-breaking, or suggesting that the King had gone too far in denying the country's liberties. The men and women punished for such nefarious law-breaking were by no means few. Within three months, the executions of the Council of Blood numbered 1800.

To assist the Duke in his ensanguined work, Philip on February 26, 1568, confirmed a decree which, as John Lothrop Motley remarks, was "probably the most concise death-warrant that was ever framed" (though in our own more advanced century it has been surpassed).[1] Only a few of all the inhabitants of the Netherlands were excepted from the automatic death sentence—a sentence that disposed of all encumbrances of trial and evidence, and permitted almost anyone to be seized and hauled without formality to the execution chamber. In its actual workings, even though it victimized the poor and the humble along with the great and the noble, this law reminds us of the worst of the proscriptions that disgraced the ancient Roman Republic: many a man was seized for no apparent reason except that his wealth was worth confiscating; many were dragged away with their tongues screwed into iron rings and seared with hot irons to prevent outcries that might disturb the streets.

As if such ruthlessness did not suffice to stir up fear and fury, the Spaniards went on to incite further frenzy by executing two leading Dutch noblemen, Count Egmont and Count Horn, who were condemned with little or no excuse by the Council of Blood, tried for treason after their fate had been secretly predetermined, and publicly beheaded at Brussels on June 5, 1568. Since nobody believed that the unfortunate noblemen had been guilty of any offense, the whole country was shaken with terror and rage. It was as if Alva had gone out of his way to scatter dynamite.

By this time resistance was becoming more organized. The spearhead of dissent was William, Prince of Orange, known as "the Silent," although he was an eloquent spokesman. A temperate and tolerant man, who had striven to bring peace among embattled religious groups, Orange had been under no illusions as to the nature of Philip's rule; having antagonized the sovereign, he maneuvered deftly against him while keeping out of reach by fleeing the country. In February 1567, realizing that he was in effect making a declaration of war, he refused to take the loyalty oath to Philip's government. Then, after disposing of his offices and valuables and joining his family in Germany, he learned that he had been condemned as a traitor, his property had been confiscated, and his eldest son had been kidnapped and carried off to Spain, where he would be trained to loathe the principles for which William was giving his life.

In league with other fugitive noblemen, Orange now raised an army at his own expense to fight the oppressors. There is a quaint ring to the commission which he gave to his brother Louis, in which his pretense of loyalty to Philip remained, although his basic purposes are stated clearly enough:

> To show our love for the monarch and his hereditary provinces, to prevent the desolation hanging over the country by the ferocity of the Spaniards, to maintain the privileges sworn to by His Majesty and his predecessors, to prevent the extirpation of all religion by the edicts, and to save the sons and daughters of the land from abject slavery, we have requested our dearly beloved brother Louis Nassau to enroll as many troops as he shall think necessary.[2]

Elsewhere—in a statement of August 31, 1568—Orange again shows why he met violence with violence:

> To few people is it unknown that the Spaniards have for a long time sought to govern the land according to their pleasure. Abusing His Majesty's goodness, they have persuaded him to decree the introduction of the inquisition into the Netherlands. . . . We are unable . . . to look with tranquillity any longer at such murders, robberies, outrages, and agony. . . . We summon all loyal subjects of the Netherlands to come and help us. Let them take to heart the uttermost need of the country, the danger of perpetual slavery for themselves and their children, and of the entire overthrow of the Evangelical religion. . . .[3]

vii. Rebellion

Here was explicit, open rebellion. Yet here was no guarantee that the country would rise up against the dreaded Spanish despotism. William the Silent—an astute and courageous political leader, but a poor general—fought valiantly against the trained followers of the Duke of Alva, took his way from disaster to disaster, watched his unpaid and mutinous army go to pieces in France, and finally, sick and discredited, fled to Germany.

But though faced with overwhelming difficulties and seemingly further than ever from the full support he so badly needed, he persisted doggedly. And in 1572 he gained new hope from the success of the buccaneering Beggars of the Sea, who captured the city of Brill and later took Flushing, while the revolt spread, several new cities joined the rebels, and William was formally given command of the insurgent army and navy.

Victory, however, was still far away. But the Spaniards, with arrogant blindness and in part owing to the passions of a rebellious, hate-filled, greedy, lustful soldiery, would provide the missing links in the chain of revolt. "The Spanish Fury," the eruption was called, when in 1576 it struck Antwerp with massacre, fire, and rapine, at an estimated cost of 8000 civilian lives. But in other cities, such as Zutphen and Mechlin, the same sort of outrages had descended during the preceding years.

An example was to be seen at Naarden in 1572, when 500 inhabitants were called by the tolling of the bells to the Gast Huis Church. Imagine the people's terror when a priest entered and called out, "Prepare for death!" Immediately, amid the nightmarish tumult, the door burst open and Spanish soldiers rushed in, fired into the crowd, and attacked with swords and daggers. Cornered and weaponless, the victims were struck down to the last man, woman, and child. Then the church was set on fire, the town was looted, and most of the remaining inhabitants were murdered, tortured, or violated. And as a mad climax, the death penalty was ordered for anyone succoring any of the few miserable escapees.

It is not surprising if such terrorism, along with the continual shock, rage, and dread created by the inquisitors, produced a traumatic effect that sharpened the spirit of revolt. Yet it is ironic that, as in Wat Tyler's rebellion nearly 200 years before and in the American Revolution two centuries later, the spark that set off the major explosion was connected with nothing spectacular such as slaughter or torture or the looting and burning of cities, but with mere prosaic taxation. This, however, could be or seem to be a matter of life or death to the commercial populace—a fact of which the Duke of Alva evidently lost sight when in 1572, being chronically in need of money, he imposed various new methods of draining the tills of the Netherlanders. Merchants and tradesmen were now called upon to pay not only a one percent property tax but 5 percent on all goods, and 10 percent on all sales—and this could turn out to be much more than 10 percent, since the tax would be added with each transaction, raising prices so enormously that trade would be all but impossible.

Beneath such an encumbrance the taxpayer was certain to grumble. And when his neighbors likewise grumbled, and when they raised a commotion all about him and burghers everywhere refused to pay the tax, he might well join the resistance movement. In city after city the people would not pay. Shops and factories closed; men and women bartered for food on the streets; so severe was the disturbance that Alva, on June 24, 1572, was driven to abolish the taxes in return for the promise of a yearly income of two million florins.

If taxation had really been the issue, the revolt should now have ended. But ensuing events proved that taxation, by stirring up long-smoldering anger and resentment, had been a mere incentive to the outburst, the spark rather than the cause. Hence opposition to the Spaniards did not end with the cancellation of the excessive taxes; the rebellion rumbled on and on, while the Estates of Holland met in response to the summons of William of Orange, who had raised an army in Germany and called upon the people of the Netherlands for contributions. The fact that contributions did flow in, including money, gold, precious gems, furniture, and silver plate, is eloquent of the awakened spirit of the people.

That spirit, having been aroused, could not easily be put to sleep. It would support a war which, though the Netherlands began as a seemingly helpless underdog, would continue tenaciously in the face of defeats and discouragements, would not be quenched even after its protagonist William the Silent had been felled by an assassin's bullet, and would persist for 80 years before at last Spain was forced to acknowledge the independence of the northern provinces. The insurrectionists, though this may not have been their intention, had won a great battle in the continuing war for human freedom.

viii. Some General Conclusions

From the revolt of the Netherlands, certain general conclusions are evident.

First of all, there is the old, often observed fact that hatred breeds hatred, violence breeds violence, and brutality breeds brutality; that forcible suppression, unless it extirpates the dissenters, may defeat its own ends; and that the harsher the repression, the fiercer the probable rebound. Even so, however, the experience of the Dutch provinces shows that an outbreak of the disgruntled may be deceptively slow in starting: the most dangerous insurgency may gradually gather underground, like the explosive force of a volcano; blow after blow may be endured with but little resistance, and then the people may erupt at some comparatively minor imposition. Meanwhile a small but determined minority, perhaps scorned or ignored at first, poses insuperable problems for the rulers, and forms a nucleus for revolution.

In all this it is not the size of the insurgent sword that counts so much as the inner force with which it is wielded; the strength of the human spirit may daunt that of the most powerful arm. For even the most powerful arm, reaching out for long distances from a seemingly unconquerable opponent, may be blunted in its striking force by a relative handful of thoroughly aroused men and women. This is likely to be all the more true since the overconfidence and complacency of a ruling clique, who seldom realize when they face a tiger that cannot be caught or tamed, tend to be dominant faults; such unawareness or underestimation of the revolting forces may prove fatal.

These conclusions, of course, do not apply to the Netherlands only. The same findings, as we shall see, are supported also by other insurrectionary movements, and not least by those of our own day.

4. America: The Tinder of Revolution

i. The Boston Massacre, the *Gaspee*, and the Tea Party

Along the snow-covered streets of Boston on a day in March 1770, the British troops swaggered with their muskets and bright red uniforms, staring contemptuously at the citizens who stared back at them with equal contempt and even with hatred. Insulting words were exchanged; violence in speech gave way to violence in action. From the civilian crowd, snowballs and rocks began to rain; some of the Bostonians, closing in, beat the guns of the soldiers with clubs, knocking over one of the opposition. "Fire!" they dared the redcoats. And the British, goaded beyond the breaking point, let loose a volley, felling eleven citizens, three of them killed outright, and two others mortally wounded.

Not surprisingly this event, which would be known as the "Boston Massacre," caused a great stir among the townspeople. Bells sounded, drums beat, the citizens poured forth in vociferous excitement, and companies of militia began to be martialled about the Town House. But the mob, fortunately, was held in check by Governor Thomas Hutchinson after the British had agreed to remove the soldiers to Castle William, in Boston harbor.

This was but one of the many unruly incidents providing tinder for the American Revolution. But it was an incident that would not be forgotten; for purposes of propaganda, it would be enlarged much beyond its intrinsic importance. And it would be followed by other outbreaks equally indicative of the trend of the times, such as the *Gaspee* affair of March 1772. This flare-up centered about an armed schooner, which, commanded by hard-bitten Lieutenant William Dudington, was scouring the coast of Rhode Island in search of smuggling ships. The smugglers of

Providence and Newport, whose profitable business had suffered little interference from British revenue agents until now, were incensed when Dudington developed the irritating habit of boarding and inspecting every vessel he could find, while threatening to blast unobliging captains with a broadside and to let Newport burn without lifting a finger. Such methods and such language brought forth a charge that he was "more imperious and haughty" than the Grand Turk. It was therefore with huge delight that the New Englanders learned one day that the crusty lieutenant's ship, the *Gaspee,* had run aground while chasing a smuggler. For hours, until the high tides of midnight, she would remain helpless.

Darkness had barely fallen when a drummer strode through the streets of Providence, announcing the great news. Let the citizens hurry to the home of James Sabin, where plans were under way to dispose of the *Gaspee* once and for all! With little delay, the rebels surged into action. On small boats they set out toward the stranded vessel, which they reached before the tide could set her free. Shots rang out as they drew near; Dudington fell with several bullets in his body, painfully though not fatally wounded. After pleading for his life, he was let loose in an open boat, while flames spouted from the *Gaspee,* which burned to the water line. In the ensuing enquiry, when His Majesty's government sought to place the blame and punish the culprits, all the interrogated citizens suffered simultaneous attacks of total amnesia, which prevented them from recalling what had happened, or admitting a share in the occurrence, or recognizing any of the alleged mobsters. Consequently, no one could be sent to England to be tried for his part in the sabotage.

But if this affair was eloquent of the growing rift between the colonies and the mother country, it was less memorable than the outburst of December 1773, familiarly known as the Boston Tea Party. The details have often been related: how three companies of fifty men each, disguised rather imperfectly as Mohawk Indians, made their way to the waterfront amid crowds of spectators; how they boarded the tea ships in Boston harbor, encountering no resistance and even receiving help from the sailors; and how they hauled the chests of tea from the hold, broke them open, and dropped them overboard. Here was not only willful destruction of valuable property; here was outright defiance of the government and laws of King George III. Here, too, was action that would be fruitful in consequences.

But before we note those consequences, let us observe what lay behind the Tea Party, the Boston "Massacre," and the *Gaspee* affair. Actually, all three were links in a single chain, a chain that stretched far back through the years and must be examined before we can understand what happened in the early 1770s.

ii. Mercantilism and Colonial Freedom

Europe of the 17th and 18th centuries, much like ancient Rome, was apt to look upon a colony as a treasury to be looted, or a granary for the benefit of the central power. According to the mercantile philosophy of the trading nations of the West, colonies were necessary pawns in a great international game—essential sources of raw materials and consumers of manufactures, enabling a country to maintain a "favorable balance of trade" and so be prosperous and great. Hence, although in theory the good of the colonies was considered, in practice this was not likely to be evident to the colonials, who too often were given the idea that they were sheep being prepared for the shearing.

Here was one source of the troubles in colonial America. Almost from the beginning, the mercantilist theory lay in the background; the Navigation Act of 1651 forbade the colonies to ship goods such as sugar and tobacco anywhere except to England or to other colonies, to transport them except in English or colonial ships, or to obtain foreign manufactures that had not passed through English ports. These regulations might appear repressive enough, but actually their yoke seems to have fallen on the colonies rather lightly. Only when the 18th century was well advanced did acute raw spots appear.

Even though an irritant was introduced when Parliament in 1733 imposed high duties on foreign molasses and sugar shipped into the colonies, the deepest sources of unrest did not develop until the 1760s. The year 1763 saw the end of the Seven Years' War, which had raged on the European continent since 1756, and, enlarged into the 18th century version of a world war, had sharp repercussions in the clash of the French and English on American soil. While warfare in those days was not nearly as costly in machinery or manpower as it would be amid the enlightenment of a more technological era, nevertheless it could be a bloodsucking parasite exhausting the national resources. England, while victorious, emerged from the Seven Years' War financially depleted—and was it not therefore to be expected that she would look to her colonies to pay for their own protection and defray part of the war's cost?

But to the colonies this was an insufferable imposition. They felt it iniquitous to be taxed by the Crown, taxed in disregard of their own legislative bodies, and for ends that brought them no benefits. Hence the opposition was much greater and more stubborn than England had expected.

To understand the outcome, we need not delve deeply into the tax laws themselves, though it may be helpful to glance at them in a general way. Consider the "Sugar Act" of 1764, which placed duties on a variety of articles, including cloth, sugar, and indigo, and provided that iron and lumber loaded on a Europe-bound ship must land in England. In the attempt to prevent fraud, this law entangled the captains in an infuriating amount of red tape, while it particularly enraged the colonials by a provision for trials which, reversing the usual practice of the common law, saddled an accused man with the burden of proving his innocence.

Another prime irritant was the Currency Act, also passed in 1764, with the aim of forbidding the use of paper money south of New England, in disregard of the economic realities of a land where circulating gold and silver were scarce or nonexistent. Then there were the Indian regulations, which, although they seem fair and enlightened from the present-day point of view, struck the colonials as unduly repressive in their attempt to control the purchase of Indian lands, to checkmate the great land companies, and protect the rights of the aborigines.

And yet none of these enactments, however they may have added to the rebellious mood of the colonists, were as provoking as the Stamp Act of March 22, 1765. In the reactions to this statute, we can hear premonitions of the rattling of the guns of Concord and Lexington.

iii. The Stamp Act and Mob Violence

In the perspective of more than 200 years, it is easy enough to see that the Stamp Act represented a monumental British political blunder, which provoked flares of unexpected violence and at the same time did much to unify the colonies. Actually, however, the measure was neither extreme nor iniquitous; taxation by means of stamps was nothing new in Britain, and the amount that was asked—no more than about a third of the proceeds of a day's labor per year—would not have borne down with an unendurable weight. To its supporters, the impost seemed entirely fair; later it was revealed that it was expected to raise only 60,000 pounds a year, or barely more than a sixth of the estimated cost of providing for the British troops in America. And what if the Americans did object to bearing this small share of the burden? Proponents of the bill such as Prime Minister George Grenville, with the usual foresight of political prophets, seemed not to doubt that the colonists would yield. Would they not be appeased by the knowledge that the lucrative post of stamp master, bearing a salary of 300 pounds a year, would be reserved for the colonists? Even so astute a man as Benjamin Franklin, having unavailingly opposed the measure, sought his share of the patronage by obtaining the position of stamp master of Pennsylvania for his friend John Hughes.

But the advocates of the Act had overlooked several factors, and most of all those that concerned the American state of mind. They seem not to have realized that the stamp tax, which was to be placed on almost all documents, licenses, and legal papers as well as on newspapers, newspaper advertisements, pamphlets, and almanacs, was obnoxious to the colonies less for the sums it sought to extract than because of its inroads into popular liberties. Let us not forget that a tax of the same nature, if imposed today by our own government even for ends held to be meritorious and necessary, would be infuriating to millions of Americans. To the colonists, however, the Stamp Act was more objectionable than any measure of a home government was likely to be. It represented the first attempt of Parliament to clamp down a direct tax; it flung a challenge at the American traditions of local liberty and of the people's right to levy all taxes through their own duly constituted bodies. If the Act were permitted to operate, who could say where the exactions might not end? Wild rumors circulated that the British were plotting to wipe out all American liberties; and these rumors, however exaggerated, did have a basis in possibility since the power to tax is the power to control and even to ruin.

Partly for these reasons, along with the fact that all taxes arouse opposition by their very nature, the Stamp Act was like a brand of fire not only to the more unruly and radical elements in America but even to generally staid and conservative citizens.

Soon riots became the order of the day. An organization known as the Sons of Liberty—self-styled patriots whose clubs ranged from Boston as far south as Charleston—became the center of the uprisings amid turbulent scenes, drunkenness, mob violence, and the threat of violence. Focusing their fury against the Stamp Act, the Sons of Liberty and the rabbles they aroused quickly taught the stamp masters some frightening lessons.

These officials, though they might be patricians of the bluest dye, were most cordially hated—so much so that their property and even their lives were in danger. The home of more than one appointee was torn down; more than one fled at top speed with the mob in full pursuit. Many of the men, preferring discretion to peril, resigned with impetuous haste, as when William Coxe gave up his post in New Jersey without attempting to perform any of his official duties. More unyielding was Maryland's Zachariah Hood, who paid for his courage in defying the mob: his store was demolished, his life was threatened, and he rode so hard to escape to New York that his horse fell dead on the way. In Massachusetts the stamp master, Andrew Oliver, was burned in effigy; later, the crowd tore the pickets from the fence around his house to make a bonfire, entered the house, broke a number of windows, and then, according to some reports, hastened to regale themselves in the wine cellar. Governor Thomas Hutchinson and the sheriff, upon rushing to the scene, were pelted with stones, and had to retreat ignominiously.

Little wonder that Oliver gave up his post next day. But Governor Hutchinson, who had aroused the rage of the pack by his attempt to aid the stamp master and also by various other complaints piling up against him for four years, now had to face a new ordeal. Rumor, disdaining as always to look at the facts, circulated the preposterous charge that it was he who had written the Stamp Act. But the multitude drew no fine distinctions between accusation and proof; one August night it gathered, crying "Liberty and property!"—the usual prelude in those days to an attack upon liberty and property. First they went to the home of the marshal of the admiralty court, Charles Paxton, who had the good fortune to be away; then, after being appeased at a tavern to which the owner of the building took them for a barrel of punch, the throngs proceeded to the house of the deputy register of the admiralty court, wrecked it, and burned the court records. Next they ruined the sumptuous interior of the mansion of the comptroller of the customs; and still not having destroyed enough for one night, they paid a visit to the Governor, and, in Hutchinson's own words, "the hellish crew fell upon my house with the rage of devils." Wishing to accompany his daughter, who refused to leave without him, he fled, while the mob stormed on until nothing remained "but the bare walls and floors" of "one of the best finished houses in the province." Furniture smashed, doors broken, money and silver stolen, clothing and pictures filched or destroyed—these did not complete the list of the depredations. Perhaps most outrageous of all, to Hutchinson's mind, was the damage to the second volume of the valuable history of the colony which he had been writing, and which was thrown into the street (but, fortunately, was recovered).

To present the picture in fairer perspective, one must record that many of the citizens of Boston were appalled at this mob violence, and expressed their "utter detestation" of the night's proceedings in a town meeting which they called next morning. But one should likewise note that, though the Governor and council ordered the arrest of the mob leader, the shoemaker and fireman Ebenezer Mackintosh, the sheriff set the prisoner free after being advised that there would otherwise be no military guard in the town that night. The fact seems to be that Mackintosh, who was head of the South End gang, was protected by certain well-placed citizens who feared that he would disclose their participation in a previous riot.

It was by no coincidence that some of the worst violence occurred at Boston. Violence had long been a tradition of the community, particularly for the North End and South End mobs, who met in a tumultuous affray each November 5 on Guy Fawkes' Day. In 1764, for example, a small-scale battle had broken out with the aid of sticks and staves, some of the heads of the participants had been broken, and a hapless five-year-old boy had been killed despite all the efforts of town officials to end the fighting. Here, then, was precedent for attacks such as those against stamp master Oliver and Governor Hutchinson. But note this distinction: in the clashes of the North End and South End gangs, only the rowdy and ruffianly elements were involved, but in the assaults on the stamp officials some of the well-to-do and "better" citizens were implicated—merchants, magistrates, men of position, who encouraged and even participated in and led the riots.

Not that Boston enjoyed the distinction of being the only center of violence; New York City was not far if at all behind.

On October 23, 1765, a mob of 2000 confronted a stamp-bearing English ship upon its arrival at the docks, and thereafter for some days tension gripped the town. On the night of the 31st, no less than three mobs trailed through the streets, accompanied by shouts of "Liberty!", the crash of shattering windowglass, the splintering of lamps, and the yells of patriots who threatened to bury alive the commander of the British fort, Major Thomas James, who was guarding the stamps. And the following night, conditions had hardly improved. Several thousand rioters, demonstrating until four in the morning, swarmed before the gates of the fort as if to take it, even though the soldiers might have massacred them; they then streamed through the city with Governor Cadwallader Colden's carriage, hung effigies of him and of the devil upon a gallows, burned the effigies, gallows, and carriage in defiance of the gunners at the fort, and made an uninvited visit to the Major's house, which was soon resounding with the noise of windows battered, shutters being pulled down, and furniture wrecked, while James's clothes, books, silverware, wine, and other possessions were borne away by the plunderers.

On November 2 Colden capitulated, but the mobs continued to demand a bonfire for the stamps, which were still in the fort. Sixteen days later a new governor, Sir Henry Moore, arrived to find his predecessor awaiting him tremblingly behind the fort's barred doors. Only by refusing to take any measures to carry out the Stamp Act was the new administrator able to restore peace.

Thus, through mob violence, the coveted end had been achieved; the Stamp Act, being impossible to enforce, became a dead letter, and the British were left with no reasonable course except the humiliating one of repeal. But one cannot help observing that, as when too powerful a drug has been applied, the violence had its side effects. And one of these was in the precedent which it provided for the Sons of Liberty, who saw in the use of force an instrument for their own political purposes. In New York, for example, when certain young lawyers approved mob action, they were seeking nothing more revolutionary than to overturn the Stamp Act; but having achieved their aim, they found that the movement had gained a momentum beyond their control; command of the mobs thenceforth would be in the hands of much more radical proletarian rabble-rousers. It is doubtful, however, whether many observers understood how mob violence was leading toward revolution and war.

iv.   Further   Friction   at   Boston

Now that the Stamp Act was out of the way, one clear fact had been flashed before colonial eyes: Britain was not invincible. By their own united protest, the Americans could gain their objectives.

This did not mean, of course, that the protest need always be violent; a long period of persistent, rancorous, but mainly non-violent strife ensued. And meanwhile the home country, by a series of ill-advised measures, continued to exacerbate colonial feelings, and the Americans struck back with attempted economic reprisals, such as the poorly coordinated nonimportation arrangement in which, beginning in 1765, the colonies agreed not to import British goods. By the so-called Townshend Acts, including the Revenue Act of 1767, new grievances were inflicted on the subjects, who were challenged in some of their basic liberties by taxes on the importation from Britain of articles such as paper, paint, glass, and tea. Likewise, an assault was made on the democratic institutions of New York by an act suspending the colonial Assembly—by implication, a blow at the freedom of all Americans.

But one of the most notorious of all the British enactments was the Tea Act, passed in 1773, three years after the resistance of the colonies had caved in; it was this law which stirred up the bitter feelings that led to the Boston Tea Party. The Tea Act, with its provision for the direct shipment of tea to American merchants appointed as agents, can best be understood if we remember that it was in part an attempt to combat the deep losses from the flourishing American smugglers of tea, and came at a time when the East India Company, the producer of the tea, was staggering beneath a gigantic debt and seemed near bankruptcy. But such considerations meant little or nothing to the smugglers who objected strenuously to the Tea Act, nor to the honorable businessmen who saw in the new law a threat to free trade. Yet, as John C. Miller points out, had the commissioners of the Customs succeeded in eliminating smuggling, "there would have been no necessity for the Tea Act" and consequently no Boston Tea Party.[1]

And had there been no Boston Tea Party or equivalent act of defiance and destruction, the subsequent history of the colonies would almost certainly have been very different. There might have been no Declaration of Independence, no Revolutionary

War, no separation from the mother country; what we now know as the United States of America might have become a dominion of the British Empire. Among all the events leading toward the Revolution, the series of riots and insurrections had possibly the most decisive long-range influence; and this may be said even though they may in many ways be regarded as effects no less than as causes. But few, except perhaps certain agitators such as Samuel Adams and Patrick Henry, appeared aware of the direction the road was taking. Moreover, it seems unlikely that the destination would have been war and independence had the British not unwittingly lent their assistance.

In part that assistance was provided by the example of England in her own not infrequent riots, as when mobs in 1768 attacked the prison where the popular politician John Wilkes was confined, threw rocks, and were fired upon by the soldiers, with the loss of five or six lives and other casualties. But the greatest British contribution to the cause of American separatism is to be seen in the home country's efforts at repression, particularly after the Boston Tea Party.

It was to be expected that the news of this demonstration would evoke cries in Parliament. Here was something far worse than the mere destruction of property; here was a challenge to the King's power and sovereignty, a challenge that must not go unrebuked—not unless England was willing to let go entirely of the reins of the colonies. Even the friends of America, such as William Pitt (Lord Chatham), were shocked. What was required now, if ever, was deliberation and diplomacy; but what was forthcoming in Parliament was bias and passion. The outrage was held by many to be the more iniquitous since it had been committed by Americans—persons regarded in certain quarters as of an inferior breed, low-born second-class scum not meriting the full rights of Englishmen. Action against these felons, obviously, must be taken, the more so since the dastardly act had occurred in the very hotbed of militant resistance—Boston. There were some who, during the subsequent debates, would have paused at no extreme. A certain Mr. Van went so far as to demand that Boston be treated as Rome had treated Carthage (which had been obliterated). In a later debate, he amplified his position: "I would do as was done of old, in the time of the ancient Britons, I would burn and set fire to all their woods, and leave their country open to prevent that protection they now have. . . ."[2]

He was not alone. Others also thought it best "to blow the town of Boston about the ears of its inhabitants"; some of these relentless avengers even wished to hang a hundred or so of the citizens. Still others, not going quite this far, thought that the Americans should be treated with the severity with which Spain or France would have dealt with rebellious colonials. Even the apostles of relative restraint, who included Prime Minister Lord North, advocated stern measures; and stern measures were adopted, of the sort that a country might aim at a wartime enemy in a moment of fury, when the impulses of humanity had been forgotten. On March 25, 1774, the House of Commons passed the Boston Port Bill, which encountered no resistance among the Lords and was signed on March 31 by King George III. By this law, which was really an antiport bill, Boston ceased to be a maritime center. Until its people paid the East India Company for the tea dumped overboard by the Tea Party and made good the losses in revenue and also gave definite other proofs that they had reformed, the docks of the city were to remain silent; no ship was to sail in or out of the harbor aside from some coastal vessels which, under specific restrictions, might carry food and firewood.

Considering that Boston was nothing at all if not a seaport; considering that salt water was its very lifeblood, and that water-borne commerce and fishing were at the core of its being, here was chastisement not with a light rod but with a club. Without its ocean trading, how could the city exist? To the stunned citizens, the answer must have seemed plain: it could not exist. They would be not only jobless and financially ruined; they would be starved. But this was evidently just what the lawmakers had planned. It would not be long, they must have assumed, before the rebels would be coerced into bowing their necks and submitting to everything their masters asked.

But the legislators, in voting for the punitive bill on a wave of emotion, had fastened their gaze upon the outer and material realities, to the neglect of the forces moving within men's deeper beings. And the same was true of the other Coercive Acts or Intolerable Acts that a vengeful Parliament proceeded to pass, one of which provided for the quartering of troops upon the colonists, while the Quebec Act (which had much merit, though not from the colonial point of view) decreed restrictive border regulations, and the Massachusetts Government Act, passed in May 1774, provided that the councilors of the province would be chosen by the Crown instead of elected as in the past by the local House of Representatives.

By such impositions, Parliament evidently hoped to crush and disunite the colonies. But what it actually did was to bolster them, to draw them together, to provide a spur for still more serious uprisings, and to feed a militancy that pointed toward revolution and war. In regard to the Boston Port Act, Lord North had said that if it brought on a rebellion, "those consequences belong to them, and not to us. . . ." But events were to show how disastrously wrong he was. The consequences did indeed belong to the colonies, but by no means to them exclusively. To a large degree, they also belonged to Great Britain, and to the world.

v. The Road to War

The troops of the British General Gage were encamped on the Boston Commons despite the Quartering Law which required the local authorities to find immediate accommodations for them; and there they were to remain for months. Meanwhile the life of the whole community had been chilled almost to a halt. Along the streets few carts creaked; in the bay the tied-up ships made a forest of swaying masts. Shops lay empty; the bakers' stands were without bread; sailors and clerks, masons and carpenters slouched along bleakly, in forced unemployment. Over them all, and over their families, stretched the shadow of impending famine.

Yet not all was hopeless. Throughout the colonies, demonstrations had erupted on June 1, 1774, the day when the Boston Port Act became effective. In New York, effigies of Lord North and others were burned; in Connecticut, a public burning of the Port Act was held; in Philadelphia, flags hung at half-mast, shops were closed, and the bells of Christ Church tolled solemnly at intervals during the day. Practical help, also, was forthcoming—sheep and fish, flour and money from the other colonies, so that the Bostonians might be not only saved from starvation but fortified in their resistance by the proof that they were not alone. The King and his councilors were to learn the sad lesson that an insurrection only half-suppressed was an insurrection that might smolder on all the more savagely:

For by restraint that piled on cruel restraint
He poured out oil to feed the whole complaint.

In Boston itself, resistance took various forms: passive, when
men stood by with hands in pockets, seeming not to hear the
General's call for workers to build barracks; active, when sabo-
teurs stole out in the dark to break carts and bridges and scatter
the invaders' brick and straw. Even if Boston was beleaguered, it
was certainly not subdued.

Meanwhile, though disturbances continued in other colonies,
Massachusetts remained the center of the uprising. It was there
that a leading man, Peter Oliver, broke out with a despairing
cry: "I never knew what mobbing was before. I am sick enough
of Confusion and Uproar. I long for an Asylum, some blessed
place of Refuge."[3] It was there also that, at Great Barrington,
the courthouse was invested by a crowd of farmers, who stopped
judicial proceedings; in Berkshire County the protesters went so
far as to pull down the bench. More and more the mounting
waves of antagonism seemed to move toward a great crisis.

In this crisis the British, for all the differences in methods and
provocations, had followed a course whose effects would be in
some ways similar to those of the Japanese in their attack upon
Pearl Harbor more than a century and a half later. By the vehemence of their onslaught, they aroused psychological waves they
had not foreseen, and brought cohesion and unity to a people
who had seemed hopelessly disunited. The rivalries among the
colonies could now be buried beneath the greater antagonisms
and the frightening differences that had developed between them
and England, and now seemed to threaten them all alike.

Thus it came about that, from September 5 to October 26,
1774, Carpenter's Hall in Philadelphia witnessed a telltale episode. The First Continental Congress, drawing up a Declaration
of Rights and Grievances, proclaimed the right to "life, liberty,
and property," stated its objections to the Intolerable Acts, and
declared that Americans could not submit to these infringements
against freedom. Here was a step at once radical and dignified,
and it was reinforced by what we today would call "economic
sanctions"—beginning in January 1775, no goods would be imported from Great Britain or British possessions outside America;
the slave trade would be abolished; no British products, after
March 1, would be consumed; and after September 10 nothing
would be shipped to Britain. Since trade between the colonies

and the mother country had been of major importance on both sides of the Atlantic, this was in effect close to a declaration of war.

But matters, as we know, did not stop at this point. Following passage of the Intolerable Acts, tension had been mounting constantly, while militant dissent was developing into military dissent and gradually a spirit of armed resistance had appeared. Thousands of Massachusetts farmers, having obtained guns and ammunition, were ready to fight the redcoats when, on September 1, 1774, General Gage's men seized some stores of powder near Cambridge. Fortunately, Lieutenant-Governor Thomas Oliver, having rushed to Boston, persuaded Gage to hold his troops in town—the alternative might have been the slaying of all the redcoats. Thus the Revolutionary War might have begun in 1774.

An armed outbreak now seemed only a question of time, particularly as those usual sparks and preludes to war, military preparations, continued throughout the latter half of 1774 among the farms and towns of New England. In September delegates from two Massachusetts counties, convening at Norwich, proclaimed the need to arm immediately for a military emergency; in the following month, the colonial assembly moved to prepare the militia. In January 1775, in South Carolina, a convention recommended military training for all the people; in Virginia volunteer companies had been formed, and before the end of 1774 George Washington was asked to command one of them; other colonies, such as Pennsylvania and Maryland, took various other defensive measures. Then, early in 1775, following the news that the English Parliament had declared that Massachusetts was in a state of insurrection and that four regiments would be sent from Ireland, the pressure mounted for the establishment of a provincial army. "The people are clamorous for an immediate commencement of hostilities," reported a spy for General Gage.

Although the people were actually divided and a large percentage remained loyal to King George's government, the direction of events should have been evident. From lesser violence to greater, from the spirit of minor opposition to one of major resistance, from protest to revolution, the current was plunging on and on, and no one seemed able to check its precipitate sweep forward. Given the militant turn of mind of the colonists and England's punitive and uncomprehending mood, it was merely a matter of detail that the first armed clashes in the War of

Independence occurred in 1775 at Concord and Lexington instead of at points now unrecognized in the annals of war.

vi. Behind the Revolution

"The revolution," John Adams wrote to a correspondent, "was in the minds and hearts of the people." This, of course, is an oversimplification, yet it does express the essence of the uprising as well as is possible in a few words. Not only was the revolution in the minds and hearts of the people; the long series of rebellious strokes and counter-strokes, including the innumerable riots and minor insurrections, was in the minds and hearts of some of the people, and often of many. For a revolution, like a human being, cannot be born without progenitors, and in this case the ancestry, as we have seen, reached back with many diverse shoots, of which the strongest were not physical in nature but psychological.

"But how can this be?" one will ask. "Was the outburst not kindled by matters such as trade regulations and taxation, and therefore was its origin not economic?" So, on the face of things, it would seem; and yet, as so often, the face of things does not reflect their soul. Economic necessity, clearly, is one explanation that cannot be urged, since there was no economic necessity. The period from 1765 to 1775, when the revolution was brewing, was not characterized by economic deprivation but by prosperity and expansion. Business was buzzing, especially in the seaports; in parts of New England, it was said, you could not easily find a man who was not well off; in New York trade was growing at such a rate that, between 1762 and 1772, the number of vessels increased from 477 to 709. Consequently, there is no evidence of any economic compulsion to revolt.

The economic restrictions, nevertheless, were important, for they affected political rights. In the celebrated phrase "taxation without representation," the key word is not the first; the key words are the concluding two. It was not taxation in itself that was under attack; it was, as we have noted, that the taxation was levied in a way that intruded upon the people's liberties. The colonies all had their representative assemblies, and held that these alone had the right to tax them; and when the British, during the decade before Lexington, imposed direct taxes and restrictive regulations, the Americans thought that they must either protest or be enslaved. How in any event could self-respecting free men, accustomed to hewing their own paths in the wide spaces of the New World, bow to the will of a royal master 3000 miles away?

"This means," one will go on to argue, "that the causes of the revolution were really political. It was in pursuance of political goals—the goals of free government—that the 13 colonies were inflamed against England." This conclusion is indeed warranted, but it accounts only for the superficials; once again the face of the matter is misleading. Why did the colonists seek the political rights which they so ardently claimed? Because of the philosophies which they had absorbed, and most of all because of John Locke and his doctrine of a state of nature, which could not be invaded by government without producing tyranny; according to this philosopher, a government which did invade the state of nature did not deserve to exist. Here was a creed that seemed made to order for Americans—proof of the unrighteousness of the repressive measures and direct taxes of King George. And here was vindication for colonial resistance, even violent resistance. Locke, besides, had recognized that an oppressed people might legitimately rebel when their natural rights had been trampled upon.

Subsequently, although not until after the first cracklings of war, the English-born propagandist Thomas Paine, in his pamphlet *Common Sense,* gave wings and fury to the views that had moved the militants of many years. "Society in every state," he proclaimed, "is a blessing, but government even in its best state is a necessary evil; in its worst state an intolerable one. . . . To the evil of monarchy we have added that of hereditary succession; and as the first is a degradation and a lessening of ourselves, so the second, claimed as a matter of right, is an insult and imposition on posterity."

It was ideas like this which, entertained with ebullience and conviction, lent truth to the statement of John Adams, quoted above, that the revolution was "in the minds and hearts of the people." But it may also be said that, in a reverse sense, the revolution was in the minds and hearts of those British lawmakers who, by their repeated inflammation of American feelings, reinforced the view that the English had indeed passed the bounds of rightful authority and were fastening chains about American liberty. When the colonists demanded greater self-government, and when their masters felt that this must be denied because it would lead toward independence, the British encouraged the very consummation they aimed to avert, and fell into this blunder because they so disastrously misread the minds of the governed. Their misreading was particularly noticeable in the strokes that led to the Boston Tea Party and the various Intolerable Acts; with a clearer insight, and freed from blinding rage and vengefulness, the lawmakers might have adopted a course pointing away from revolution.

But was revolution inevitable? Certainly not—not if we consider only the external circumstances, in which there was nothing unsusceptible to the peaceful processes of negotiation and compromise. History shows us examples, though not very many, of political entities amicably split apart, as in the bloodless separation of Sweden and Norway, and, more recently, in the slicing off of various parts of the British and other modern empires without gunfire, even though sometimes, as in the case of India and Pakistan and in parts of Africa, the separation has been followed by violent internal disturbances. It is notable that most of the spokesmen for the American colonists, though Samuel Adams may have been an exception, did not foresee that the rebels were moving toward independence. A statement of John Adams makes strange reading today. "We cannot in this country conceive," he wrote on October 4, 1775, months after Concord and Lexington, "that there are men in England so infatuated as seriously to suspect the Congress, or people here, of a wish to erect themselves into an independent state."[4]

But though the hope of reconciliation was still entertained in high quarters, the possibilities had gradually been undermined, not because they need have been, but because the currents of men's minds did not flow toward quiet readjustment. It was these currents of mind that underlay the outbreaks of violence, which in turn had led to further and even greater outbreaks in a self-renewing sequence. Had the exactions of the Stamp Act been answered otherwise than by the pursuit and persecution of stamp masters; had the protests been confined to passive resistance and civil disobedience, a sore and difficult situation would still have ensued, but it would have been susceptible to solution without leaving a legacy of torn feelings and a precedent of militancy. Even so, the Stamp Act might have been repealed, thus securing for the colonists what they most sought. And in that case, by following the example they themselves had set, they might have gained other ends in later confrontations; the lawlessness of the Boston Tea Party might have been avoided, along with all its bitter consequences, including the Boston Port Act and the various other coercive measures that went so far toward kindling a revolutionary situation. More than that—had there been no Tea Party and no Port Act nor any Coercive Acts at all, the pugnacity of farmers and townsmen in New England and elsewhere might not have been aroused; they might not have been goaded into military training and preparation, no new troops might have been poured into the colonies to increase resentments and the danger of clashes, and revolution and war might never have become more than remote possibilities.

Yet this does not mean that the colonies need have relinquished their objectives of complete self-rule and freedom from foreign tyranny. It only means that they might not have felt compelled to enforce their will at the cannon's mouth.

All prospect of a placid solution was destroyed, however, by the passions of mutinous mobs, whose leaders evidently did not perceive that the paths of riot led to revolution. Thus the colonies moved toward an end which, however beneficent its overall effects may appear, had been planned by few if any on either side of the Atlantic, was desired by few if any, and might eventually have been achieved without a collision that shook two continents and had mighty repercussions upon the far greater blast that exploded in France a few years later.

5. Conflagration in France

i. The Fall of the Bastille

The streets of Paris on the 13th of July 1789, were in a tumult. Barricades had been thrown up; the shops of gunsmiths had been stripped of weapons; a pushing, shouting rabble looted the grain supply of the Saint-Lazare monastery, set fire to tollgates, raided the King's armory, forced open the debtors' prison, and plundered the home of the chief of police. But this was a mere curtain-raiser to the drama of July 14, when an estimated multitude of 7 or 8 thousand seized some cannon and 32,000 muskets from the Hôtel des Invalides. "To the Bastille!" they yelled. "To the Bastille!"

Not that they seem to have had any clear idea of taking the ancient fortress or releasing its prisoners, who numbered only seven, though they did covet the powder known to be stored there. But the grim notorious prison, the symbol of long-smoldering wrongs and century-old sufferings, was a proper target for their hatred.

At first, however, they followed methods of peaceful negotiation rather than riot. The governor of the Bastille, the Marquis de Launay, received a people's deputation who sought surrender of the gunpowder and removal of the guns from the battlements. And while he apparently did not yield to all the demands, he did promise not to fire unless fired upon.

But his nerves, on that storm-stricken day, were evidently under severe strain. He had no reason to fear that the mob, which surrounded the building in a black mass, could cross the 75 feet of water in the moat and scale the 90-foot walls. But when some of the bolder intruders did climb the walls and cut the chain to the drawbridge, giving them access to the outer court though not to the fortress itself, de Launay showed signs of panic, forgot his promise, and ordered his men to fire. Several of the crowd fell dead; others retreated with cries of "Treason!"; those who were armed fired back; soon the Bastille's cannon were booming. And thus began a battle in an undeclared war, fought on a most unequal basis; only one was hit out of the Bastille's garrison of 95 pensioners and 30 Swiss guards, but the attackers left 98 dead on the field, and 73 were wounded. How then could they, before the day's end, take the seemingly impregnable stronghold?

The turning point came with the arrival of two detachments and five cannon of the Gardes Francaises, under command of an officer named Hulin. While the rebels shielded themselves behind whatever shelter they could find and aimed their cannon at the main gate, the distracted de Launay, despairing of being relieved, threatened to blow up the fortress. Dissuaded from this mad idea by the garrison, he did an about-face and lowered the central drawbridge under promise of safety for his men and himself—a fatal mistake for him and some of his followers. His enemies equalled him in bad faith; de Launay was dragged away to the Hôtel de Ville and slain; three of his officers and three of his men were likewise murdered, as was the provost of the merchants, Jacques de Flesselles. Then the mob, with the tang of victory on their tongues, trooped through the streets of Paris bearing the heads of the slain officials upon pikes. As for the Bastille itself—it was demolished, and its stones were scattered throughout France as souvenirs of an event whose savagery and brutality became transmuted into a legend of heroism and glory.

Thus ended an episode which, while not of major importance for any intrinsic accomplishments, is outstanding for what it signified. For it ushered in one of the great revolutions of history. Nothing in France or the Western world would ever be quite the same again.

To many who stared dazed and bewildered at the conflagration, it must have seemed that what they witnessed was a convulsion of nature. It must have been a little as when, in some long-settled countryside, startlingly the earth quakes, a volcano explodes, the skies take fire, smoke and steam and sulphur choke the air, streams of boiling lava seethe down over once-tranquil villages and plantations, and all who cannot save themselves by flight are overwhelmed.

Yet a volcano is a phenomenon of nature, and one that is beyond control. And what happened in the French Revolution was due not to any external force but to the strange, troubled currents within man's own being. This, however, may be why this type of disturbance is in some ways more complicated and harder to understand and scarcely less difficult to combat than the outburst of a Vesuvius or a Krakatoa.

ii. The Privileged and the Poor

A riot can be the sparkplug of revolution, yet many riots do not amount to revolution. What, then, is the mysterious force that converts a seemingly minor disturbance into a major eruption? The taking of a Bastille may offer some evidence.

We should not be deluded by the fact that a stormy mob surrounded the fortress, eager to break through its barricades. This was, indeed, indicative of deep popular unrest, but this in itself need not have opened the gates to revolution. Had the central authority been able to muster a capable resistance; had military units been on hand to scatter the crowd or at least to hold it in check; had the commandant of the Bastille not feared that the government would not relieve him and thus have been intimidated into surrender, the fortress and its garrison would not have capitulated, no officials would have been slain and no heads carried on pikes, the monarchy would have remained secure at least for the time, and the tempest about the Bastille would have been remembered as no more than the gale of a moment. The line of demarcation, the crucial boundary between riot and revolution, was passed when control slipped from the hands of the state to the hands of the mob.

But why was control permitted to slip from the state? Here a number of factors were at work, some of them psychological, including official irresolution, shortsightedness, and timidity. Other elements were the weakness of the state itself, the slowly accumulating ills that had been undermining it like termites burrowing in the dark, the deep and widespread popular resentment, and, perhaps not least, the disaffection of the army (which, on the eve of revolution, contained 35,000 officers including 1,171 generals as against 135,000 men whose loyalty in an emergency could not be guaranteed). It is an irony that troops had been concentrated about Paris, kindling popular fears of an attack. Had Louis XVI been able to count upon this force, he need not have dreaded the rabble that invested the Bastille.

But let a rabble once make inroads, let it realize its own strength, let it swallow the exhilarating drug of victory, let it provide an example and a legend, and above all let it show that the supposed rock-walls of the state are only paper ramparts—let all this happen, and revolution will not only be invited, revolution will have begun, as in France in that pervervid July of 1789. Yet this is only a partial explanation. No matter what the preliminaries, there could have been no conflagration had the fuel not been waiting and accessible. And the fuel was to be found in a variety of forces that affected French society from top to bottom. The aristocrats no less than the masses were involved, and, indeed, were to be of major importance in the opening stages.

The crisis had been slowly building up due to the recklessness, the improvidence, the gross incompetence of Louis XVI and Marie Antoinette and their profligate predecessor Louis XV. The monarchy was face to face with the workings of the old law that you cannot eat your cake and have it too; Versailles had been gulping down cake until none was left—and when it cried out for more and could not get it, the day of reckoning was at hand.

The situation, with privilege lounging on couches of rose petals while poverty and toil were taxed to the last bead of sweat, approached the unbelievable. Three hundred and fifty princes, dukes, marquises, and counts, immune from state levies, were drawing four and a half million livres a year from the treasury in return for nothing at all; a flock of some 15000 drones, consuming the wealth of the land, were supported in luxury at the court, whose extravagance is suggested by the fact that the month-old daughter of Louis XVI was served by no less than 80 attendants. The clergy, like the nobility, paid no taxes; army posts were multiplied for the benefit of titled sycophants; the costs of warfare, and particularly of aid to the Colonies in the American Revolution, had piled up a burden too great for the shoulders of the state. All the while, the government was living beyond its means; able and even outstanding officials like the economist Turgot and later the people's hope, Necker, were discharged when they pressed down too hard on the toes of privilege; and at the same time the public debt was mounting continually. During the reign of Louis XVI, it trebled, until the problems could no longer be hidden behind official smoke-screens. This led, as a measure of desperation, to the convening at Versailles on May 5, 1789, of the States General, which had not met within living memory, and which became transformed into the National Assembly, a major instrument of the Revolution, involving both the nobles and the Third Estate, or Commons.

But not only was the convocation of the States General like the flashing of a red danger signal in its acknowledgment of the financial crisis; it combined with other influences such as food scarcities and high prices to produce an incendiary situation, which was reflected by demonstrations in Paris in the days immediately before the fall of the Bastille, and was gravely aggravated after the Bastille was taken. Now long-slumbering evils joined with present complaints to blow the lid off the volcano.

iii.   Behind the Explosion

Behind the explosion we can see the convergence of a miscellany of such forces as have rarely come together at one time. First, in the cities and among the literate classes and the intellectuals, there were the ideas of the thinkers: Montesquieu (1689–1755), who, though not aiming at revolution, mercilessly revealed the evils gnawing at French society; Voltaire, who in 1764 wrote that "Everywhere the seeds are being sown of an inevitable revolution"; Encyclopedists such as Diderot and Condorcet, with their liberal outlook; and, above all, Rousseau, who spoke of a "century of revolution" at the same time as he opposed a bloody upheaval, and yet, by exalting the will of the people, evoked the tyranny of those who claimed to represent the people. These ideological seeds, supplemented by the practical demonstration of the American War of Independence, would produce a bristling outgrowth and give the Revolution some of its peculiar features. Yet they could have had little effect in a soil not already prepared.

That soil had been fertilized by various other converging forces. There was, as suggested above, the flabbiness, the gross incompetence of a government eaten away from within by ancient privilege. There was also, as we have noted, the financial crisis that forced the aristocracy and the clergy into action against the royal government and led to their alliance with the masses and the creation of a Constituent Assembly that defied the monarchy, as in the knife-edged challenge of Mirabeau: "We will not stir from our seats unless forced by bayonets." There was the fact that the middle classes, roused by the rebellious nobility, rallied to the call for action, and struck out against the favored groups. There was the discontent among city workers in response to unemployment and the high cost of living; for example, in early July 1789, the jobless artisans of Lyons rioted and burned toll-gates and tollhouses. And, not least important, there was the revolt among the peasantry.

Any one of these factors, taken alone, might have produced a dangerous, even a convulsive situation. But, in combination, they added up to much more than the sum of their parts, and blew up a storm-gale such as the world had not seen before.

Despite all the wrongs the peasants had suffered, and despite the fact that rural disturbances had seethed for more than half a year before the fall of the Bastille, one wonders whether the peasants would have been swept on to revolution had it not been for the distress signals that they saw all about them from other classes. In many ways, their situation had been improving. Their landed possessions had, in some districts, increased enormously; the dues they paid, while still onerous, had been shrunken in fact if not in theory by the decline in the value of money; the individual farmer might work his own patch of ground; compared with the peasantry of certain other European countries, their position was a favorable one. But for these very reasons, and perhaps not least because of the taste of freedom they had already enjoyed, they craved a fuller, more satisfying life. Such things as forced labor and the iniquitous tax on salt, which was levied on the commoner without regard to his actual consumption while clergy and the lords and officials bought salt at cost price, were like thorns driven into the flesh of the countrymen, who could not help knowing that, in the minds of their masters, they were much what peasants had always been—two-legged beasts of burden, to be driven for whatever was in them.

We moderns, in our society of ease and high wages, can hardly comprehend the misery of a French peasant under the old regime. It has been calculated by the French critic and historian Taine that, while a laborer on the prerevolutionary farms could buy 959 litres of grain with a year's wages, his descendant in the 19th century could purchase 1851 litres. His descendant, besides, was not taxed as he was, nor subjected to conscription to perform the unpaid roadwork of the *corvée;* nor had his way of life been overturned by the landowners, who exemplified enterprise and progress by cutting down the forests where the peasants had obtained their wood, and barring the sheep and cattle of the peasants from newly cultivated land. While rents and other prices were rising, some of the poorest country workers were obliged to pay for items such as wood which they had never had to buy of old. More and more, as the common land shrank beneath the claws of the great and powerful, the farm workers were crowded to the wall. Meanwhile, living in windowless hovels with the earth for floor, usually without shoes, often lacking even furniture, and sometimes tottering on the edge of famine, they had little to lose from any change, however revolutionary—little, that is, except their misery.

Even angrier, however, was the mood of their more fortunate kindred who possessed their own small strips of land. For these men felt still more severely the demands of the tax agent, who did not act by genteel means like notices in the mail, but might burst into a man's house at night, rousing him from bed, overturning the whole place, and threatening to drive him out unless he paid forthwith. Little wonder if, spurred on by such outrages, some of the farmers sold their holdings and drifted to the cities, while other emigrated, or became vagabonds, poachers, smugglers, or brigands. Little wonder if some of the villagers rose up en masse, broke into town halls, and plundered storehouses. Here, certainly, were the germs of a major convulsion. And when the microbes were scattered on the winds that began to roar throughout France, inevitably the countryside became infected, and the uprising became not merely a Parisian disturbance but the revolution of an entire people.

iv. The Peasant Demonstrations

Demonstrations in the French countryside had been erupting ever since December 1788, when consumers had struck out against granaries, millers, and the wagon trains of wheat. From this violent beginning the attacks expanded to include threats to the châteaux and flare-ups against taxes and feudal dues as well as against the hunting and game laws. These outbreaks were encouraged, of course, by the example of the revolutionaries at Paris—rebellion enjoys company. And yet the urban object-lesson would have meant little had it not confirmed preexisting inclinations, old half-muffled rages, and the long-suppressed impulse to hit back at the oppressor.

Following the stirring news of July 14, 1789, many country districts began to fume and crackle with one of the strangest outbursts ever recorded. The "Great Fear" it has been called, and fear was indeed its keynote—fear that amounted to terror, and terror that flew on wings of madness. Dread of a "counter-revolutionary plot" evidently underlay the movement, along with rumors that the "brigands" were coming—whoever they were, for no one seems to have known. Hysteria swept many of the villages. At the small farming community of Creil, according to the reminiscences of a woman who endured the ordeal as a child, the tocsin was rung, and the houses were filled with stones to be hurled at the expected enemy. Women boiled oil or collected ashes to throw into the eyes of the intruders; bands of men rushed about with hoes, pitchforks, and scythes, looking for the foes who had often been reported but somehow were never found. Children, with their mothers, took flight; girls were barricaded in attics, along with food to last for days.

Here if ever, was insanity. And it was insanity that could not pass without leaving tremors behind it. Even today we cannot be sure how the rumors originated, nor whether they had been meant to arouse revolutionary passions, although if there had been an organization it must have been widespread as well as secret, since the disturbances radiated from no less than six or eight sources. In any event, the countryside had been violently stirred up, the emotions of the men had been excited; they had taken up arms with the intention of using them, and having been inflamed against a phantom enemy, they were in a mood to strike against the real enemy they had so long resented. Apparently provoked by deliberate fomenters of rebellion, some of whom bore orders falsely ascribed to the King, peasants throughout the country moved against the *seigneurs*. Châteaux were torn down or given to the torch, while the manor-rolls that recorded the feudal obligations were burned, sometimes by agitators who imagined that they were carrying out the royal wishes. On the whole, however, the outbreaks were not bloodthirsty; what the peasants sought, in most cases, was not the life of the *seigneur* but the end of his feudal power.

They had moved at the strategic moment. So long as the old regime was still perched on its studded seats, the uprising might have accomplished no more than the peasant revolts of earlier centuries. But now that a revolutionary government had seized power, the rumblings from the countryside could not be ignored, particularly in a closely knit country like France, where every wind that swept the provinces stirred the air of the capital.

Providentially, the peasants found allies among the liberal nobles at the National Assembly. The Vicomte de Noailles, who had seen service in America, called for abolition of the feudal system. The Duc d'Aiguillon asked the aristocrats voluntarily to renounce their feudal revenues. And such pleas, on the night of August 4, led to the surrender of privileges by dozens of deputies; at the same time, the Assembly provided that peasants, by specific payments, might buy their freedom from certain of the old feudal dues (as it happened, the landlords would never be paid by the militant farmers, and the Convention, in July 1793, would abrogate the debt).

Meanwhile, on the memorable night of August 4, 1789, other exactions were abolished, including ecclesiastical tithes and the forced labor of the *corvée*. Equality of punishment, the equal rights of all to public office, and freedom of worship, were among the other measures voted. Thus the final decree of the session, which lasted until August 11, was justified in its declaration that "The National Assembly destroys the feudal regime in its entirety."

But the National Assembly did not deserve the full credit for destroying the feudal regime. That honor was shared by the people who had risen against the ancient order, and not least by the disgruntled and rebellious peasants.

v.   The March of the Market Women

The tempest at the Bastille was but the greatest of a series of disturbances in Paris and the surrounding areas throughout the summer and early fall of 1789. Food had been scarce not because of a poor harvest (the harvest had actually been good) but because a protracted drought had prevented the millers from making flour. For the same reason, there were speculations in food prices. Even though the cost of bread was twice reduced following the events of July 14, the shortages led to bread riots in which a municipal officer and a baker were killed by the mob and other persons were threatened. Women along with men participated in the disturbances, particularly after mid-September; the market women of Paris were central actors on October 5 in one of the crucial outbreaks.

This incident flamed up after Louis XVI, in a show of resistance to the August decrees of the Assembly, ordered the Flanders regiment to Versailles. A banquet to welcome the new arrivals was given by the royal lifeguards, who, toasting the queen, and singing, "O Richard, o mon roi," made a noisy demonstration of loyalty to the monarchy. This prompted flamboyant reports in the "patriot press," which claimed that the national cockade had been trampled upon; exaggerated stories told of the luxuriance of the affair in contrast to the deprivation of the people; and cries were sounded for "revenge," while rumors circulated the alarm of an impending *coup d'etat*. The whole provided a perfect example of a crisis whipped up by propaganda and high-flown emotionalism.

But what is most important is the episode that followed. It has been called "the march of the women," yet men in women's clothes are said to have participated, and the demonstration was headed by a man, Stanislaus Maillard, a sheriff's officer who had been conspicuous in the taking of the Bastille. That the stroke was spontaneous is highly questionable; it bore the evidences of planning by radical journalists and agitators, and all that we know tends to support the views of the Commune of Paris that the insurrection "was premeditated." In any case, there had been a call by Camille Desmoulins on October 4 to bring the King from Versailles to Paris, and the outbreak seems to have been at least in part a response to this appeal.

On the morning of Monday, October 5, women from the Fauberg St. Antoine and from the central markets broke into the Hôtel de Ville at Paris. "We want bread!" they yelled. "We want bread!" But they also wanted arms, of which they seized all that they could find. A strange procession, with pitchforks, pistols, and a pair of cannon, set off in two columns for Versailles in defiance of a steady rain. "Let us fetch the baker, the baker's wife, and the little baker's lad!" they chanted. Two hours later, they were followed by 20,000 National Guardsmen, reluctantly led by Lafayette; upon being joined by a crowd of civilians bearing muskets, pikes, and clubs, they made a formidable array, a veritable insurrectionary army. To meet the challenge, what was the King to do?

It is easy to speculate what some other king might have done. Perhaps he would have fled, and carried on the business of state from some safer retreat than Versailles. Or perhaps he would have called together whatever armed forces were available, bolstered their wavering loyalty by a rousing speech, and ridden forth in full uniform to meet and defy and possibly overawe the intruders. Perhaps, again, he would have found ways to conciliate the opposition, and would still have sat as king, even though in a limited monarchy somewhat like that of England. Weak, irresolute, and impercipient Louis XVI, however, made none of these choices. What he actually did was one of the worst things of all—nothing.

Drenched to the skin by the persistent rain, the tired and hungry women reached Versailles in midafternoon after a trek of more than four hours. "Long live the King!" they cried. "We want bread!" Munching at whatever crusts could be found for them, they pushed their way among the men of the Flanders regiment, urging desertion; they surged into the Assembly and asked to see the King, who had been recalled from his favorite pastime of hunting. Led by a deputation to the palace, they interviewed the faint-willed monarch, who promised everything they asked, including the dispatch of food to Paris, endorsement of the democratic Declaration of Rights, and approval of the Assembly and its abolition of the feudal system. One can imagine his relief when the deputation finally left. Perhaps he could still have saved himself—saved himself, at least, from the executioner's blade and the long series of preceding humiliations—had he taken the advice that was urged upon him to leave with his family and transfer the center of government to Rouen. But, as usual, he vacillated—and, by the next morning, the opportunity was gone.

At about six A.M. on October 6 a serious new outbreak exploded. In some unexplained way, one of the palace approaches had been left open, admitting the mob. In vain they were challenged by the King's bodyguard; during the ensuing affray, two men were killed. And then the rabble, pouring up the stairs, along the hallways, and into the rooms, slew a soldier who stood in their way, frightened the half-dressed Queen into running for refuge to the King's apartments, and might have slaughtered the remaining members of the bodyguard except for the timely arrival of Lafayette and his men. "To Paris!" the women shouted. "Bring the King to Paris!"

And to Paris the King went—a captive of the people. As the long procession made its way out of Versailles, the carriage bearing Louis and Marie Antoinette was surrounded not only by the throngs of women but by National Guardsmen, pike-wielding workers, and Swiss Guards, while some of the women bestrode the field guns or went singing and dancing along the way. High over them on pikes were borne the heads of two slain soldiers.

vi. The Rabble and the King

The march of the women on Versailles, and the demonstrations that expelled the King and Queen to the palace of the Tuileries at Paris, had driven another nail into the coffin of the monarchy. Now that Louis XVI was no longer a free agent but was confined at the people's will, the road lay open to his deposition and death. Even so, he might have retained his life and perhaps some remnants of his pride and place except for a series of events in which he himself was implicated. Not the least of these was the flight to Varennes in June 1791, when he and his family stole away by night in an effort to flee the country, but were apprehended near the border and brought back to Paris under heavy guard after five days, while menacing crowds swarmed about their coach and went so far as to murder a nobleman who came to greet the monarch. The violence of these incidents was indicative of the abyss into which French royalty had fallen. It is generally held that the attempted escape, and the unhappy light in which the whole sorry affair showed the King, signified the impending overturn of the monarchy.

Nevertheless, some semblance of Louis's authority did linger for a time, as in the declaration on April 20, 1792, of war against Austria—a conflict in which Austria was promptly joined by Prussia, and which began disastrously for France. Likewise, Louis and Marie Antoinette, and especially the latter, were connected with conspiracies to summon foreign powers against the revolutionary government—and the very suspicion of such treason, even before anything had been proved, deepened the shadows about their reign.

Thus the way was shown to further demonstrations, wherein Parisians moved an alarming distance from their old reverence for the sovereign. One of the outbursts occurred on June 20, 1792, beginning with the march of sword-swinging and pike-bearing citizens, who, attended by artillerymen with cannon and by crowds of onlookers, had gathered in defiance of an official prohibition. Toward noon an estimated 8000 advanced upon the Assembly, which consented to let the people pass through the Chamber after hearing a customs clerk declaim in a long speech that "The will of twenty-five million men must not be subject of that of one man." One can picture the motley throng of the intruders—variously clad, diversely armed, some of the men drunken, some singing and dancing, some jeering and threatening, while above them rose their standards—a pair of torn trousers on a pole, and a pike that bore a calf's heart, and the explanation, "The heart of an aristocrat." By that inrush of the masses into premises previously sacrosanct, the prestige of the Assembly was seriously impaired.

At about four in the afternoon, when the mob was ready to disband, something put it into the leaders' heads to visit the King at the Tuileries. Not that there was any reason for a visit, except possibly that the rebels wished to intimidate the monarch. In any case, who can argue with a rabble? Off to the Tuileries the thousands trooped, where an unbolted door, admitting them, played the part of fate. While the National Guards stood by without resisting, the mob battered down the inner doors, and, carrying a cannon, streamed upstairs into a great hall, where they found the King and a few of his attendants. With an immense clamor, they shouted their conditions: he must reinstate three recently discharged ministers, sign two of the Assembly decrees which he had vetoed, and put an end to the veto power. To use the verbiage of a later day, the demands were non-negotiable. "We shall not go away," the dissidents threatened, "until you sign the decrees!"

Denounced as a traitor and addressed as mere everyday "Monsieur" instead of "Sire" by a butcher named Legendre, the King was forced to listen for two hours to the railing crowd as it pushed its way back and forth amid the fumes of the hall, while he retained his composure and told the citizens that he would do what the Constitution required, but that they too must obey the law. Fortunately for him, his visitors were not blood-bent; fortunately, also, he remained calm enough not to add heat to their emotions. The denouement was comical, even clownish. Louis received from a woman a flower-decked sword and a tricolor cockade, which he waved, exclaiming, "Vive la nation!" From others he took a red cap, and, from still others, an offering of wine; and, to loud applause, he uttered a toast to the people of Paris and of France. "Long live the King! Long live liberty!" the invaders shouted.

But while the King emerged physically unscathed, his escape was only momentary, as was suggested when a member of the crowd roared a threat that he would be dethroned should he not yield. Actually, the demonstration of June 20 was but the prelude to a costlier uprising a little more than a month and a half later.

vii. The Monarchy Collapses

It was the outbreak of August 10, 1792, that brought down the rickety monarchy. While the regime of Louis XVI was probably doomed in any case, the immediate causes of the August disturbance were varied, and not least was the pressure upon the French threatened by the Duke of Brunswick, the Austro-Prussian commander-in-chief in the newly declared war. As frequently happens with exponents of force and intimidation, he produced exactly the reverse of the desired effect when on July 25 he promised Draconian penalties, including destruction of all cities that stood out against him, punishment as rebels of all arms-carrying National Guardsmen, eternal vengeance for the "slightest outrage" to the royal family, and the clamping down upon Paris of "complete military subjection and martial law."

This blustering proclamation, which took no account of the psychological processes of the enemy, was nothing less than a demand for unconditional surrender, and so left the revolutionaries no halfway goal to aim for, no possibility of compromise. Thenceforth they must see the King's very existence as a threat to themselves. The reaction against Louis, consequently, was sharp and not long delayed. The surprising fact, indeed, is that he still survived for a while; had the insurgents at that time been as ruthless as soon afterwards under the Terror, the entire royal family might suddenly have dropped out of history, as did the Romanoffs in 20th-century Russia. What Louis actually obtained, however, was a reprieve and not a pardon.

Confusions and agitations meanwhile had been shaking the Assembly; some members wished to overthrow the King, though many were opposed. But the extremists slowly made headway. At two in the morning of August 10, some of the sectional representatives, guarded by workers armed with pikes, pushed themselves in the people's name into the Hôtel de Ville. Other agitators forced their way into the Municipal Council; Mandat, head of the National Guards, was shot to death after questioning by the Council and after radicals had usurped power in the body. At the same time, a crowd composed of miscellaneous elements, including sansculottes or revolutionaries of the poorer class, began action against the King.

The Tuileries Palace was now protected by 950 Swiss Guards, 16 battalions of National Guards, and around 200 richly clad noblemen whose pomposity chilled any inclination to fight on the part of the National Guardsmen. At about seven in the morning, when the first of the insurrectionists began pounding at the doors, it was not the King but the Queen who urged a fight to the finish. After a session with his confessor, Louis seems to have concluded that further bloodshed would be useless. What, then, could he do? He would seek safety in the Assembly. And so he and his family, defended by Swiss and National Guards, managed to make their way through the muttering, ugly crowd to the projected refuge. "I have come to prevent a great crime," he told the Assembly. He could not have known, nor is it likely that he would have cared had he known, of the scorn his surrender had aroused in an obscure artillery lieutenant, who happened to be looking on amid the crowd, and whose name was Napoleon Bonaparte.

Meanwhile riot was spreading. In a guardhouse, some prisoners were slaughtered by an insurgent mob led by a female terrorist Théroigne de Mérincourt; at the Tuileries, the Swiss Guard fired upon the closely packed throngs, and for several hours shots were exchanged in a guerrilla war. Later, mounted men-at-arms and National Guards, instead of defending the palace, joined the swelling masses of rebels. The climax came with an order from the King to the Swiss Guards to cease fire and return to their barracks. Now, in a fury, the mob swept into the palace, raiding, burning, and dealing death to the resisting Swiss, to aristocrats, to royalist suspects, and even, it is said, to some unoffending porters who had the misfortune to be known in the jargon of the day as "suisses." A short while later still others, who had sought refuge in the Assembly or who had been arrested, were slain by the rabble.

Although he had saved his life for the moment, this for all practical purposes was the end of Louis XVI. True, the Assembly still did not vote explicitly to dethrone him, but it declared his functions to be suspended—thenceforth he and his family were "hostages." Six weeks later, a new National Assembly completed the process by dethroning him and proclaiming a republic. Had he been endowed with prescience as he and his family forced their way out of the Tuileries on that crucial August 10, he might have heard the thud of the guillotine rising above the shrieks and howls of the mob.

viii. The Final Accounting

A country riddled with insurrections is a country that is sick, and from the disease all manner of aberrations can spring. In the French Revolution, the aberrations tended to be extreme, and included not only the Terror and the regicides but the foreign wars, military conscription with the portentous precedent it established for Europe and the world, and the rise of a military dictator who would lead the nation through some of the most sanguinary wars ever fought until that time—wars which would not end until 1815. For better or worse, the results of 1789 are with us yet; the world today is much different than it would be if armed protesters had never risen against the government of Louis XVI.

The enormous benefits of the Revolution cannot be denied— liberal reforms, the shattering of chains, the demolition of old walls, old corrupt practices, old favoritism, old religious discrimination; the encouragement of free thought, free speech, and democratic institutions. As against these badly needed gains we must place the radical stimulation of those two great banes of the modern world, nationalism and militarism, which, by threatening the very race of man, may prove that the Revolution, for all its gifts to the world, has cost far more than even the most magnificent contribution could be worth.

To say this is to emphasize the fact that violent dissent, at least when widespread and long-continued, tends to follow tracks that not even the wisest can foretell. At the same time, we are bound to ask whether the main benefits might not have been achieved by peaceful and nonviolent processes, without the monstrous penalties inflicted by the Revolution on successive generations. Remember that the neighboring country of England had also been subject to the tyranny of the great lords and of royalty, yet had emerged into the light of democracy; liberalizing influences already in operation in France gave reason to suppose that in 1789 and subsequent years she would have followed a road similar to the English had the representatives of the old regime been less unyielding, had they not clung to feudal dues, and had they accepted a limited monarchy in which popular rights were represented as in the British House of Commons.

The obtuseness and blind stubbornness of the ruling classes, however, do not by themselves explain the Revolution; ruling classes in other countries have been equally stubborn, equally bemused by delusions of grandeur, and equally or more oppressive without bringing down the palace walls about their own heads. What, then, did produce the convulsion?

We have seen the Revolution developing and drawing strength

from scattered insurrections, as when the Bastille was taken, and
when the women marched on Versailles. We have also noted that,
for generations, the soil of revolution had been fertilized by
abuses against the common man, who was often treated as less
than a man; but we have observed that conditions, while still
bad, were in some ways improving. We have taken account of
the philosophical doctrines of the century preceding the outbreak—doctrines of liberalism and of freedom that blew through
France like invigorating gusts; and we have seen how the American Revolution provided an example of the application of those
doctrines in practice. We have glanced at the part played by
parasitism and privilege in undermining political institutions
and producing the grave financial crisis. We have remarked that
a central difficulty lay in the drains of past wars and especially
the American Revolution, which France had supported beyond
her means; and we have identified another main source of the
trouble in the weak and impercipient leadership of Louis XV
and Louis XVI. We have also noted the convergence of forces
that led to simultaneous urban and rural rebellions including
an uprising of the Parisian aristocrats and bourgeoisie.

These were all among the factors that turned scattered insurrections into a major outbreak; but these do not fully explain
the tumults of 1789. There were also other ingredients, some of
them elusive and difficult to assess. One was the element of planning, which was to be observed in the deliberations of the Assembly, and, as we have seen, appears to have had a covert part
in the women's march on Versailles and in the Great Fear that
shook the countryside. And planning, in its turn, was linked with
organization, as among the radicals of the Jacobin Club, while
another molder of events, undoubtedly, was that great arbiter
of so many affairs, chance.

But it seems to me that, beyond all these influences and perhaps dominating them, there was one great continuous force—
the subtle, intangible lever of men's psychological reactions. It
was this that, producing a deep and resolute and at times an
angry opposition to the old regime, had created a state of mind
favorable to revolution. This state of mind, blown upon by liberal philosophies, inflamed by ancient hatreds and resentments,
and exasperated by current miseries, might have endured for
generations, as indeed it did endure, without producing an eruption. But as soon as it was fortified by the spur of an inspiring
example, and by the precedent of militant flare-ups and especially

successful flare-ups, all the old inhibitions were whisked aside and the lid was lifted off long-hidden furies. Now the provocative taste of freedom on the common man's palate, the exhilaration of new ideas, and the excitation of emotions by incendiary groups such as the Jacobins and their offshoots the Girondins, resulted in increasing riots and demonstrations in the face of the monarchy's obvious inability to resist. And once the fuel had been piled up, an organized handful of flame-scattering leaders was enough to start a chain reaction that set fire to the multitude, while the revolution blazed on from its comparatively mild opening to an ever fiercer heat and glare, sporadic small upheavals became merged in one immense convulsion, and the country and indeed all Europe was shaken by an explosion that no one had fully foreseen, few desired in the form in which it occurred, and none was able to check or contain.

6. The Black Revolution in Haiti

i. Toussaint L'Ouverture

You might not have been impressed had you seen him driving the coach of M. Bayon de Libertad along one of the back roads of Haiti in the 1780s. He was a small Negro, not more than five feet two in height, with a triangular face and vivid close-set eyes, thick lips, uptilted flat nose, sharp white teeth, a long pointed chin, and a look that has been described as one of sardonic cruelty on a face crowned by a yellow handkerchief woven about his head as a sort of turban. Yet here was a man who was to make Negro history.

For this was Toussaint L'Ouverture (the last name was an assumed one, taken after someone remarked that he "opened" things up). He had been born in slavery (evidently in 1744), but in so far as that spirit-wounding institution can press down lightly on any man, he had been one of the less unfortunate; the manager of his plantation was one of the most enlightened of his kind, and went so far as to hold the unorthodox view that slaves should not be denied an education. Thus, unlike most Negroes, Toussaint had an acquaintance with books. Nevertheless, during the years when he stooped in the labor of the fields or in the exhausting grind of the sugar-mills, seeing the lash snap out at the backs of fellow slaves, resentment brooded beneath his sorrowful eyes. Then, in 1777, at the age of 33 or 34, he was given his virtual freedom, although theoretically he was still the property of his old master, in whose service he remained—a good and apparently a tractable coachman, who enjoyed exceptional trust and privileges and was commended by the whites for his loyalty.

Deep inside him, however, unhealing wounds festered. In 1758, as a teen-aged boy, he had witnessed an incident that did incalculable violence to his inner self: Macandal, a notorious black rebel, had been captured after running away from his master, fighting against the landowners for 18 years, and being accused of poisoning a number of whites, including entire families. His captors, wishing to make an example of him, sentenced him to the excruciating torture of being burned alive; and the memory of that scarifying event, including the jests and raillery of the white men as the victim writhed in the flames and agonizingly struggled to escape, was never to be erased from Toussaint's mind. Within him were planted seeds of rebellion that were not to sprout for many years. "Every day," he wrote to the French Directory in 1797, "I raised up my hands to God to implore him to come to the aid of my brethren."

But he was discreet enough to keep his feelings secret, though his anger was fed by the daily sight of his fellow blacks laboring like cowed dogs beneath the whip. He could not have failed to notice the contrast between the luxury and display of the well-to-do whites and the abasement of the Negroes in his native Saint Domingue; and word surely reached him of the execrable cruelties, representing sadism at its most debased, which some of the masters practiced upon offending and even unoffending slaves. Other writers are in agreement with Hilliard d'Auberteuil, whose book on Santo Domingo was published in 1776:

> Negroes die daily in chains and under the lash. They are beaten, strangled, burned to death without any legal formality. Every act of cruelty against them remains unpunished.[1]

Although the Negroes were naturally prolific, the treatment they received was such that their birth rate declined by an annual average of $2\frac{1}{2}$ percent—which meant that in time they would have followed the Indians of the islands into extinction had their numbers not been augmented by fresh imports. Their appalling death rate (which, doubtless not without considerable exaggeration, has been computed as high as 11 percent a year) proceeded not only from cruelty for its own sake but from a commercialism which, like that of practical old Cato in ancient Rome, made the landowner consider it cheaper to work his slaves to death than to prolong their lives by treating them humanely.

None of this, of course, could have been unknown to Toussaint. Had he lived in an earlier period, he might have passed his days futilely cursing and muttering in secret. But in the late

18th century, after the unspeakable barbarities inflicted upon the slaves for 300 years, new currents were stirring in the world.

Those currents had been created first of all by the American Revolution, and even more decisively by the greater outburst in France; the Negroes had learned of these from the masters themselves, who, in their disdain for the slaves, did not hesitate to speak in their presence of the exciting events abroad. Thus a fiery message had been flashed to the lowly and abused: that man might strike out in defense of freedom; that tyranny might be overthrown; that the downtrodden, no longer treated like bricks or stones, might rise to the seats of the mighty. To the oppressed Negroes of Saint Domingue, as to freedom-loving men throughout the world, the meaning was clear. Hence rebellion smoldered and crackled, particularly after 1789.

Yet the situation was complex and confused, and was complicated by racial lines within racial lines. The various part-breeds —mulattoes and others of differing degrees of white blood—held themselves aloof from their hundred-percent colored relations, and constituted in effect a distinct caste or a series of castes, overshadowed by the whites but feeling superior to the full blacks. The whites, on their side, accepted this self-appraisal of the mulattoes over those of wholly black descent, and in fact most part-breeds enjoyed relative favor; they were not treated as actual slaves, and were even educated and protected by their white fathers, or at the worst were set free upon reaching the age of 24. Even so, they had militant claims to press, most of all after 1789, although they still tended to act with an aristocratic aloofness from the mere slave. This was notably the case in the revolt of Vincent Ogé, which erupted in 1790.

ii. Ogé, Boukmann, and Jean Francois

Ogé, a young quadroon, appears to have been a man of culture and intelligence. His wealthy father had sent him to Paris to be educated; subsequently, following the outbreak of the Revolution, the freed slaves of his native island had chosen him to present their claims before the French Assembly. Thanks to the efforts of a group with which he had associated himself (the Society of the Friends of the Blacks, founded in 1778), the French Assembly, in March 1790, passed two decrees recognizing equal political rights for the ex-slaves. Nothing was said, however, about the emancipation of those who remained in subjection, and whose interests continued to be opposed by the great landowners. Even in regard to the freedmen, it was found that it was one thing to pass decrees, and quite another to get them obeyed. Accordingly, in October 1790, Ogé returned to the New World, and went before the Colonial Assembly at Cap Francais with an appeal for recognition of full equality for mulattoes as decreed by the French legislators. But he was met, as he might have expected, by a flat rebuff—equality for men of African blood was not to be considered. Angrily he charged that the resistance of the Assembly to the French decrees was rebellion, but all that he accomplished was to enrage the President of the Assembly, who ordered him thrown from the building. Doubtless the official did not realize that he was setting off the trigger to a pile of explosives.

The methods of the forum having ingloriously failed, the freedmen decided that their only alternative was violence. Still holding himself apart from the hundred-percent Negroes despite the warning of a more liberal friend that cooperation of all the blacks was essential, Ogé led about 200 armed part-breeds, who presented an ultimatum to the colonial Assembly—they must assent to the decrees of the French National Assembly, and assent at once!

Unfortunately, Ogé had overestimated the power of his aroused minority. However just his case, he was but a pygmy challenging a colossus; the colonial legislators, gathering together about 1500 men along with artillery, defeated the rebels in a few days, and exacted a terrible retribution. Thirteen were condemned to the galleys by a court of the landowners, 21 were sentenced to be hanged, and Ogé (who wept on hearing the judgment) was doomed with his chief collaborator to be broken on the wheel. The frightful scene of the public execution, when the screaming rebel leader could not endure the bone-crushing torture, must have branded itself upon the mind of a nonparticipant, Toussaint L'Ouverture, whether or not he was physically present. And thus he may have been driven another step toward his own better-prepared uprising.

Still more profoundly, he may have been inflamed by the revolt of Boukmann, an ill-famed former slave who had killed his master, and had lived ever since in hiding in caves and among the thick bushes of the mountainsides, leading bands of looters, incendiaries, and murderers in strokes that spread terror across the land. With his grim, twisted face, he had gained the reputation among his fellow Negroes of being a great magician. Although several factory strikes which he had inspired among the slaves had won nothing except dire reprisals, the idea of a general rebellion was in his mind.

And this rebellion was fanned into reality on an August night of 1791, when, goaded by a refusal of the landowners to grant the slaves the extra day a week they desired to cultivate their own patches of earth, he held a mass meeting of the Negroes in a forest hideout under circumstances of weird color, pageantry, and melodrama. It was a night of rain and wind, when the lightning flashed in scintillating zigzags, the thunder crashed, and huge trees were blown about and uprooted. In the shelter of a great rock an immense fire, fed with resin, was burning; and behind the fire was a leaf-crowned altar, against which Boukmann stood in the palpitating light, dressed in a red sacrificial robe, and wielding a long sword. Chanting an appeal for aid from the hidden powers of heaven, he played upon the superstitious feelings of the crowd, which were further provoked by the ensuing ceremonies. These, if the reports are to be believed, included the successive sacrifices of a gazelle, a pig, and a goat, and led on to the death of a naked black virgin, whose song and dance wove a hypnotic spell, until snapped short by the effects of the poison she had been made to swallow. Then Boukmann knelt and uttered a prayer: "God God . . . protect and save us from what the white men do to us. Good God, the white men do crimes but we do not. God God, give us vengeance, guide our arms, give us help. . . . Good God, grant us that freedom which speaks to all men!"[2]

It has been reported but is not positively known that Toussaint was among the hysterical hundreds, who, weeping and crying, attended the meeting; in any case, the influence of the gathering did lie heavy upon him. Without doubt, he was one of the most interested witnesses of the ensuing revolt, even though, still holding his privileged position while biding his time, he had the discretion to remain aloof.

But such was the rush of events that his own hour to strike could not be far off. On the night of August 22, frenzy like the blast of judgment day burst forth. Led by Boukmann, a swarm of Negroes burst over the countryside, intoning their barbarous songs while the night sparkled and glowed with the red of burning sugar plantations, the mansions of the great went up in flames, and the crazed mob spared no man, woman, or child. A French writer, whose words I translate below, has described the outbreak:

> At this time, more than a hundred thousand Negroes were in revolt in a single district of the North; these bands, organized for massacre and arson, had no weapons except torches, sticks, knives and other sharp tools, some sabres, and some guns pillaged from the devastated houses; but they had a weapon more powerful than all the others, the fury to destroy.[3]

According to an unlikely-sounding story, the insurrection was hatched by the French officials, in the effort to warn any independence-seeking colonists that they faced the peril of a slave revolt if they detached themselves from the mother country; but unhappily the blacks, having gotten the idea of rising, were moved to a delirium of looting, arson, raping, and murder in no way envisioned by the original plotters. However this may have been, it is certain that the rebellion actually accomplished little except in killing, in spreading terror and havoc, and in ruining the local economy. Reinforced by troops from France, the whites were able to defeat the revolutionaries and to slay Boukmann, whose head was displayed on a stake; but the revolt went on under another runaway slave, Jean Francois, who possessed an imposing physique, great daring and courage, exceptional cruelty, a pronounced taste for medals, silken gauds, and embroidery, and little military ability. He and his lieutenants Georges Baissou and Jeannot, the former a drunkard and the latter a murderer, carried on the campaign and waged guerrilla war against the whites. But with these enemies the mulattoes eventually reached an agreement that led to the betrayal and deportation of some of their black allies, the "Switzers," who were placed on a pontoon at night and cast into the sea after being stabbed.

Toussaint meanwhile, still watching from the sidelines, viewed these events with evident bitterness, as was shown when, six years later, he wrote in self-defense to the French Secretary of Navies and Colonies:

> The white men, fearing universal freedom, sought to separate the mulattoes from the Negroes. . . . The mulattoes, having achieved their aim, and afraid of freedom for the Negroes . . . cut themselves off from their comrades-at-arms and companions in distress . . . and allied themselves with the white men to trample the Negroes down. . . .[4]

iii. The Emergence of Black Leadership

Now the turning point had come for Toussaint. He had held off long, but not because he had not contemplated action. With an almost mystical sense of destiny, he remembered the words of the Abbé Raynal predicting the coming of a black Spartacus: "Where is the great man to be found? . . . He will appear, we cannot doubt it; he will show himself to raise the sacred standard of Liberty and to gather round him his companions in misfortune. More impetuous than the mountain torrents, they will leave behind them on all sides the ineffaceable signs of their just resentment."[5]

In the course of time, if not from the beginning, Toussaint apparently came to identify himself with that "great man." There is a story, though its truth is naturally a matter of conjecture, that one night Toussaint had a vision: he saw a maiden riding toward him on a crimson cloud, while invisible trumpets rang out and the damsel informed him, "You are the Negro Spartacus whom the Abbé Raynal foretold!" Even if some such dream did occur, one need not interpret it as anything more mysterious than the vivid embodiment of the dreamer's own thoughts, which, built up through the years, were impelling him to strike out at the whites.

In any event, a time did come when Toussaint, already middle-aged, abandoned forever the privileged, sheltered life he had led as a coachman of Bayon de Libertad, and joined the insurgents under Francois and Baissou. Unlike certain other black rebels—notably Nat Turner in his Virginian uprising of 1831—Toussaint did not turn upon his former master, but, on the contrary, saw that the Libertad family made their way to safety. Then, in his alliance with Francois, he found himself brushing shoulders with a great miscellany of Negroes of various types, sprung of a multiplicity of stocks in the Congo, Dahomy, Libya, and widely scattered other parts of Africa. Almost instinctively these men began turning to him as their leader, though at first he was much impeded by the need to collaborate with inferior commanders. But by 1791 he had emerged at the head of the Negroes.

Inconsistently, deserting France for a while, he found it necessary to work with the Spaniards, even though they, in their bitter opposition to the principles of the French Revolution, were foes of the very liberty for which Toussaint was fighting. From the Spaniards he received his commission as a general; then, on

May 6, 1794, he turned upon them treacherously and destroyed many in a merciless slaughter. Now he cooperated with the French, and on August 17, 1796, the Directory confirmed his appointment as general of a division. Thenceforth, for ten years, he stirred up insurrection by going to the plantations, notifying the workers that they were freed, and preaching their escape under his banner. During the same ten years, he led his poorly armed, scantily equipped army through the Haitian mountains and jungles, fighting by turns not only the Spaniards but the French, the British, and the mulattoes, while living on the country, until he had come to dominate French Haiti and Spanish Santo Domingo.

Later, like so many successful military commanders, he set himself up as a dictator. Strangely, he abolished slavery under a constitution that made the farm laborer virtually a serf, while his recommendation for an increase in the island's labor force sounded curiously like a call for an extension of the slave traffic. In the end he clashed with Napoleon, who sent 54 ships and 23,000 men to put an end to his power—this was accomplished only after the French had been hard pressed not merely by Toussaint's army but by yellow fever, and after the black leader had been captured by treachery and carried away to die in an Alpine prison.

Through all his operations, Toussaint's avowed principle had been the right of the Negroes to rule themselves. His feeling for his abused kindred cries out in his complaint, "It is always the blacks who suffer the most," and likewise in one of his proclamations:

> O you Africans, my brothers! you who have cost me so many fatigues, so much labour, so much worry, you whose liberty is sealed with more than half of your own blood![6]

Because these brethren of his had cost him "so many fatigues, so much labour, so much worry," Toussaint won the confidence of the downtrodden thousands, with the result that "among a people ignorant, starving, badgered, and nervous, his word by 1796 was law—the only person in the North whom they could be depended upon to obey."[7]

This is not to say that, because Toussaint's power was rooted in the support of the black masses, he was more scrupulous than most great popular leaders in the pursuit of his objectives. As one of his biographers puts it,

His whole adventure was a mixture of frankness and deceit, cruelty and kindness, temerity and prudence. Dedicated entirely to his dream of redeeming the Negroes, he paid no heed to the propriety of the means he employed: even crime seemed to him legitimate when it was for this purpose.[8]

iv. Aftermath

In leading the way to the independence of Haiti, Toussaint not only proved himself to be one of the most remarkable of the Latin American liberators, but provided an example for later emancipators operating on a wider stage. Yet the unhappy subsequent history of the island of Hispaniola forces one to ask: Was the country in his day ready for independence? And just what advantages in the long run had the various uprisings brought to the oppressed people?

Let us glance at the record in swiftest résumé. Toussaint was followed in power by General Jean Jacques Dessalines, an illiterate middle-aged ex-slave, who on January 1, 1804, celebrated the island's delivery from European shackles, yet promptly clamped down shackles of his own after ordering the slaughter of most of the island's remaining whites. The peasants, even as they rejoiced at their escape from French domination, were forced by the new ruler (whom they knew as "Emperor Jacques I") to labor in the very plantations where they had endured their old servitude, under conditions as burdensome as those they had congratulated themselves upon escaping. After two years, the brutal rule of this black Napoleon was ended when a bullet felled him in a popular outburst.

But Dessalines, tyrannical as he had been, had at least been efficient. As much could not be said for his successors, who presided over a nation which for a time was split as by a carving knife. In the north the one-time revolutionary general Christophe, crowned as "King Henri I," ruled with great panoply for 12 years in an ornate palace which, along with other edifices, he built by means of conscripted labor, while thousands toiled in the fields under military compulsion. In 1820 the disgruntled people revolted, and King Henri I, now completely paralyzed below the hips, found his way out by shooting himself.

If Christophe, like Dessalines, had been oversevere, the president of the southern "republic of Haiti," the mulatto Alexandre Pétion, erred in the opposite direction. Permitting his people a freedom of action without precedent in their experience, and for which they were unprepared, he was to be sadly disillusioned by the results: in the countryside little in the way of crops was produced, while the nation's finances suffered disastrously. This incompetent but beloved ruler was succeeded in 1818 by another mulatto, Jean Pierre Boyer, who reunited the country two years later, and in 1822 annexed what had been Spanish Santo Domingo. But Boyer, like Pétion, governed with a mildness for which the people were not ready. "Poverty and degradation," reported the visitor Jonathan Brown in the 1830's, "stare one in the face wherever he goes . . . the population . . . is without sustenance or a disposition to make exertions to obtain it."[9]

But Boyer, after a bruising experience, changed tactics. Since a lenient administration had brought financial embarrassment and difficult relations with France, he resorted to force. And once more the peasants, laboring under the eyes of armed guards, must have asked wherein their lot had been improved since the day of the white taskmasters. Then, in 1843, Boyer was driven out by his fellow mulattoes, while a separate nation, the Dominican Republic, was established in Santo Domingo.

Now Haiti was to be ruled by unlettered Negroes, 22 of whom issued their dictatorial decrees during the next 72 years, while the masses became more wretched than ever and the very land degenerated under erosion and neglect. Although three of the nearly two dozen presidents did show some competence, there was on the whole little if any progress; even the caste system, one of the iniquitous features of white dominance, had not been eliminated but had merely been changed—the elite were no longer the whites but in most cases the mulattoes, whose infusion of Caucasian blood elevated them to a patrician rank. In Santo Domingo meanwhile the record was equally bleak, especially during the years between 1882 and 1899 under the black dictator Ulises Heureaux, whose rule of luxury, spying, and murder reminds us of one of the more debased of the Roman emperors such as Caligula.

But we need not consider in detail the history of the tragic country: the period of the United States occupation, lasting from 1915 to 1934, and the subsequent era of dictatorship, when Duvalier ruled in Haiti and Santo Domingo was stamped under heel by a power not less cruel than that of the old Spanish and French landowners (as was evident in October 1937, when Rafael Trujillo ordered the massacre of thousands of Haitians). Nor

need we enter into the events following the assassination of Trujillo in 1961, when civil war broke out in 1965 between backers
and opponents of the overthrown president Juan Bosch, and
United States marines intervened. The fact most worth noting is
that, to this day, the overpopulated and undernourished island
has not escaped from the economic, political, and social morass
in which it has struggled during the entire era of independence.

And this arouses questions as to the island's whole liberation
movement, in which Toussaint L'Ouverture played the most
prominent part. It is possible to accept a biographer's suggestion
that it is "no rash assumption that but for the treachery of his
own generals, the Liberator of Haiti might have become the
liberator of the West Indies."[10] And yet, while Toussaint's role
was the age-old one of the incensed rebel striking out at long-
festering evils, and while he lays special claim on our sympathy
for his strokes against tyranny, and for being the only slave leader
ever to captain a successful insurrection, nevertheless a review
of the sequel causes one to wonder whether he did not merely
chop off one dragon's head while causing another or even two or
three others to sprout. Liberty and equality, surely, were sadly
deserved and outrageously overdue, yet these were not actually
obtained even after an explosion of violence had led to the expulsion of the Europeans. The caste system remained in another
form, dire poverty remained, forced labor remained, and social
disruption entered in new ways, while foreign intervention (by
the United States) occurred on more than one occasion.

The Haitian revolution had in fact shown, as had many another uprising, that revolt is not enough, even in the face of the
cruellest evils; a way must be prepared for a favorable future.
Such a way had indeed been opened by the common purpose
and homogenous nature of the people when the Dutch rebelled
against Spain, and when the American colonies struck at England;
but such a way had not been cleared, if indeed any thought had
been given to it at all, when the unschooled, abused Negroes of
Haiti hacked, slew, and burned their way to freedom under their
black leader. In this respect, unhappily, the Haitian revolt was
not exceptional, but rather was typical of most of the militant
movements into which men have been blindly propelled by their
own unleashed emotions, by an impassioned leadership, and by
the goad of scourging old wrongs.

7. Further Storm-Blasts in Latin America

i. Hidalgo

In the church of Our Lady of the Sorrows in the village of Dolores about 100 miles northwest of Mexico City, the bells tolled and tolled on the morning of September 16, 1810. Obedient to the summons of the well-loved priest, Father Miguel Hidalgo y Costilla, the ragged and barefoot inhabitants assembled. The jail was emptied; the prisoners and many workmen were given weapons, until the building and the churchyard were packed with armed Indians. All listened as their leader, generally known today simply as "Hidalgo," preached a revolutionary sermon. Did the people wish to be free? Then the time had come for a new dispensation. Three hundred years before, the Spaniards had stolen their land—would they not try to recover it?

To this emotional appeal, the crowd roared its approval. "Long live our Lady of Guadalupe!" hundreds of voices shouted back. "Death to bad government! Death to the Gachupins!" (a term of contempt for foreign-born Spaniards). Then Hidalgo, whom we may picture in the usual curate's costume of the place and times, including long black cloak, short trousers, and round sombrero, began marching at the head of the motley multitude—a rabble composed mainly of Indians augmented by mestizos or half-breeds and a few Creoles or men of pure Spanish extraction but American birth. As in the rebellion of Wat Tyler, the weapons were strangely varied; some of the men carried bows and arrows, others bore miners' picks, lances, pikes, swords, slings, and rocks, in addition to machetes and a scattering of guns. Above them as their symbol they carried a picture of their patron saint, the Virgin of Guadalupe, torn from the sacristy of a chapel. "Long live religion!" they raised their rallying call. "Long live our most holy Mother of Guadalupe! Down with bad government!" Followed by the Indian women, who scoured the land for food and cooked the meals at night around uncountable campfires, the marching crowd bore closer resemblances to a horde of Goths or Vandals than to an army in the modern sense of the term. Yet they were out for blood, of which they were to have their fill.

Hidalgo, a mild man with scholarly interests, a Creole and a humanitarian who had struggled hard to improve the lot of the Indian, had apparently not realized what a storm he was letting loose. He could not control the uncorked passions of men who had not only built up personal resentment against their scornful white abusers but whose hatred of the Spaniard had been transmitted by word of mouth from their fathers and mothers, who in turn had received it from their own fathers and mothers, and so on for a dozen generations. It may well be that Hidalgo himself was among those most appalled when the murderous frenzies of his followers seemed to halt at no extreme. Consider the fate of the city of Guanajato, where barricades against the approach of the rebellious masses were thrown up, while 500 soldiers guarded the great public granary, the Alhohdiga de Granaditas, where the Gachupins had taken refuge. Aided by the embattled poor of the city, the lunatic mob battered down the doors of this stronghold, and not one of the 600 men, women, and children was spared. Hidalgo and his aides, unable to check the slaughter, lost 2000 of their own number.

Then, for two days, the city was sacked as by Avars or Huns. Buildings were demolished, and everything that was valued and transportable was hauled away. Iron grills were wrenched from windows to make weapons; silver plate was carried off after the protecting partitions were broken down; treasuries were looted of coins and silver bars, and meanwhile in the country cattle were stolen in the *haciendas,* and farm lands were appropriated.

After such demonstrations, followed by further havoc at San Luis Potosi and elsewhere, Hidalgo might have been expected to hesitate when, with a host of some 80,000, he stood on the mountains high above Mexico City and could presumably have swept down and taken the capital. With the memory of blood-streaked halls and crimsoned paving stones and the cries of the wounded and dying still fresh in his mind, what humane man would not have shrunk from the prospect of the still greater horrors which his invasion of the capital might inflict? In any case, like Hannibal encamped before the walls of Rome, Hidalgo approached his goal but withheld his attack.

And thus his revolution passed its crescendo. Gradually a substantial part of his army deserted him, while the barbarities of his enemies equalled those of his own most savage followers. But he still hoped that, out of all the fury, a beneficent crop would sprout; a proclamation which he issued at Valladolid on December 15, 1810, called for a congress of all the cities and villages, which would enact benevolent laws, treat all men as brothers, overcome poverty, stimulate industry and agriculture, and promote the best use of the land.

His position, in fact, had been enunciated months before, on September 23, only a week after the start of the rebellion, when he called for the surrender of the opposing general:

> On the plains near Celaya, the large army which I command elected me to be captain-general and protector of the Mexican nation. The city of Celaya, in the presence of fifty thousand men, ratified this selection—an example which has been followed by all the towns through which I have passed. . . . In brief, this project is: the proclamation of the liberty and independence of the Mexican nation. . . .[1]

Despite this magnificent idea, a few tumultuous months sufficed to bring Hidalgo to the end of his road. His uprising had degenerated into anarchy spiced with brigandage and bloody reprisals; it had become a war of classes more than of political factions. In March 1811, he was caught by a ruse; and on the following July 31, after conviction by a military court, he met his death before a firing squad.

In a direct way, his revolt got nowhere at all; all the terror, all the destruction, all the loss of life had been fruitless. Hidalgo, therefore, is one of the most tragic figures among all of America's would-be liberators. Yet in the annals of the Mexican movement for independence his name has been placed above all others; he has become a national hero; the date of his uprising, September 16, is his country's Independence Day.

What, then, were the forces behind his abortive rebellion? We have noted the Indian's inherited resentment against his white conqueror, but this requires more specific explanation. After the original thrust of conquest and the relentless exploitation and tragic depopulation that ensued, the Spanish government aimed to follow an enlightened policy toward the Indians. It was not, however, always able to regulate their affairs at its great distance, and it treated them as virtual wards of the state, somewhat in the way of minors entrusted to the supervision of a court; it denied them the rights of white men, forbade them to assume a debt of more than five pesos, and prohibited their use of firearms, branding irons, and European clothes. But at the same time it favored them in some ways, as in exemption from the heavy tax of the *alcabala* (though not from tribute), and in relative immunity from fines, imprisonment, and execution.

Nevertheless, the Indian might be subject to the forced labor of the *encomienda* (in which his work was farmed out to Spanish colonists), or he might be oppressed by a sort of *corvée* or conscription of labor, the *repartiemento,* despite official attempts at suppression. But whatever the theory, the Indian's back might be striped by the lash; and though he could not legally be enslaved except for rebellion, in practice this exemption might mean little to one groaning in agony as the hissing brand seared his brow. On the dukedom of the hacienda or great landed estate, in the mine, or in the sugar mill, there was not much to hinder the arbitrary treatment of the worker by the overseer. And even when nominally free, the Indian might be entangled from generation to generation in the web of debt peonage, in which he was caught, literally, like a fly in a spider's coils. He could not even flatter himself upon being a second-class citizen; he was not a citizen at all, and the knowledge that he was regarded as less-than-man inevitably scorched its way into his spirit even more gallingly than the red-hot iron had eaten into his skin.

Yet in general, despite some sporadic exceptions, the Indian did not revolt. For the most part he remained aloof from the whites, sullenly nursing grievances that most members of the master race would have been astonished to learn about. In the more than $2\frac{1}{2}$ centuries between the Mixton War of the early 1540s and the revolutionary movement of 1810, no serious Indian uprising occurred in central Mexico. Yet the ingredients did exist, somewhat as in Peru, where in 1780 a descendant of the Incas took the name of a more famous ancestor, Tupac Amaru, arose at the head of a largely unarmed Indian force of 70 or 80 thousand men, and was captured after about six months and slain with extreme cruelty.

In Mexico as elsewhere in Latin America, complicating factors were presented by the man of mixed blood: various part-breeds, mestizos and mulattoes, and other mixtures of different racial strains, which, when too hard to identify, were lumped together under the general name of *castas*. These persons, rejected by whites and Indians alike, might suffer the disabilities of both and enjoy the privileges of neither: mestizos had to pay the *alcabala,* were subject to military service and the full severity of Spanish punishments, but could not take political office, practice certain professions such as the law, wield the branding iron, nor live in certain urban residential districts. Yet they constituted a large and growing element, a disruptive ingredient in society, which could not be permanently subjugated. Meanwhile the *castas* dwelt in city slums ("ghettos," we would call them, with our common misuse of this term) , and occasionally they erupted in violence—riots known as *tumultos* led to general looting and killing, to occupation of government offices and to burning of buildings, as when the mobs in 1624 and in 1692 fought with the police and the army. And in the country regions some of the *castas,* scornfully known as *leperos,* resorted to banditry, especially in the area between Mexico City and Veracruz, where they made any unguarded journey perilous.

Here, certainly, was not the organized substance of revolution. But here were its raw materials, which needed only the proper time and a well-directed leadership to fuse them into major combustibles.

And this brings us to possibly the strangest fact of all about the revolutionary movement in most of Latin America. The outbreaks were not precipitated by the Indians, the mestizos or the *castas,* despite all their long-endured grievances, though all these groups would play their parts once rebellion had broken out. Surprisingly, the initial strokes against European power were captained by white men.

For the whites themselves were rifted by a sharp social division. At the top there stood the *peninsulars,* whom we have already noted under the belittling name of *Gachupins*—the persons born in Europe and claiming special privileges by virtue of their place of birth. And beneath the *peninsulars* stood the Creoles, whose hundred-percent Iberian blood did not save them from the disdain and discrimination of their brothers who first saw the light across the Atlantic. We have seen, for example, that Hidalgo was a Creole, though his followers were mostly Indians. We have witnessed how he aroused the mob, which clamored against the

Spaniards with cries of "Death to the *Gachupins!*" This does not mean that Hidalgo desired a class war, nor that his detestation of the *peninsulars* was as great as his love for the common people. But it does mean that, in his opposition to the Spanish-born whites, he was making use of the material he found at hand. He was but one native-born white leader in a wave that had begun to swell all over Latin America. The clash of Creoles against *peninsulars,* however, may be seen more sharply in the case of other insurgents, such as the celebrated liberators Bolivar and San Martin.

ii. Bolivar and San Martin

With curly black hair and piercing black eyes, black mustache and beard, sun-tanned lean face and sharp nose, a small thin form and an animated manner, Bolivar early in life manifested energy, agility, and swift-changing moods. Born in Caracas, Venezuela, on July 24, 1783, the son of a colonel who owned rich copper mines and haciendas, he was not one of the underprivileged except in the most relative sense of the term. Having lost his father and mother at an early age, he came under the guardianship of an uncle, who in 1799 sent him to Europe to finish his education, and thereby crucially influenced his whole life. The young man's first trip abroad was followed by another, which lasted three years beginning in 1804; and during this period, it seems, revolutionary ideas were burgeoning in his mind.

These ideas, apparently, came from two main sources, and first the sense of injustice which he shared with many Creoles who felt oppressed by Spaniards of European birth. Here, to be sure, were not the abrasive basic wrongs that rankled in the hearts of beaten Indians or despised mestizos; but here were grievances that seemed serious enough to proud and ambitious men who saw themselves unjustly scorned and overlooked. For while the Creole might be the possessor of rich mines and lands, he had small hope of elevation to the higher, more coveted positions of state and church under a government that favored the Spanish grandees to administer the affairs of America while native Americans were blandly ignored. It was true that, from the Spanish point of view, this seemed just as it should be; men trained in the home country, they thought, were best qualified. Besides, it was necessary to reward the King's faithful servants, and colonial appointments were easy and recognized means. Viceroys, governors, captains-general might thus be sent overseas for brief periods—long enough, however, to enable them to return home with treasure chests bulging. One might have expected that the Creoles would resent such practices, yet the home government seldom saw justice in the complaints of Americans that they too deserved a chance.

At the same time, another cause of discontent was the mercantile policy of Spain, which was built upon the ancient thrust-and-grab philosophy that we have noted in the English imperialists of the 17th and 18th centuries. Spain, like England, clung to the idea that colonies were gifts of nature to be tapped by the home country regardless of their own requirements, somewhat like maple trees being drained of their sweet sap. And this will explain why, in the early 19th century, tariffs on goods leaving Spain for America ranged from about 9½ to 43 percent, while smuggling was general and corruption flourished. This will also account for various minor outbreaks, such as one that occurred in New Granada in 1781, when the rebels decried the tobacco monopoly and various burdensome taxes including the *alcabala*. Two years later, when some conspirators in northern South America solicited the aid of England for a contemplated revolt, the government at Madrid might have done well to take warning.

Thus the discontent of the Creole as well as of other Americans continued to mount, until toward the end of the 18th century it was reaching the breaking point.

But even if Bolivar was one of the most prominent of those who made a striking arm of this dissatisfaction, he was by no means the first to move, even if we except the revolutionary currents in Mexico. He had been preceded by Francisco de Miranda (1750–1816), a misguided idealist who visited Europe and the United States before he led a short-lived rebellion in Venezuela, then was defeated and denounced, was seized by Bolivar as a traitor, and was handed over to the Spaniards, and sent to die in a prison in Cadiz. Also before Bolivar, there had been the Brazilian leader "Tiradentes," physician, dentist, and minor army officer, who in 1788 headed a revolt against the Portuguese rule, demanding such radical ends as the establishment of a university, the abolition of slavery, and independence from European rule; in 1792, his rebellion was crushed, and this courageous crusader was beheaded. But though he, like Miranda, had failed, he too showed in which direction the wind was blowing.

Now to return to Bolivar. The second great force that swept

him on was ideological. The Spaniards might clamp down a civil and ecclesiastical censure of books, but they could no more prevent the circulation of ideas than they could block the tides of the Atlantic. Ideas, invigorating and germinal ideas, were pouring into Latin America, the very ideas that underlay the American and the French Revolutions. Montesquieu, the Abbé Raynal, Voltaire, Rousseau—these writers among others provided the fresh airs of inspiration for Bolivar and his fellow revolutionaries, perhaps the more so because they raised forbidden standards. At the same time, there was the stimulation of the successful revolt of the North American colonies, and the even more inspiring example of the great upheaval in France, the fall of the regime of Louis XVI, and the rise of the people over their one-time oppressors. Then, nearer home, in 1806 and 1807, there was a spur to the pride of all Latin America in the repulse of two successive British expeditions into the great estuary of the Rio de la Plata. However the Americans may have objected to Spanish rule, they were in no mood to exchange it for that of any other foreign power. Led by a Frenchman, Santiago Liniers, they speedily defeated the invaders, and so inevitably aroused new hope in the minds of all patriots: if England could succumb, why not Spain?

Meanwhile events in Europe were having powerful repercussions in America. Many in the New World, who would ordinarily have remained loyal to the Spanish Crown, felt released from their obligations in 1808 when a foreign interloper, Napoleon, removed the Bourbon King Ferdinand VII from his throne in Madrid, and when, two years later, he seized the continuing centers of royal resistance, Seville and Cadiz. Shock and confusion filled the New World at word of these strokes; the universe as the Latin Americans had known it was crumbling, somewhat as the universe today would crumble for North Americans were a foreign power to occupy Washington. What, therefore, could the colonists do? It is significant of the tendencies of the times that in Buenos Aires a *cabildo abierto* or town meeting was summoned for May 22, 1810, to discuss the necessary measures, and decided to establish a "provisional junta of the Provinces of the Rio de la Plata, governing for Ferdinand VII." Playing a leading role in this junta was the brilliant young creole lawyer Mariano Moreno, who desired independence from Spain and fought for this end energetically in the face of strong opposition. It was a great loss to the cause of freedom that, a few months later, sailing on a diplomatic mission to England, Moreno died at sea.

All this should make it clear that the activities of the greatest of the liberators, Bolivar and San Martin, were not isolated phenomena; these men moved with the strong tides of their times, even if they did push further out with those tides than most others. They had not only a more and more manifest desire to throw off the reins of Spain, but an increasing realization that this was possible. Nevertheless, there was no unity of aim among the fighters for freedom. The Creoles were eager for greater rights for Creoles, and what they craved was primarily political equality, political independence. But to the great masses of downtrodden Indians and mixed breeds, what seemed most desirable was economic and social reform—a plot of land, a full bin of corn, freedom from outside control, the right to live without payment of tribute or forced labor.

These specific motivations, it is true, may have seemed to drop out of sight during the course of the uprisings. But when the fighting had ceased and attempts were made to restore order to the dismembered land, the objectives of the rebels were of prime importance. Had they been moved by one dominant purpose, even to the same extent as the English colonists some years before, their revolution might have swept on to a unified, continent-wide achievement. As it happened, however, the Creoles were, in general, content after shaking off European control, whereas the underprivileged peasant or city worker remained in the same gruelling poverty as before, if not even crueller destitution owing to the afflictions of war. And the sufferings of much of South America therefore continued throughout the 19th century and into our own day.

Unfortunately, liberation—which is to say, deliverance from the authority of Spain and Portugal—was often accompanied by means that defeated the stated aims of the insurgents. Warfare was the method—warfare that was often daring and sometimes brilliant in execution but that left in its train a grievous brood of evils. As in many civil conflicts, terror was more in evidence than restraint; dedication produced fanaticism; the inflictions of both sides reached monstrous depths of inhumanity. Consider how Bolivar, on June 15, 1813, issued his celebrated proclamation of war to the death against the Spaniards: "Spaniards and Canarians, count on death, even though you are neutral, if you do not work actively for the liberty of Venezuela! Americans, count on life, even though you are culpable!" No middle course was to be tolerated: what Bolivar said was, in effect, "Spaniards and

Americans, either you are with me, in which case I will excuse all your crimes, or else you are not with me, in which case I will kill you!" Nothing could have divided the people more sharply, offered a more atrocious foundation for a revolution, set a more disastrous precedent, or promised worse for the future. Bolivar had fallen into the blind error that has entombed more than one other apostle of righteousness—the error of tying men's arms in order to make them free.

When a man launches such a program, he is like a daredevil racing down a steep mountain road, unable to check his reckless course. And so it is not surprising that, in retaliation for the savagery of his Spanish opponent José Tomas Boves, Bolivar on February 8, 1814, issued another infamous command, one not unique in the annals of war: all Spanish prisoners in the dungeons and hospitals of Caracas and La Guaira must be shot. More than 800, accordingly, were massacred.

Yet the Bolivar who ordered this ferocious act was the man who, not long before, had proclaimed his desire "to free the oppressed, and to give liberty to all." Apparently, like most men, he could lock conflicting ideas in "watertight compartments." And this made it possible for him to hold humanitarian views, and at the same time to take a road of terroristic aggressiveness. In the beginning, indeed, the old, often discredited doctrine of the strong arm seemed to justify itself, as did the corresponding notion that barbarous means can achieve idealistic ends. Bolivar did, after agonizing warfare, make northern South America politically independent of Spain; but he did not weld it into a cohesive whole, he did not insure orderly or just government, needed social reform, or economic equality, and he did not save the area from continual turmoil, nor prevent it from going deep into the 20th century as one of the world's deprived and troubled regions.

Whether or not the country might not have prospered at least as well or better under continued Spanish rule is an open question. Bolivar himself recognized the difficulties, particularly near the close of his life, with the failure of his grandiose scheme to unite Venezuela, Ecuador, and New Granada in a new state. Then, in despair, he spoke of constitutions as being "printed matter; elections, battles; freedom, anarchy; and life, a torment." It was in this defeatist mood that he pronounced America to be "ungovernable" and declared that the revolutionaries had "plowed the sea." But perhaps the great lack of the rebels had been their want of a common feeling, a unifying tradition, a sense of oneness sufficient to overcome the divisiveness of classes, races, and geography. That lack was one which no militants, however determined, were able to counteract.

It was much the same with José de San Martin, the liberator of southern South America. Here was a man of a markedly different type, as was proved when the two leaders briefly met but failed to harmonize; San Martin was basically the military commander, though one with much less than the usual quota of personal ambition—perhaps as near as one could come to the pure patriot seeking the freedom of his people regardless of self-exaltation. An outstanding strategist and military planner, he was as brave and daring as he was resourceful; his surprise descent upon the Spaniards in Chile, after a crossing of the Andes at such an elevation that some of his troops died from the cold or from lack of oxygen while more than half of the pack animals perished, must be listed among the extraordinary martial adventures of all time. To make this possible, he had built a powder factory, an arsenal, and a textile mill, and imposed special taxes. At the same time, he received devoted and courageous aid from the populace at Mendoza, his headquarters in Argentina, where the men labored to produce cannon and ammunition, boots and uniforms, while the women offered their jewels and heirlooms. The tall, black-eyed, black-haired, bushy-faced, olive-complexioned leader, with his military bearing but kindly and simple manner, stated his position to the English traveler Captain Basil Hall: his desire was not for military glory or for a reputation as the conqueror of Peru—his one aim was to free his country from oppression. Day by day, he thought, he had been gaining "fresh allies in the hearts of the people," the only allies he considered important in a war of independence.

Yet San Martin, like Bolivar, did have his doubts as to whether the ends he sought were fully attainable. Although he believed in republican government, he early began to question whether the people of the la Plata provinces were ready for republicanism; later he appeared to veer toward monarchy as the solution, and went so far as to write to his associate, the Chilean dictator Bernardo O'Higgins, in regard to Peru and Chile, "I believe that you will be convinced of the impossibility of erecting republics in those countries." All that he desired, he said, was a government adapted to the circumstances and able to avoid anarchy.

But such a government was to elude him. Disaffection flamed

up within his army, where many of the officers and soldiers opposed his policies; severe dissension broke out between the *portenos* or "port dwellers" and the men of the back country; his own health was affected by a disease of unknown nature; and in 1824, following the death of his wife, he sailed with quiet self-effacement for England, accompanied by his young daughter, to pass his remaining 26 years in Europe in poverty and neglect. Thanks to his efforts, much of South America had indeed been released from foreign control. But he, like Bolivar and like the liberators in Mexico and elsewhere, had not sufficiently learned one great lesson: a country can no more plunge unprepared into self-government than an inexperienced swimmer can safely make a high dive into a stormy sea. In his case also, militancy was not enough; even the sacrifice and the heroic struggling were not enough. The ground had to be plowed, the rocks and brush had to be cleared away if a suitable edifice were to be erected. To the lack of preparation, which had its roots hundreds of years in the past, we can attribute much of the long-continuing turmoil and suffering of the regions which San Martin had delivered from the Spanish rule.

iii. Diaz and Zapata

For almost a decade and a half, from 1910 to 1924, Mexico was shaken by revolution. Yet there was really not one uprising so much as a series of uncoordinated, often conflicting outbreaks under various leaders, some of whom fought one another, while others concentrated upon the social structure. The hallmark of the period was anarchy; the tormented nation was riven by violence that seldom ceased, and whose trail was marked by lifeless bodies dangling from trees, the charred remains of haciendas, the remnants of railroad tracks torn from their ties, the ruins of sugar mills, and weeds that grew thick where farms had flourished. Meanwhile sharply diminished agricultural production brought hunger; the country's finances sank into chaos; and the population, during the period from 1910 to 1921, diminished to an extent that can only be estimated and yet was certainly large: Charles C. Cumberland, for example, gives figures which "suggest that from all causes the nation lost about two million citizens."[2]

Just what lay behind the long-continuing agony? After all, the preceding regime—the dictatorship of Porfirio Diaz, lasting more than a third of a century from 1876 to 1911—had brought at least superficial prosperity. Business had flourished; the onerous old tax the *alcabala* had been dropped; the nation's finances had been put into order and its budget balanced; the country had earned great favor abroad. And when, in September 1910, Diaz celebrated his 80th birthday and the centennial of Hidalgo's rebellion at Dolores, thousands not only from his own country but from foreign lands joined him in commemorating both events. What reason, therefore, could there be for violent uprisings? What grounds for revolution?

Unfortunately, Mexico was like a building with a brilliant facade and rotting underpinnings. The merchant, the banker, the industrialist, the owner of vast lands and rich mines might bask in affluence, but the poor Indian in the cornfield or sugar plantation, the toiler in the ore-pit or the mill was helped not at all by the glitter and the luxury. True, his misery was of ancient lineage, and he had grown accustomed to it, but lately he had been made more aware of his deprived condition by preachers of anarchy and radicalism from abroad, largely from Spain, who organized strikes that Diaz put down with a bloody hand. A liberal paper established by Ricardo Flores Magon, after being suppressed in Mexico, was published irregularly in the United States, while various underground groups worked for the overthrow of Diaz and for a miscellany of reforms in state and church, education, labor, and agriculture. All this need not in itself have produced revolution, yet it did show that revolutionary tides were rising.

The contrast between wealth and poverty, more evident than ever now that money poured into the coffers of the well-to-do, has seldom been expressed more bitingly than by Emeliano Zapata, the scion of a poor but respected family in the state of Morelos. This man, in every way a son of the people, had by turns worked his own land, sharecropped the land of others, bought and sold horses and cattle, and driven mules. Having passed several weeks in charge of the stables of a wealthy sugar planter in Mexico City, he returned home to the village of Anenecuilco with a remark that would ring through the corridors of the revolution: The horses of Mexico City, in their tiled stalls, were better housed than any workman in all Morelos. In this statement the illiterate farm worker expressed the bitterness, though only part of the bitterness, that underlay his raids when, as a captain of guerrilla horsemen, he sacked the haciendas of his native state and of Guerrero, seizing horses and guns, and leaving a trail of ash and blood behind him.

To understand the violence of his outburst we must glance at the countryside in his day. Though the white man's oppression dated back to the 15th century, of recent years it had shown new features beneath the international competition between the growers of sugar cane and of sugar beets. The cane planters of Morelos, aided by new rail lines, new machinery, and lobbying that won them reduced taxes, had planned to found modern economic empires, and had encroached more and more on the domain of poor free labor. Company towns had been established, each housing from 250 to almost 3000 permanent residents, and offering services ranging from police to schools, and from stores to powerhouses.

Thus, perhaps not so much by design as by the familiar sort of economic growth which looks to size, power, profits, and "prosperity" rather than to long-range social effects, the people's traditional life was being crushed beneath a machine-like regimentation that was honored with the name of progress. Once-flourishing towns ceased to grow; many villages disappeared, as may be seen in the fact that there were 118 pueblos in Morelos in 1876, and only 105 eleven years later; an example of the reduction, although an extreme one, occurred in the case of Tequesqitengo, which, as a plantation owner's retaliation for a grievance or supposed grievance, was flooded with irrigation water until only its church spire was visible. The workers of such a community, as well as of many villages that remained physically intact, might desperately try to support themselves by sharecropping on the most unpromising land, but in the end they might have to accept service among the plantation gangs, and would be fortunate if not driven into permanent peonage by their mounting debts.

Meanwhile the rank and file of the peasants, whose hunger for land was like that of peasants the world over, were being frustrated more and more by the growth of the great plantations, the expansion of industry, and the concentration of wealth. The situation was most unhealthy when as much as a quarter of the total soil of Morelos, including most of its choice land, had come into the hands of 17 proprietors. From the economic point of view the new developments may have seemed efficient, and therefore necessary and desirable. But economic incentives—which, in practice, are often difficult if not impossible to disentangle from the incentives of private greed—may also be motivations to revolution, especially when they intrude upon human needs and take no account of human psychology.

An example of the current abuses was provided by the wealthy planter Pablo Escandon, later for a time Governor of Morelos. Much as the common land of England in previous centuries had been enclosed by private encroachment, some 3500 acres of common land in the Yautepec district were fenced off by this Mexican land-baron in 1903. And when the excluded cattle found a way back into their old grazing grounds, Escandon's agents impounded the animals, sold some of them, returned others after being paid a heavy fee, let some of them starve to death, and threw some of their owners into jail on charges of permitting trespass. Thereupon one of the farmers, Jovito Serrano, was reckless enough to go to court on behalf of the other injured peasants. Unhappily, the decision of the local bench went against him. Serrano then appealed to the district court, and was worse than rebuffed—the plaintiffs not only lost the case, but had to pay a fine of 100 pesos! Yet the courageous crusader, undaunted by this piling of injury upon injury, took the case to the Federal Supreme Court, while leading a delegation of villagers to present their side to President Diaz. On June 21, 1904, the court handed down its ruling—the verdicts in favor of Escandon were sustained! Nor was this the whole story: Serrano had been arrested in Mexico City, and sometime later his family received their last word from him—somehow he had smuggled out a letter as, with 35 other refractory farmers, he was being hustled off to a labor camp at Quintana Roo, where he died the following year.

Let us ask ourselves: what if you and I had been among the farmers expelled by force from lands that had traditionally belonged to the people? What if we found it impossible to obtain justice in the courts—found it as dangerous to oppose the landholders as to attack a fer-de-lance with bare hands? And what if we knew that Serrano's case was no solitary one, but had witnessed other outrages, as when the cattle of villagers were seized at a roundup and kept without compensation, and when the courts sided with a hacienda that had ruined a community by diverting river water needed by the orchardists for their fruit trees? How would we react to all this? And how would we feel when the timber of the people was taken by corrupt business interests, and when rice growers put heavy drains on the drinking supply of a city? If such injuries did not infuriate us sufficiently, would we not grow even angrier at reports of the palatial elegance displayed by our exploiters, the extensive racing stables, the wide landscaped grounds with their palms and fountains, the elaborately furnished houses? If we did not nourish a secret desire to revolt, we would hardly be human. This, then, will explain why leaders in the country districts found so many followers for plundering, burning, and killing.

iv. Madero, Carranza, and Others

Among the insurgents ushering in the revolution, one of the most remarkable was Francisco I. Madero, who, astonishingly, had sprung from a great landowning family; for a time, after the abdication of Diaz in 1911, he became President of Mexico. This black-bearded, flat-nosed, sallow-faced, fiery-eyed leader, with his bulging forehead and diminutive form, enacted the part of an evangelical preacher more than of a political rebel. To the bedazzled throngs that greeted his passage from town to town, waving palm leaves and singing hosannas, he was almost like the Lord come down to earth. "Viva Madero! Viva el Immaculado!" rang out the cries of the multitudes for whom he was more-than-man—a faith healer into whose presence the sick were carried, so that their sores and pangs might be cured by his magical touch.

Beyond question, Madero was a good man, an honest man, a man of burning earnestness. There is no reason to doubt the sincerity of his beliefs, including his conviction that spirit messages proved him to be foreordained to his task—such an idea was surely no more far-fetched than the faith of many a king that he was the special appointee of God. Unfortunately, however, mystical persuasions and practical politics do not ordinarily mix. While Madero was swept into the Presidency on a surge of popular feeling, he came unprepared for his high office. The problems of the country were not solved, despite his deep interest in the people; small insurrections kept cropping up during his short term of office. To the beneficiaries of the old regime his moderate proposals for reform seemed wellnigh revolutionary, while to the abused peasants, who craved instant land reform, he appeared to move at a snail's pace. Thus he fell between two classes, satisfying neither, and accomplishing little.

Madero had held office for no more than about a year and a quarter when, in February 1913, violence broke out in the capital. For ten days the city thundered with cannon fire; Diaz's former aide Bernardo Reyes and his nephew Felix Diaz had started a bloody coup; Madero's brother Gustavo was slain, he himself and his Vice-President were made palace prisoners, and the Presidency was taken over by the ruthless Victoriano Huerta, who had fought against Indian rebels and against Zapata's militant farmers, and whose favorite hangout was a bullet-marked saloon, from which he passed down decrees to be enforced by his gunmen. It was by no coincidence that, on February 22, Madero and a companion were shot to death by the guards on their way to the penitentiary.

Although at first Zapata had tried to work with Madero, this visionary was too slow and ineffective and too far at heart from the rural movement to satisfy the peasant leader. After a time Zapata condemned the new President as "inept, a traitor and a tyrant," and issued a clear revolutionary challenge: the men and the villages that had been stripped of their land should reoccupy them; one-third of every great estate should be appropriated (though their owners should be indemnified) in order to supply land for the people.

Here was in effect a battle call, and one that sent wild pulsations through the countryside. In August 1911, an order was given for "the active pursuit and arrest of Zapata," who was now an outlaw. Hunted by General Huerta, he contrived to escape, while the latter unwittingly brought recruits to Zapata's cause by the terror and fury of his assaults in his quest of "bandits"—his name for the villagers of Morelos. Thus, while the people of the huts and fields were being armed, Zapata's forces occupied more and more villages, and the revolution continued to spread.

Its subsequent course, however, was checkered, uncertain, and up and down—sometimes more down than up. And this can be traced to various causes, not the least of which was the worldwide influenza epidemic, which took a heavy toll in Mexico as elsewhere, and which, along with emigration, reduced the population of Zapata's native state of Morelos by a fourth in the single year of 1918. But another reason for the devious history of the revolution was that its leaders were men of widely differing types, aims, and principles; they included the opportunist President-to-be Venustiano Carranza, who was assassinated in 1920 after fleeing the Presidential palace with a trainload of bullion; Carranza's great enemy the brigandly Pancho Villa, whose murderous thrusts into the United States prompted President Wilson to send General Pershing across the border in pursuit; and General Alvaro Obregon, who became President after the death of Carranza, and showed a practical understanding of the land-craving peasant, the laborer, and the businessman. But Zapata dominated all the others in the impetus he gave the revolution, until in 1919 he and some companions were treacherously shot to death at the instigation of Carranza, who had put a price on his head.

A little more than two years before, in February 1917, the hopes of the revolutionaries had seemed to be coming true. A new constitution was promulgated, announcing major reforms: the right to all land was held to be originally vested in the state, and private exploitation of natural resources was therefore to be restricted and controlled; labor was to have a new deal, including the eight-hour day, wage control, the outlawing of child labor, and increased responsibility of employers; and the Church, in confirmation of laws more than half a century old, was to be divested of her great estates, denied a share in public education, and subjected to other limitations including regulation of the number of priests. But these provisions, while embodying the thought of Zapata, Obregon, and their followers, were to have little practical effect for many years. Though the revolution was over in 1924, the condition of the average worker had improved only slightly if at all; Charles C. Cumberland is apparently justified in concluding that "The mass of the population probably had less to eat than they had two decades earlier, their educational opportunities had improved not at all, and they had no greater political rights."[3]

While the figures of other authorities suggest that the real wage of peons and farmers was slightly more in 1934 than 40 years before, the improvements had been almost imperceptibly small. Likewise very slow had been the redistribution of the land, a major objective of Zapata; by 1934 no more than about 20,-000,000 acres had been redistributed—which may seem a huge amount, though actually it was small compared with the hundreds of millions of acres remaining in private hands. The situation was considerably better, however, in Morelos, the center of the peasant revolution; according to statistics for 1927, "Provisionally at least 80 per cent of the state's farming families had fields of their own, which altogether amounted to around 75 per cent of the arable land."[4] Yet only after the rise in 1934 of Lazaro Cardenas, one of Mexico's most progressive presidents, were the revolutionary aims given their strongest thrust toward fulfillment. Under his determined leadership, nearly 45,000,000 acres were transferred to the villages; but even so, nearly a third of all Mexican workers labored for a pittance on other men's land, and immense difficulties continued to obstruct the effectiveness of the Constitution.

The efforts to implement the Constitution were themselves the causes of severe sporadic violence; for example in the twenties, the clergy revolted against the government's attempt to close religious schools and to curb ecclesiastical functions in various other ways. In 1926 a strike of an unusual nature was called—a strike by the religious authorities. Beginning on August 1, the church bells were to be silent; no baptisms, marriages, burials, or masses were to be held; no priest would officiate, though the churches would remain open under the supervision of the lay officials. Unfortunately, the religious nature of the protest did not mean that a sanctified calm would be maintained. Military groups, or so the government claimed, arose under the captainship of priests (and the Church never condemned the fighting, but merely alleged that the priests served as chaplains and not as soldiers).

But no matter what palliating words the prelates spoke, a veritable religious war ensued. With cries of "Viva Cristo Rey!" ("Long live King Christ!"), the insurgents rushed into battle, burned schools and other buildings, wrecked any property they could lay hands on, and slew teachers, government officials, and progovernment labor leaders as well as prisoners. And the state, in its turn, committed atrocities—hanged men, seized hostages, and uprooted the people of entire villages. Finally, after a railroad train had been derailed and more than 100 hapless passengers had died in gun and fire attacks led by priests, matters came to a crisis; President Calles held the Church responsible and ordered the remaining bishops and archbishops expelled. During the three years following the failure of the strike, and before an accommodation was reached with the Church, the revolt shook the country with banditry; retaliatory blows were struck as in a blood feud; and thousands of lives were lost.

This prompts one to ask: how much good did the Revolution accomplish? Were the gains worth the costs in life, havoc, and suffering? It is true that, after all the troubled decades, substantial progress was attained; Mexico did make her way to a better-integrated national existence; the lot of large sections of the people was improved; the land as a whole was mercifully free of disturbances such as had marked the era of Huerta, Zapata, Villa, and Carranza. Nevertheless, might not these results have been possible without all the agony and the loss? In other countries vast social improvements had occurred without violence; slavery had been peacefully abolished in the British dominions and elsewhere in America (unfortunately, not in the United States); child labor had been controlled or ended, the labor of women had been subjected to severe restrictions, and hours and working conditions for all had been radically improved—not always, indeed, without strife, even bloody strife, but never with violence on the Mexican scale. Even in Mexico, however, might not the ameliorating action of time, aided by determined, well-organized, nonviolent social pressures, have accomplished everything that the Revolution achieved, and accomplished it without slashing and tearing the country?

Whatever the answers to these questions, I believe it is clear that a revolution so generally unorganized as the Mexican, and with so many fountainheads, is certain to be inefficient, if not immensely wasteful in its methods. It is like a dragon with many heads, several of which are constantly biting one another, while the body bleeds profusely. Mexico, like such a dragon's body, bled for years from innumerable cuts and gashes; and much as she suffered, she was fortunate in not emerging even more mangled. Partly it was by mere good fortune—the accident of obtaining presidents like Cardenas and some of his liberal successors—that the country was able finally to reach some of the central revolutionary objectives. But again, as in other lands, history and forecast did not agree; not Madero, nor Zapata, nor Obregon, nor any of the rebels were able to foretell the bends of the road they were following; they took their way more or less blindly, as all men must. But this they might have known: that a legacy of violence, in almost all cases, would leave a legacy of violence, terror would lead to terror, destruction to destruction, and chaos to chaos. It was not by chance, but through the natural workings of the forces set into action by the insurgents and counter-insurgents, that the storm raged with a fury destined to outlive many of the spokesmen of change.

8. 1848: All Europe Crackles

i. Italy and Central Europe

On New Year's Day 1848, the city of Milan took fire with one of the strangest insurrections on record. Much as the rebels in Boston had struck out at tea three quarters of a century before, the Italian insurgents aimed their attacks at a commodity—tobacco. No citizen was to smoke; the man seen with a lighted cigar was met with an instant protest, "Put it out!"—and if he was prudent he did put it out, else he would feel the fury of the mob. After three angry days, while innocent passers-by no less than the guilty were in danger of arrest by the police, the streets echoed to the tramp of Austrian troops, whose lips closed defiantly over smoking cigars. The riots grew worse; bloodshed followed; six were slain and scores wounded. But just what did all this mean?

It meant a phase in the growing hostility between the Milanese and the occupying Austrians. It meant that patriots were asserting themselves in the name of independence, seeking to show their power at the same time as they protested against the state revenue from tobacco. It meant, furthermore, an exacerbation of the relations between the citizens and the foreign soldiers, whose brutality in putting down the outbreak aroused fierce resentment. Most of all, it represented one of the opening manifestations of the revolutions of 1848, which were to erupt throughout Europe.

But although attended by tragedy, the Tobacco Riots represented little more than a flexing of the muscles, a warming up for the outbreak of March 18 to 23, 1848, the "Five Glorious Days," when the populace of Milan arose almost as one man against the forces of Austrian Marshal Radetzky. Citizens of all ages and both sexes participated—old men and young women, youths and children, boys and girls, armed with weapons as strange as were ever seen among the peasant rabbles in the *jacqueries* of past centuries. Kitchens had delivered up their meat knives, museums their ancient spears and guns, while more modern equipment had been seized in the barracks into which the people fought their way. On the streets curious obstructions arose—barricades erected of paving stones and furniture from the houses, sofas and tables and pianos. Unseen on the roofs, sharpshooters took aim at the Austrian soldiers; in the barricades the mob was driven from one stronghold only to take refuge in another, and continued the fight until the Austrians saw no choice but retreat.

Thus, in a remarkable popular surge, the Milanese cleared their city of the foreign oppressors. And similarly another northern city, Venice, wrested itself free of the conqueror. But these triumphs did not lead to the dreamt-of Italian unity, principally because the Italians were not sufficiently one at heart. As so often in an insurrectionary movement, all the heroism, all the bloodshed, all the sacrifice were of little avail because of inadequate planning and the lack of a unifying determination and design.

But precisely why did the people revolt? The answer is graphically presented in the Manifesto of the Provisional Government of Milan after the expulsion of the Austrians. While too long to quote here in entirety, this document mentions such grievances as "immoderate taxes"; the foisting upon the people of "shoals" of foreigners who acted as their judges and administered their affairs without knowing their language or customs; an intricacy of foreign laws which forbade the growth of commerce and industry; a harrassing control over municipal institutions; the enchaining of religion and even of public charity; the seizure of property; the shackling of the arts; the restrictions upon the printing or importation of foreign books; the persecution of distinguished men; the organization of "an army of spies"; and the granting to the police of "full power over liberty, life, and property." One would scarcely need a broader list of abuses. The wonder is that the rebellion was so long delayed.

Meanwhile uprisings were occurring elsewhere in Italy and Sicily. One noteworthy though short-lived upheaval shook the Sicilian city of Palermo early in 1848. Here again the incitement was a detested foreign rule—that of the Neapolitans. Avoiding the secrecy of most revolutionary moves, the rebels on January 10 announced that they would strike on the 12th. And strike they did; citizens of all ranks fought side by side, the aristocrat along with the plowman and the priest, and within two weeks the army of the Kingdom of Naples had been beaten—a triumph that, while only temporary, lent impetus to other revolutionary moves throughout Italy.

The nature of the uprising in Palermo is evident in this account by Guiseppe La Farina, a Sicilian historian who became a member of the committee of war and later the minister of defense in Sicily:

> . . . Small bands were forming themselves here and there. They had neither rules, orders, nor plans; they did not barricade the streets; they did not make trenches . . . troops of children preceded them, dancing and singing. . . . In the night the insurgents were recruited from the country districts and the neighboring communes. . . . By the next day Fiera Vecchia contained about 300 men armed with guns, and as many more armed with scythes, billhooks, knives, spits, and those iron tools which the popular fury changes into arms. The fortress of Castellmare bombarded the city; the artillery of the royal palace was dragged along the Cassero; but the insurgents attacked, stormed and destroyed the police commissariats and made themselves masters of the military hospital of San Francesco Saverio; the soldiers who remained prisoners were embraced as brothers.[1]

Elsewhere at about the same time, the blows were aimed in many directions. The professional revolutionary and ardent republican, Mazzini, had his moment in the sun as one of a short-lived triumvirate which the revolution established to rule the Roman state. Garibaldi, the adventurous captain of irregular troops, made his daring march across Italy with 4000 men in the cause of Italian freedom rather than lay down his arms to a foreign enemy. In Germany riot roared and blood spilled into the streets when mobs in Berlin protested the King's failure to grant needed reforms. In the inquisitorial police state of Austria the almost legendary figure of Metternich, who had stood like a concrete block in the way of progress, was driven in one day from his apparently impregnable perch and fled for his life when students and professors led the rioting against his rule. In Bohemia the hopes for Czech liberty were blasted out of existence when on June 17, 1848, the cannon of Prince Windischgratz blazed out against Prague. And in Hungary the revolution was sparked by the brilliant oratory of Louis Kossuth, who attacked the "stagnant bureaucratic system" and "the pestilential air from the Vienna charnel house," and demanded parliamentary government. Copies of the speech containing this inflammatory material were widely distributed and incited flaming agitations among students and others, against whom the police at first made no move, although later the troops were ordered out and fired a volley whose chief effect was to unite the previously disconnected demonstrators.

But the Hungarian hopes were not to be long-lived. Kossuth, whose demands had been granted for a time, was proclaimed President of a Hungarian republic; but in April 1849, the illusion of independence was blasted away with the aid of Russian troops—Kossuth was fortunate to escape with his life by slipping out of the country while other revolutionaries were executed.

One notes that most if not all of these movements originated in riots that escalated, usually escalated rapidly to revolutionary dimensions. One also notes that outbreaks in any country might provide an example to rebels in other lands, particularly since the revolts in Austria, Hungary, Germany, etc., had this in common: in all a military and monarchical tyranny was opposed by liberal or democratic forces. That these forces generally did not succeed is perhaps of less overall significance than the precedent they established—a precedent which would not be forgotten in the far more devastating outbursts of the 20th century, when they would advance democracy less than Communism while giving impetus to the world-upsetting ideas of Karl Marx.

But one of the most momentous rebellions of 1848 occurred not in Italy nor Germany nor Austria-Hungary but in that perennial storm-center, France, where it differed in many ways from that in any other country.

ii. Confusion in France

A curious fact about France in the early 19th century is that the Revolution, which seemingly had extirpated the monarchy, led to the rise of a new monarch under the title of First Consul and then of Emperor, and later made way for official restoration of the old royal line under fat, gouty, unimpressive Louis XVIII, followed by his brother, the still more unimpressive elderly onetime rake now turned religious, who took the name of Charles X. Then, when the Revolution of 1830 with its mob demonstrations drove Charles into exile in England, he was succeeded by the generally unobjectionable but unimposing Duc d'Orleans, Louis

Philippe, who became a familiar figure as he walked the streets of Paris, gray-hatted and umbrella under arm. Under his "Constitutional" rule France flourished materially, but the regime was a bourgeois one without kingly flash or pomp. Perhaps the most damning charge ever hurled against Louis Philippe was that he bored the people, but it was significant that he and his celebrated minister Guizot stood out against reform when reform was badly needed. On the one hand, he was confronted by the rising wave of liberalism and even radicalism in popular thought, the demand for political reform and for improvement in the lot of the urban worker; and he made little effort to meet these challenges. And, on the other hand, he faced a revival of the Napoleonic legend, the myth of military grandeur which flourished in an invigorating atmosphere now that the monstrous losses and sufferings of the long series of wars were fading out amid the hazes of remoteness and inspiriting fiction—fiction that would favor the elevation of the scheming, unheroic Louis Napoleon to a hero's post under the title of the Emperor Napoleon III.

Here are facts which, although their implications may not have been clear to the King until too late, must be remembered if we are to understand the Parisian tumults of 1848. Yet some observers did have premonitions of things-to-be; one was the poet Heinrich Heine, who has vividly described what he saw in Paris in 1842. In particular, he noted the incendiary material in the reading matter of some workmen in the factory district of Saint-Marceau—speeches by Robespierre, pamphlets by Marat, "Cormenin's poisonous little works," and other writings that smelled "of blood." "The songs which I heard them singing," he goes on to say, "seem to have been composed in hell and have a chorus of the wildest excitement. . . . Sooner or later the harvest which will come from the sowing in France threatens to be a republican outbreak."[2]

Other intellectuals also could see clearly enough the faults of the country and the evils of its materialistic preoccupations. In the business world of his day, the searching eye of Balzac discerned "a basket of live crabs seeking to devour one another."[3] Content with its traders' and bankers' code of prosperity, as expressed by Louis Philippe's policy of "Peace and Industry," the regime in its foreign affairs could lean toward the backward-looking Metternich, while on the home front it sat back in a complacent conservatism, indifferent or blind to such matters as

the low average wage of the workingman and the continual rise
in the rate of poverty-induced crime. France of the Constitutional Monarchy was not unique in the modern world in em-
bracing the illusion that if all is well commercially, then all is
well with society, and that the prosperity of the upper and middle
classes, by some mysterious process of social osmosis, will seep
down to the less favored elements. Such a philosophy, however,
in France of the 1840s no less than in America of a later day,
proved to be not without its dangers.

It may be that the factory workers of France were not, on the
whole, so badly off as their cousins in the execrable mills and
slums of Birmingham and Manchester, even though conditions
in Alsace and in the textile heart of Lille were inhuman and
degrading. These industrial abysses, however, afflicted fewer people than did the growth of poverty and the spread of public relief
in Paris, where in 1847, it was said, a third of the city's million
people were recipients of charity, while criminal gangs increasingly exploited the community. Bad harvests, not least the potato
blight, complicated the situation; political scandals and crimes
in high places added to popular distrust; unemployment among
the poor contrasted with orgies of speculation among the mon-
eyed; and meanwhile nothing was done to alleviate the growing
sickness of society. Thus the prosperity of a business administration, even as that which American conservatives were wont to
acclaim in the halcyon days before 1929, was in reality nothing
but a mirage behind whose roseate sheen revolutionary pressures
were accumulating.

Contributing to those pressures, there were radicals and liberals of all tints and hues: communists, socialists, utopians, and
plain level-headed analysts who saw the rifts in the social structure, and demanded, if not drastic reform, at least the removal
of that fortress wall in the way of progress, Prime Minister Guizot. But Guizot, and likewise his master the King, remained
grandly self-assured and stolidly unaware that they stood on
crumbling pillars. In his insensitiveness to the forces battering
away at the regime, Guizot could go so far (in a speech of December 28, 1847, ghost-written by him, though Louis Philippe
was its mouthpiece) as to accuse his opponents of "blind and
hostile passions"—which meant, obviously, that their claims, however reasonable, could expect scant consideration.

Yet Guizot's position, seen through his own eyes, may have
looked impregnable. While he remained in office, the reformers

would have about as much chance as the serfs of Russia had to win freedom under Czar Peter I. And he would remain in office as long as the vote was left to the "stockholders" of what Alexis de Tocqueville has pointedly termed the "business company" of the government of Louis Philippe.

The spokesmen of the opposing forces, enraged at the speech of December 28, arranged for a public banquet (banquets were at this time a common device for appealing to the public by means of stirring orations). As nothing more than an orderly protest seemed to be intended, a compromise was reached by which the government permitted the meeting, until it was revealed that a public demonstration was also planned, and that members of the National Guards had been invited to attend in uniform with the aim of "defending liberty by protecting order and preventing interference by the police."

Without delay, Guizot acted against this rebellious move by prohibiting both the demonstration and the banquet. But if he still did not perceive that he was staggering on the brink of a smoking pit, he might have been warned when, in mid-morning of February 22, 1848, knots of workmen began to gather at the Place de la Concorde, from which they crossed the Seine to the Chamber of Deputies. Joined by students from the Latin Quarter, they began to yell, "Vive la Réforme! A bas Guizot!" until a contingent of soldiers forced them back to the Place de la Concorde.

Even now the King apparently did not realize that his throne was tottering. But next morning he again called out the troops, since the mobs still milled about and had even started to throw up barricades. Now came a critical moment; the National Guards, summoned by Louis Philippe to aid the regular army in holding threatened points against the rebels, disobeyed orders and joined the crowd that continued to shout, "Vive la Réforme! A bas Guizot!" And the King, a rarity among monarchs, yielded in regard to the Prime Minister. "I have seen enough blood spilt," he said.

Unfortunately, it was too late. Bloodshed was not avoided; the sacrifice of Guizot only whetted the mob's appetite for further concessions. Soon after sunset following the Prime Minister's dismissal, a crucial incident occurred. A procession of demonstrators, making its way down the Boulevard des Capucines with torches and a red flag, was confronted by a detachment of the 14th regiment on guard duty before the Ministry of Foreign

Affairs. A shot rang out; the horse bearing the commander of the troops fell with a broken leg; and this caused the men to panic, in the belief that they were under attack. In the ensuing volley, 50 or more persons were hit (52 were killed, according to the contemporary historian Elias Regnault, while another account lists 35 dead and 47 wounded). The inexactness of the numbers, however, did not affect the usefulness of the massacre as propaganda. Some of the dead, piled into an omnibus and paraded before the multitude, had the effect of oil upon smoldering faggots.

At about this time, in an effort to meet the growing crisis, the King added ineptitude to ineptitude by making two appointments that virtually cancelled one another: the conciliatory journalist Thiers and the militaristic Marshal Bugeard. But the latter proved ineffective and was quickly discharged after General Bedeau, a hero of the conquest of Algiers, had vainly tried to negotiate with the rabble, who were now yelling, "Le peuple est le maître. Á bas Louis Philippe!" (The people rules. Down with Louis Philippe!).

On the morning of February 24, the 75-year-old King decided to confront the agitators, and rode forth from the Tuileries with Bugeard, Thiers, and a few others. After hearing encouraging cries of "Vive le Roi!" he faced a demonstrating legion of the National Guards, whose shouts roared in his ears, "Á bas les ministres! Á bas le système!"—which was much as if a mob in our own time clamored, "Down with the government! Down with the establishment!" Some of the men, flourishing their weapons, swarmed about the monarch, confronting him with the sort of test that may make or unmake a man. If he was ever to show who was the king and master, now was the time. But portly, genial Louis Philippe was not built in an heroic mold. He was no Caesar or Alexander to win men's hearts by the power of his personality, the magnetism of his eloquence; he was only a timid old man, who meekly turned and rode away, not even pausing to review the waiting troops. And that, for all practical purposes, was the end of Louis Philippe.

After this spectacle, not even his most loyal followers could be expected to fight for him with enthusiasm. The one course he had left himself was to abdicate, and this he promptly did, under the illusion that he would be followed in his high office by his young grandson. But never again would anyone of his line rule in France. He was fortunate to escape with his life after the crowd had stormed into the Tuileries; he and the other members of the royal family boarded three carriages and eventually made their way to England.

iii.   The Barricades of Paris

A vivid account of the insurrection of February 23 and 24 has been preserved for us by Marc Caussidière, a socialist who was himself involved in the fighting and was among those who seized the Prefecture of Police. He tells how the insurgents had come into the streets with their work tools on the 23rd, and, in preparation for the next day's fighting, "cut down the beautiful trees of the boulevards," and "demolished the railings of the monuments, the lamp-posts, fountains and sheds, and everything that might serve to hinder the passage of troops; they carried on to the pavements materials from houses under construction, beams, blocks of stone, planks, and carts; and all this was built round with formidable walls of paving-stones."[4] Axes crashed down, weapons clashed, detonations rang out in the darkness, the monotonous notes of the tocsin sounded, and soon the rebels, guarded by sentinels, might have been seen manning the newly made barricades, squatting around sparkling braziers, molding bullets, collecting weapons, quietly smoking their pipes, or rushing from barricade to barricade with the glorious news of the King's downfall. The narrator proceeds:

> The passage of the Porte Saint-Denis was closed by an enormous barricade, and the principal entries into the insurgent camp were equally defended by insurmountable barriers. In the little streets of the center . . . barricades succeeded each other almost every ten paces, and the fighters moved about enthusiastically in this labyrinth of little citadels. . . . To see the exaltation of the people . . . to hear the shouts of *vive la republique*, made by men, women, and children, made one feel that the revolution would be accomplished.[5]

Heinrich Heine, in a letter dated March 3, 1848, offers further pictures of what happened:

> I had a good seat from which to watch the performance—as a matter of fact, a reserved seat, as the street in which I found myself by chance was closed by barricades at either end. . . . I had full opportunity of admiring the talent of the French in building barricades. Those lofty bulwarks and fortifications . . . were here im-

provised in a few moments. They spring as if by magic from the
ground; one would think that the earth-spirits had a hand in the
game.[6]

The writer goes on to give further details and in particular to
comment on the absence of stealing:

Many objects were demolished by the people in their anger . . .
but there was no looting. Only weapons were taken, whenever they
could be found—and in the royal palaces the people were allowed
to help themselves to provisions.[7]

Despite the violence of the outbreak, one notes some favorable
contrasts with certain insurrections of a later day.

One gets the impression, furthermore, that as in the case of
the greater revolution that had broken out 59 years before, not
everything had fallen into place of its own momentum. As one
of the historians of 1848 tells us with evident understatement,
"there was a handful which acted on the night of February 23
with remarkable discipline and unanimity,"[8] making it "not certain to what extent the February uprising was a spontaneous
movement."[9] And in this we can perhaps divine the hidden reason
why there was a major outbreak in Paris in February 1848, and
why, having erupted, it took the particular form known to history.

iv.   The Provisional Government of Lamartine

In the Provisional Government that replaced the monarchy,
the dominant figure was the Minister for Foreign Affairs, 58-
year-old Alphonse de Lamartine, who has made a double entry
in the history of France, first as poet, and then as politician. Had
he never ventured outside the doors of literature, he would be
remembered for his lyric and epic poetry; and he was well known
for his prose. As the author of a *History of the Girondins* (1847),
he did much to arouse republican sentiment, even though scholars have complained that his book was poorly documented. This
history, a liberal work in which he exalted Robespierre, was in
part responsible for his rise in 1848; but as far back as 1833 he
had been a deputy, and with great seriousness had exchanged the
robe of the Muses for that of the legislator. He possessed, indeed,
many qualifications of the successful politician, including great

personal magnetism and attractiveness, a magnificent voice, and an eloquence that made him eminent among the orators of his times. His popularity was immense; in that eventful February of 1848 when Louis Philippe was overturned, the name of Lamartine was among those shouted by the crowd in its quest of new leaders. Acting as the people's spokesman, he had led the throngs that crowded into the Hôtel de Ville, and had drawn up the proclamation of the Provisional Government. It was the brilliance of his appeals to the masses that kept the Government alive regardless of threat after threat during its shaky first days.

And yet his situation, in the face of the surging, riotous rabble, was inconceivably difficult. By the rush and force of his ideas, the inspiriting flow of his rhetoric, he was able to prevail over a heckler who challenged his right to take over the government. But he faced a graver problem on the morning of February 25, when a crowd of workers forced its way into the Hôtel de Ville, its leaders fingering guns and calling for a proclamation of the right to work—a guarantee of employment for all. Again Lamartine turned on his flow of words, but for once words did not suffice. There came a sharp interruption: "Assez de phrases comme ça!" (Enough of that kind of talk!). The most that the people would concede was a three-month period of preparation. After that time (as embodied in a decree drafted by Louis Blanc, a socialist member of the government) work would be guaranteed to every citizen.

This assurance, published apparently without the knowledge of Lamartine or other moderates, placed him indeed in a dilemma: to accept socialism as an accomplished fact, or to resign. He thought, however, that somehow he could maneuver a way around the difficulty, and continued hopefully in office. But his problems would only grow with the months, the more so as the workers of Paris were beginning to taste the sweets of seemingly unlimited power. The opposition had hit upon a secret which more recent demonstrators on college campuses and in the heart of great cities seem not to have forgotten. To the protesters, as one commentator puts it, "the art of politics was delightfully simple. It consisted in getting up a demonstration for whatever was wanted, and, provided the demonstration was noisy and threatening enough, Lamartine and his friends would always give way."[10]

Yet for some months the poet-statesman would still prevail. Lord Normanby, the British Ambassador at the time of the downfall of Louis Philippe, has given us in his journal an example of the oratory by which Lamartine subdued the mob. The particular incident occurred on the afternoon of February 25, when the workers, sweeping into the Hôtel de Ville with the red flag uplifted, demanded that this symbol be taken to represent the new order. But Lamartine, to whom the red flag signified anarchy, could not yield. Although aware that they might not emerge alive, he and two other members of the Government went out to confront the mob.

"Citizens," he said, "you have power to lay hands on the Government, you have power to command it to change the banner of the nation and the name of France. If you are so ill advised and so obstinate in error as to impose upon it the republic of a party and the standard of terror, the Government, I am well assured, is as determined as myself to perish rather than dishonor itself by obeying you. As for myself, never shall my hand sign such a decree! I will reject, even to death, this banner of blood, and you should repudiate it still more than myself, for this red flag you offer has only made the circuit of the Champ de Mars, dragged through the people's blood in 1791 and 1793, while the tricolor has made the circuit of the world, with the name, with the glory and liberty of your country."[11]

Normanby proceeds to tell how Lamartine was "interrupted by almost unanimous cries of enthusiasm," and how he "fell from the chair which served him as a platform into the arms stretched out to him from every side." Routed, the rioters shrank back. "Vive Lamartine!" they clamored. "Vive le drapeau tricolore!"

But it would take more than oratory to preserve the insurrectionary government.

v. Street Fighting and Terror

Rebels, like other men, often overreach themselves, defeating their ends through the shortsightedness of their methods. Thus it was when the socialist Louis Blanc, applying pressure on the Government, maneuvered it into a position in which it either had to guarantee work for every man or face the peril of overthrow. By this he did nothing for the long-range improvement of the worker's lot; all that he did was to guarantee a political crisis within a few months, and one that the Government proved unable to survive. Whether it could have survived in any case is, to be sure, highly questionable; but Blanc's move swept away its last chance.

The issue concerned the National Workshops, which the Provisional Government had established two days after its recognition of every man's right to a job. The next day, February 28, Minister of Public Works Marie announced the organization of "important operations," and said that any workman might apply to take part in them. But the young republican, Emile Thomas, the Director of the Workshops, had no idea of providing everyone with work; what he did was to propose a Labor Exchange which would distribute doles after registering the men by their trades and their sections of the city. Within a few days, 17,000 had been registered, of whom about 3000 were put to work on what we nowadays would call "public works projects" such as repairing roads and terracing the Quai de la Gare, while an additional 6000 were engaged by the Ministry of War—which meant that nearly half of the original 17,000 remained jobless.

But this was far from the worst. The numbers of unemployed continued to swell, even though the employed increased to around 120,000—in less than four months, or by June 20, the Workshops had closed their doors against 49,000 applicants. At the same time, splits were appearing inside the Government, which had not gone far enough to suit its more radical members, and was accused by Louis Blanc of creating a "rabble of paupers" (his charge took substance from the fact that workers who could have earned 40 sous a day on the Government program, would be paid 30 sous if they remained idle, and so were encouraged to do at most 10 sous worth of work). The situation, in truth, was one not unfamiliar in other countries that have experimented with the "dole," though added sparks of trouble were provided by an undercore of determined socialists whose minds were set upon gaining more than the authorities had vouchsafed. It was the chasm in opinion between the moderates and the more extreme elements that, more than anything else, brought down the regime.

One obvious fact is that the reforms envisaged by the "right to work" would so revolutionize society that, however justified they might be, they could be reached only by well-planned, carefully planted measures extending over a considerable period. Buffeted by opposing currents of thought under the improvised conditions of the Provisional Government, the innovations were certain to fail. Hence fuel was being heaped up for the June crisis. If the National Workshops were to be abandoned, as the prevailing sentiment of the nation seemed to demand, what should be done with the more than one hundred thousand men the program employed? The answer came on June 21 with the publication of a decree drafted some time before: Unmarried workers must enlist in the army, or be ready to go to assignments in the provinces. Already on June 22, a detachment left to participate in a drainage operation in the marshes of Sologne.

Here was the waiting and heaped-up firewood for insurrection, even for civil war. And the trouble, which was not unexpected by the Government, broke out with blazing fury.

"Bread or bullets! Bullets or work!" shouted a crowd demonstrating in front of the column of the Bastille with the cry of the desperate and hungry. Again the streets were blocked by barricades—400 of them!—and these fortifications were commanded with skill and organization by capable officers. The passion that drove the men on was described by the celebrated astronomer Francois Arago, who had become Minister of the Navy and also Minister of War in the Provisional Government. A man of strong republican sympathies, he approached one of the barricades and asked why the men had taken up arms. "Monsieur Arago," someone replied, "you have never starved. You do not know what misery is." And so there was nothing for the astronomer to do but withdraw.

The answer he received, however, came far from expressing the entire truth. Hunger, as we have seen, may have been an element in the outbreak, but another powerful ingredient was the fact that the extremists, having been overwhelmingly beaten in the April elections, saw their only chance in a resort to force. Violence, as so often, implied the failure of reasoned methods.

In escaping unscathed, Arago was fortunate compared with certain others, such as General Brea, who, appealing to the rebels to yield, was enticed inside their lines with his chief of staff, and murdered. Or consider the case of Monsieur Affre, the Archbishop of Paris, who went among the barricades crucifix in hand and clad in the resplendent robes of his calling, asking for an hour's truce; even while appealing to the mob, he was fatally shot. Hundreds of fighters and civilians—some estimates have placed the total as not less than 4500—paid with their lives in the goriest street fighting Paris had ever seen, while property valued at millions of francs was destroyed.

The savagery of the four-day contest has been portrayed by

contemporaries, including the socialist leader Louis Blanc, who tells how the fight "assumed gigantic proportions" in the Faubourg du Temple. With the falling of night, the rebels were in complete command:

> Terrible was that night—a night of expectation and grief! On the following morning, the heavy guns began to thunder once more against the Faubourg, without gaining the least advantage over the insurgents, while the troops advanced, retreated and advanced again, with alternate wrath and discouragement. Until Sunday morning, the blood of countrymen and fellow-citizens was flowing in disastrous rivalry. What was most lamentable of all, was the inexorable fury of the fight between the working men and the Garde Mobile—between fathers on one side, and sons on the other![12]

Blanc also depicts the terror of the reprisals, when prisoners were shot from air-holes as they huddled together beneath the terraces in the Garden of the Tuileries, or else were gunned down en masse in the cemeteries, in cloisters, in quarries, and in the court of the Hôtel de Cluny. For days terror hovered over the city, amid unspeakable barbarities. Nor is it much of an explanation to plead, as does Blanc, that "These atrocities were the acts of scoundrels, whom every party would reject, but upon whom, unhappily, the state of siege, the public stupor, the fear and rage of some, the consternation of others, had for the moment conferred an odious authority."[13]

This is merely to say that the uprising followed the course of many riots and insurrections, and also of many of the sanguinary episodes of warfare, from the horrors committed by Nazi occupation forces in World War II to the American massacre at My Lai in 1968, bringing out the most savage emotions, elevating the most ferocious of men to command, and subordinating humanity to frenzy and cruelty. All this should not surprise even if it does depress and horrify us. Nor should we be astonished at the sequel. The government of Lamartine and his republican associates were indeed destroyed—but of what advantage was this to the people of France? What advantage to the worker in search of a job? It may be all very well to fight for bread, but bread is not produced by bullets; the frightfulness of the methods of the rebels alienated the middle classes, which might otherwise have enlisted many sympathizers. It was not the workers who prevailed; it was the troops of General Cavignac, who restored order to the torn city after he had been given dictatorial powers.

In November, it is true, a new constitution was adopted, acknowledging the sovereignty of the people, and establishing a republic with a president and representative assembly. But what of the period that followed?

If the working classes had wrested the priceless boon of universal suffrage from the revolution of 1848, this boon had come to them under the very government they had bloodily overthrown. And if there was to be great urban and industrial expansion, materialism was to triumph; the things of the spirit would be subordinated; the rich would grow richer, and the powerful more powerful. The progress which the workers were to continue to make, as in most countries while industrialism advanced, must be set against the fact that an era of repression and class hatred had been inaugurated; in the press censorship, the controlled elections, the police rule of the adventurer Louis Napoleon upon his rise to supremacy as the Emperor Napoleon III, the laboring masses could hardly feel the same socialistic or democratic sympathies as under Lamartine.

One is entitled to ask some questions. Had the workers not revolted in June 1848, would there ever have been a Napoleon III? And had there been no Napoleon III, would there have been a Franco-Prussian War (into which the Emperor let himself be tricked by the wily Bismarck)? And without the nationalistic and militaristic incentives of the Franco-Prussian War, would there have been a First World War, at least as it took shape in 1914? Further, had there been no First World War, would the nations have been afflicted with the long and grievous succession of evils, the riots and the revolutions, the local and global conflicts, the dictatorships, the unprecedented havoc and sadism and slaughter, the conversion of great nations into armed camps, the perils of world annihilation which have fallen upon us since 1914 like the manifestations of a universal insanity?

Not all the answers to these questions can lie with the Frenchmen who threw up barricades against fellow Frenchmen on those disturbed Parisian streets in June 1848. But the fighters behind the barricades, like most rebels at most times, could have had no idea what seeds they were contributing to a dire sowing for all mankind.

9. Russia: Hotbed of Rebellion

i. Iron Czars and Peasant Revolts

In 1917, when the magnificent old capital of St. Petersburg was shaken by one of the great revolutions of all time, the explosion did not come without preliminaries. The way had been prepared by the oppression, the discontent, the violence of centuries, even though the fuse and the spark had been supplied by the disruption of a great war, added to the ineptness of a purblind and reactionary government.

Nearly a century and a half before, in 1774, the furies that were to batter down czardom might have been seen in the spokesmen of the rebellious Cossack Emelian Pugachev, who galloped across the steppes, challenging the autocracy in the name of autocracy, and circulating the claim that their leader was Czar Peter III (the husband of Catherine II, who disappeared from history in 1762 under mysterious circumstances that lent strength to the myth of his survival). Surely there has never been a stranger claimant to a throne than the nearly illiterate Pugachev, a representative not of the royalty from which he claimed descent but of the poor people and in particular the peasants, whose wrongs were deep and old, and who hoped for deliverance from the claws of the landlords, the factory owners, the government officials. He made his aims clear when, after taking the district of Kazan, he crossed the Volga and seemed to threaten Moscow. Serfdom, he announced, was to be abolished; war was to be waged against the gentry. To the ex-serfs he granted "liberty and freedom, always to be Cossacks, without recruiting levies, poll taxes or other money taxes, with possession of the land, the woods, the hay meadows, the fishing grounds."[1] Having gone on to announce the deliverance of the oppressed from "the malefactor landowners and the bribe-taker officials and judges," he proceeded pitilessly to demand that the offenders be seized, hanged, treated as they had treated the peasants. And he ended with naive hope: "With the extermination of these enemies and malefactor gentry every one will begin to enjoy a quiet and peaceful life, which will continue evermore."[2]

This pronouncement reflected the attitude of the abused masses quite as much as of their leader. It explains why Pugachev could rage across the country, a punishing fury who seemed to endanger the government of Catherine II, who slaughtered more than 1500 of the privileged classes and some 1300 other persons, and was checked only after the Empress had sent a powerful force against him under one of her best generals. Actually, the poorly armed, poorly organized, undisciplined and comparatively small rebellious bands (which never numbered more than 15,000 to 20,000 men) could not have posed a real threat to any trained, well equipped army. But the great headway made by Pugachev before his eventual capture and execution was eloquent of the power of the forces of latent dissent. Nevertheless, as the Cossack's claim to be Peter III testified, the revolt was not against czarism itself, which was generally regarded as almost sacrosanct; it was aimed at social rather than political grievances.

The same was true of a number of other uprisings in the 17th and 18th centuries. In 1606, nearly a century and three-quarters before Pugachev's flare-up, a former household serf and galley slave, I. I. Bolotnikov, had sought to install himself in a seat of power, and had led an army composed largely of Cossacks and runaway peasants—a move symptomatic of deep-seated social unrest, as were a succession of later outbreaks, including those of the Cossacks Stenka Razin (1670–71) and K. Bulavin (1707–08). The chief significance of all these rebellions is not in what they accomplished, though some of them did inflict great damage and terrorize wide areas; their chief significance is in the evidence which they give of an underlying vast current of popular disaffection.

It is difficult if not impossible for us today to put ourselves into the state of mind of a Russian peasant of the 17th, 18th, or early 19th century; in many respects his lot resembled that of the medieval peasant elsewhere in Europe. Living in filth and hovels, denied the marvelous extension of consciousness provided by learning, treated in many cases more as a thing than a person, he

was the prey of exploiting forces, increasingly fastened down by
a serfdom that differed from slavery in name rather than in fact.
His movements, more and more, were placed under fetters; he
came to be literally owned by the landholder if not by the state;
he could be sold like a horse or a plow or even gambled away; he
could be flogged almost to the point of death at his master's will;
he must submit to his master's adjudication of disputes (from
which, after 1767, there was not even the flimsiest right of appeal) ;
and he could not leave his master's land or marry without permission (usually he paid for the privilege of taking a wife) . While
a law of 1734 required the owner to aid the serf in case of need,
the very fact that such a provision was thought necessary is eloquent of the state of the times; but the practical efficacy of the
enactment remains in doubt, as does that of the limited government measures on behalf of the aged, sick, and needy.

Meanwhile, even apart from landowners, destitution, famine,
and other natural calamities, the peasant lived in fear of two
great afflictions, perhaps the more frightening of which was the
tax collector, who bore down every three years with a reign of
terror that might last two months and subject the delinquent to
the knout and even to execution. But also deeply to be dreaded
were the army officials, who, from the time of Peter I (1718) subjected the peasant to a gruelling supervision, not only in the heavy
burden of recruits which they exacted, but in checking and re-
straining the people's movements, and in pursuing and arresting
the wretches who tried to save themselves by flight.

Under these circumstances, it is not surprising if grumblings
were frequent and revolts now and then flamed forth—flamed
forth despite their hopelessness in the face of greater might re-
morselessly applied. But here were some of the distant preliminaries of 1917.

Other preliminaries were provided by the political tightening
of the screws, particularly under Peter the Great, who had wound
new impositions about the necks of the peasants, had conscripted
farm-boys and city laborers alike and forced them to drudge in
founding the city of St. Petersburg and digging the Ladoga Canal
under conditions that killed thousands from overwork, unsanitary
living quarters, maladministration, disease, and shortages of food.
Later in the century Catherine II, though supposedly of liberal
leanings, was so deeply enmeshed by the landowning class that she
too enlarged the range of serfdom and imposed new restraints,

as when she extended the right of the master to send the serf to Siberia or to dispatch him to the army or imprison him for "impudence."

Here, in the deep-rooted sufferings of the people, we do not have the precursors of inevitable armed dissent on the streets of St. Petersburg in 1917. But we do have some of the ancestral forces leading toward that dissent, which might never have occurred, at least in the form it actually took, had no grievous abuses been inflicted on the peasants and city workers by centuries of czars and whip-wielding landlords.

ii.　Further Despotism and Dissent

Russia for centuries resembled an ice-crowned volcano, beneath whose surface boiling furies were accumulating, revealing themselves now and then in geysers of steam before the devastating inevitable eruption. Meanwhile the keepers of the land, the czars and their agents, were recklessly if unconsciously adding to the danger by measures aggravating the pressures.

An example was to be seen in 1816, under Alexander I, who had shown a pretense of liberalism upon becoming czar 15 years before at the age of 24. But it was not a liberal sovereign who, influenced by the writings of the French General Servan, established a military district in Novgorod, turned its men into soldiers, subjected them to the blows and abasement of military service and also forced them to grow food for the army, while many of the villages were destroyed, the children underwent military regimentation, and the adults were assigned mates without being consulted, somewhat like animals on a farm, were told how many offspring they were to produce, and (in the case of the women) were fined if they did not contribute sufficiently to the program.

Strange to say, the unobliging peasants seemed not to appreciate the benefits thus showered upon them. Some, in token of their dissent, refused to cut off their beards as the authorities demanded; others were so churlish as to object to compulsory marriage and the obliteration of private life. Still other ingrates revolted, which led the Czar to insist that the military colonies would continue even if he had "to cover the road with corpses all the way from Petersburg to Chodov." It is not recorded that he did make corpses enough to carry out this amiable intention, but in 1819, following a revolt in Chuguiev, he did go some distance in this direction. After 275 rebels had been sentenced to die, he reduced the penalty to the running of the gauntlet of a thousand men 12 times—which actually substituted death by a particularly cruel means, as the victim's chance of survival was slight. To pleas for mercy, Alexander turned a deaf ear; he conceded that "the occasion is doubtless painful," but could see no solution except "to let the full weight and severity of the law take its course." As a result, according to the report of the French ambassador, 160 men died, 26 women were beaten and imprisoned, and 56 officers were severely disciplined.

Like most extreme measures, however, these penalties were self-defeating. They not only failed to crush dissent, they inspired it; resentment among the intellectuals and in the army was widespread; and impetus was given to underground movements, even though the time had not yet come when the rebels could organize their forces or act effectively. But here was one of the roots of the revolutionary attempt of 1825, at which we shall glance in passing.

All the while, quite aside from the incentives to revolt provided by Alexander's efforts to out-Spartan ancient Sparta, the seeds and hidden sprouts of insurgency remained alive among the peasants. This is shown, for one thing, by the fact that peasant insurrections did not end when Pugachev in 1775 was put to death in the Red Square. Although the equal of Pugachev's outbreak would not be seen again until the 20th century, it is not hard to detect the symptoms of impending revolution in the numerous uprisings of the country folk (400 of them between 1845 and 1855, the last ten years of the reign of the repressive Czar Nicholas I, while as many more occurred in the following years) :

> In twenty years (1835–54) two hundred and thirty serf-owners or their baliffs were killed; in three years before emancipation another fifty-three. The situation far exceeded in scale and intensity that of the most disturbed districts of Ireland in the eighties.[3]

Emanicipation, proclaimed by Czar Alexander II in 1861, therefore seemed inevitable if the most serious trouble was to be avoided. But emancipation proved to be no panacea. Not only did it in some ways increase the woes of the peasants, who broke out in various quickly suppressed revolts, but it fanned discontent among other classes also, including the nobles who resented the loss of their privileges, and the intelligentsia whose roots were deep in the philosophical movements of the times. Both the nobles and the intellectuals provided additional impulses toward 1917, and this, in fact, was to be seen as far back as 1825, in the short-lived "Decembrist Revolution."

This outburst was staged by liberal army officers who had been repelled by Russian tyranny and inspired by Western ideas; it aimed at various reforms, beginning with the overthrow of the recently crowned Czar Nicholas I, and ranging from the establishment of a limited monarchy to the freeing of the serfs and the guarantee of the rights of the individual. The insurrection, however, was poorly organized by men who could not agree upon most of their objectives; and it came quickly to a bloody end when the cavalry of Nicholas, carrying out his orders, fired upon the rebels on the sleety streets of the capital. Many were slain outright; many were drowned in the Neva as they attempted to flee across the thin ice; and many were captured. One hundred twenty-one, most of them nobles, were brought to trial; five were sentenced to death, including the leader Paul Pestel and the poet K. F. Ryleiev, whose hanging produced a furor throughout the country. It was apparently only by accident that one of the most renowned of all Russian poets, Alexander Pushkin, did not meet the same fate. His biographer Henri Troyat, in describing the poet's meeting with the Czar after the rout of the Decembrists, attests to his involvement:

"Would you have been taken in the December 14th uprising if you had been in St. Petersburg?"
Pushkin's eyes flashed.
"Without the slightest doubt, Your Majesty. All my friends were in the plot. It would not have been possible for me to desert them. Only my absence saved me, and thank God it did."[4]

But while it was the good fortune of Puskin and of literature that he escaped the doom of Ryleiev, despotism had clamped itself more strongly upon the Russian people, intellectual freedom was being choked more than ever, and most of the remaining dissenters had to scurry underground.

They had, however, been suppressed without being subdued, and this had made them all the more dangerous. In secret cells and hideouts, new types of rebels were developing—men with an aristocratic or intellectual background, who made revolution a dedication and a profession, ready to go to jail or to the gallows for their cause. These agitators would not only travel into the countryside to instill the peasants with revolutionary ideas; in their one-minded fanaticism, they did not disdain extremist methods: in 1880, a member of a terrorist organization, a carpenter named Khalturin, threw a bomb intended to blow up the Czar as he dined in the Winter Palace. This attempt failed, but not so the effort of March 13 of the following year, when an assassination plot resulted in the Czar's death after various other tries had come to nothing.

Here once more violence was self-frustrating. Despite all the insurgents' deep-rooted and just grievances against despotism, the military repression, and the police rule, what conceivable contribution had the murder of Alexander II made to the cause of freedom? This ruler, the emancipator of the serfs, was less of a tyrant than his son and successor Alexander III turned out to be; on the very day of his assassination he had, ironically, signed an order calling for Representative Committees as Advisors to the Council of State, and thus, while far from granting the proposed constitution, he would have provided at least one short step on the long, long road to moderate government—a step that, because of the bomb that destroyed Alexander II, was never taken. But perhaps the most important result of the assassination was the effect upon the new emperor. Doubtless a man of his disposition, suddenly elevated to the Russian throne, would have been a despot in any case; but his father's dreadful fate, not unnaturally, reinforced his suspicion, fear, and hatred of popular causes, and strengthened his adherence to the principle of autocracy. And this principle he handed down to his son Nicholas II, who clung to it with a rigidity that would make him the last of the czars. If there were any possibility of gradual evolution from czardom to limited monarchy, that possibility received a serious, perhaps even a fatal setback in the violent death of Alexander II.

But since a brutally repressive rule remained, the hidden forces of dissent were still alive in the country; revolution continued to be plotted in secret, and revolutionary techniques were developed. And meanwhile the driving force behind the various organizations was hatred of the Czar and belief in the possibility of a government based upon the peasants.

iii. The Revolution of 1905

In 1905 the voice of protest broke out in St. Petersburg in demonstrations that were like dress rehearsals for the greater act of 1917, though not so intended. Quite aside from the hardship and czarist abuse stretching back to an unremembered past, there was an impulse of contemporary origin—the impulse provided by the war with Japan, whose chief incentives had been the mining and timber rights in Korea, though the conflict had also been intended by Minister of the Interior Pleve as a "little war" that might divert pressures from the home front. But this "little war," not unlike a more recent "little war" in Southeast Asia, had turned out to be an immense struggle that swallowed thousands of men and vast resources. Worse still, the great Russian Empire, plagued by the difficulties of land transportation across 5500 miles, had suffered defeat after defeat at the hand of once-despised little Japan. Not that all this might not have been endured had the Russian people seen any need for the war; but it was hard for the peasant or worker to discover much reason for the fighting, suffering, and dying in far-distant Asia.

Consequently, instead of fulfilling Pleve's hope of relieving tensions at home, the war only increased tensions; the effort to enhance the nation's power and glory abroad had jeopardized its security at home. Pleve was not the first strategist, nor would he be the last, who picked the wrong battlefield.

The Revolution of 1905, however, took fire even before some of the worst of the Russian wartime setbacks, such as the defeat of the imperial army at Mukden and the annihilation of the navy in the battle of Tsushima in May. Quite aside from the aggravating effects of the war, the rebels had political and economic objectives: freedom of speech, freedom of the press and of assembly, freedom from dictatorial restraints on their movements, freedom from arbitrary arrest, a national assembly to represent the people. And in the economic sphere, the workers sought what oppressed employees elsewhere have generally demanded—improvement in their meager pay, and shortening of their hours. Disillusioned with a government-supported Society for Mutual Aid for Working Men, which permitted them to frame petitions to the authorities under police supervision, and to set forth but not to correct their grievances, they had concluded that only by demonstrating could they obtain their rights.

And they did indeed demonstrate, though they could not have foreseen that their protests would lead to one of the memorable incidents in Russian history. Their leader was a priest of the orthodox faith, Father Georgi Gapon, who was not a revolutionary in the traditional sense; he might not have been a revolutionary at all had circumstances not made him so. The offshoot of a peasant family, a believer in Tolstoy's creed of nonviolence, an able orator and a convinced social reformer, this black-bearded 32-year-old man had no idea of overthrowing the Czar. His state of mind was plainly set forth in the letter which, on the eve of the great demonstration of January 22, he wrote to the sovereign:

> The people believe in Thee. They have made up their minds to gather at the Winter Palace tomorrow at 2 p.m. to lay their needs before Thee. . . . Do not fear anything. Stand tomorrow before the people and accept our humblest petition. I, the representative of the workingmen, and my comrades, guarantee the inviolability of Thy person.[5]

As Gapon was the head of a workers' organization licensed by the police and had a huge following, this appeal represented more than mere words. The authorities might well have been concerned, although there is no reason to doubt Gapon's intention to protect the Czar. But Nicholas II was taking no chances; he had already removed himself and his family from the city. Had he been the man to face the crowd, had he possessed the understanding to win their sympathy, the good will to make concessions, and the eloquence to sway men to his side, then Russian history in 1905 and all subsequent years might have been considerably different. However, a vast multitude, moved by uncertain passions, is at no time predictable or easy to control; it would have taken a braver, stronger and more astute, and above all more democratic man than Nicholas to confront the demonstrators with any hope of success. However, he did not confront them, and they were answered in the worst way possible, and with results that would leave deep imprints of bitterness and horror.

It has been estimated that the crowd, which moved toward the Winter Palace in five converging columns on the afternoon of January 22, numbered as many as two hundred thousand. But whether or not this figure is even approximately correct, unquestionably the marchers were very many. They must truly have presented a frightening sight as they advanced on the Winter Palace bearing ikons and singing "God Save the Czar," while Gapon at their head carried a petition setting forth their revolutionary demands, which included an eight-hour day, a minimum daily wage of one ruble, and a people's assembly. The marchers, under the pathetic illusion that their ruler could really be made to sympathize with a people's cause, were determined to see the

Czar and explain their case. Quite a different fate, however, awaited them.

What happened was similar to what has occurred on many another tragic occasion, as in Amritsar in India, Sharpeville in South Africa, and our own Chicago, Illinois. Though the demonstrators were unarmed and gave no evidence of hostile intentions, the guards at the Winter Palace, perhaps in a panic, fired upon the undefended people. Gapon, one of the first to fall, was uninjured, but others were less fortunate; several hundred were killed, and hundreds or thousands dropped wounded to the snow-covered streets.

Thus "Bloody Sunday," as it was not inappropriately called, became a focal point in the Revolution. Instead of suppressing the agitations, the brutal violence of the troops blew down upon the demonstrators like a raging wind, stirring resentment to new life. Perceiving that they could find no haven in czardom, the working classes were united as never before; strikes spread rapidly through the country; intellectuals joined forces with workers; universities were closed; terrorism raised a dragon head, notably in the burning of manor houses and the assassination of officials, including Grand Duke Serge, Governor-General of Moscow. In June sailors on the battleship *Prince Potemkin* mutinied, and pitched their officers overboard; in the autumn one of the most effective general strikes in history paralyzed the country, halted streetcars, shut down most of the railroads, and cut off water and electricity, while physicians, lawyers, teachers, bankers refused their services, and many businessmen closed their doors.

Meanwhile the Czar, perhaps horrified at the slaughter of "Bloody Sunday," had made some efforts to recompense the families of the dead and wounded. But in innumerable Russian minds, the sentiments of Father Gapon were echoed, and would continue to be echoed as long as the throne had an occupant: "The innocent blood of workers, their wives and children, lies forever between thee, O soul destroyer, and the Russian people."

The government's reactions during the continuing demonstrations which its own agents had done so much to provoke, were shot through with fury and terror. Under Premier Stolypin, savage reprisals were ordered against the revolutionaries, who were subjected to court-martial, and executed when found guilty—perhaps four to five thousand were thus put to death during the succeeding years (the largest recorded total was 782 in 1908). Meanwhile, scapegoats were made of those convenient ancient butts, the Jews; in more than a hundred cities, although St. Petersburg and Moscow were noteworthy exceptions, the unfortunate people were attacked by street mobs and by terrorist organizations, the "Black Hundreds"—in Odessa alone several hundred died in a four-day pogrom. There is little doubt that the secret police supplied funds to the murderous bands, and that the government aimed to divert revolutionary passions, complaints, and violence from the abuses of the rulers to the mythical misdeeds of a defenseless minority.

Nevertheless, the government's counter-terrorism did not suffice. It was also necessary, the officials found, to make political concessions—or, at least, political promises. In the midst of continued strikes, riots, and mutinies, which were to include three days of street fighting in Moscow by government forces against armed workers, plans were announced on December 24, 1905, for convocation of a new Duma. Thus for a time the rebels were placated. But the legislative body, when it did meet, proved to be largely a ruse and a delusion; its influence on foreign policy, finances, and appointments was slight; the landowning class was disproportionately represented in the election that brought it into being; and it was disbanded by the Czar in two months. A second Duma, which met in 1907, was likewise short-lived, and two succeeding Dumas offered the mere shadow of representative government.

Yet the creation of this body, weak as it was, did lead to an end of the wave of uprisings, and did introduce a new political principle even though in attenuated form. The demonstrations of 1905, besides, had brought into being two important groups: the Constitutional Democrats or "Cadets," who sought universal suffrage and a responsible ministry; and the Social Democrats, under Leon Trotsky, the leader of the relatively mild Menshiviks, who was to become the head of the Petersburg Soviet after his return to Russia in 1905, when Lenin remained in exile.

Thus, though the revolutionaries may have seemed to gain little or nothing in 1905 and the years immediately following, a basis was laid for the major eruption of 1917. That basis, however, was tenuous and unstable. The police still bore down with a steeled grip, while Trotsky and other agitators were transported to Siberia; the autocracy had evidently no intention of surrendering its power, even though slow and measured progress was permitted by Stolypin up to the time of his death beneath an assassin's hand in September 1911. But despite all the potentially explosive forces still brooding underground, the country might even yet have escaped the violence of the revolution of 1917 except for violence in another form—that of warfare.

iv. The Climax of 1917

Had Nicholas II and his advisers possessed a wisdom not reached by many except in hindsight, they would have known that in 1914 their real danger was not from without. They would have realized that, despite some slight democratic concessions, the power of the Czar might have remained intact regardless of events in Austria and Serbia, whose clash was to set the continent on fire. They would have recognized that Russian control of Constantinople and the Straits, one of the evident objectives of their strategists, was unimportant compared with the ruler's grip on the throne. They would not have permitted the secret agreements, subsequently disclosed by Leon Trotsky and published in *Isvestia,* to apportion the possessions of the Central Powers among Russia and her allies. Most of all, they would have perceived the need of meeting the unrest still fuming beneath the surface of Russian life, the conspiracies of terrorists and revolutionaries. and the aspirations of a long-abused people. And they would have understood that the forces of discontent and disruption would be strengthened by the stresses, the sacrifices, the losses, the cruelties, and the despair inherent in a great war.

Nor it is an answer to say that the Czar and his councillors did not anticipate a great war, but looked forward to early victory with a blind confidence in which Russia was not alone, and in which the people shared (symptomatic of the times was the subscription of about $100,000 raised at St. Petersburg for the first soldier to reach Berlin). Nicholas's fatal misjudgment was quite in line with that of many another leader, including his own Minister of the Interior Pleve in the war with Japan. For the simple fact is that the Russian state could not bear the double burden of the war without, and the growing strains within. Something had to crack, and something did crack.

When war hits the vast land of Russia, it is likely to be of a particularly costly and cruel nature. This was true of the great invasion by Napoleon in 1812; it was to be even more strikingly true following the attack by Hitler more than a century and a quarter after Napoleon; and it would prove true a generation before Hitler in World War I. The first two years of this gigantic and futile struggle had undermined the nation in a number of ways. The enormous military waste of manpower had demanded a drainage of farmhands from the plows and sickles and of needed millhands from their machines. The huge expenditures of money had caused the ruble to totter, and ruined the country's finances. Food supplies, fuel, raw materials, railroad transport had all been gravely reduced. Yet even these losses, dire as they were, might not have brought on the revolution had war-weariness not gripped the countryside like a fever, making the peasants eager for an end to the czars as a way to peace and a full breadbin. Even among those classes that still desired to carry on the war to victory, the downfall of czarism seemed preferable to the defeat toward which czarism was leading.

And yet, although conditions were ripe for the emergence of the revolutionary forces that had been developing underground for many years, the outbreak of March 1917 (February, by the old calendar) seems not to have been expected. It is eloquent of the fallibility of human judgment that Lenin, sometime before his gateways to power swung open, had stated in despair that he did not expect to live to see the Revolution. And hardly less remarkable is this report from the memoirs of N. H. Sukhanov, an eyewitness and a participant in the Revolution:

> *Not one party was preparing for the great upheaval.* Everyone was dreaming, ruminating, full of foreboding, feeling his way. . . . Revolution—highly improbable! . . . everyone knew this was only a dream.[6]

Even on the crucial eighth of March, when striking men and women in Petrograd swarmed across the ice of the frozen Neva River with cries of "Bread! Bread! Give us bread!" and broke into the bakeshops to seize what they could, no one seems to have viewed the outburst as the prelude to a far greater drama. But on the ninth the demonstrations became more widespread, more truculent, while the marchers swung clubs and hurled cobblestones and chunks of ice. Ominous shouts began to ring out, more menacing than on the day before, "Down with the war! . . . Down with the police! . . . Down with the autocracy!" The mood of the people, as they surged in a black mass along the Nevsky Prospect—the great thoroughfare that cuts through the city almost from riverbank to riverbank and touches at one end upon the Palace Square of the Winter Palace—was becoming increasingly ugly. Spreading strikes, spurts by mounted police, the snap and rattling of gunfire—these were among the marks of that uproarious day, while the mob still howled, "Down with the war! . . . Down with the police! . . . Down with the autocracy!"

A surprising fact was that the uprising seemed leaderless, spontaneous, almost the automatic act of men and women driven to distraction by an irresistible common impulse to rid themselves of the persecutor. So long had these people suffered, so tightly had they held their grievances under cork and key, that they themselves could not have known how near they were to the bursting point. Yet so bitter were their war-born needs, so close to the surface their resentments, that it required no more than a spark to kindle the conflagration. And this apparently explains why revolution, unheralded and unplanned, broke out in those March days of 1917. A people's patience might be long-enduring, yet at last the ignition point must be reached.

But still the peril was veiled from the scornful eyes of the man most directly concerned. The Czar did not even see fit to reply when the President of the Duma warned him of the urgency of action if the regime was to be saved. With an incomprehension so profound that one can only marvel, Nicholas let his will be known over the telephone: "I command that the disorders at the capital shall be stopped tomorrow as they are inadmissible at this heavy time of war with Germany and Austria." As reasonably might he have ordered the waves of the sea not to leap or foam.

All the while, as he sat in imagined security in his crumbling house of sand, the demonstrators with their sticks and stones were spreading out across the city. Streetcars were silent, the wheels of factories no longer turned, the police and the troops began to cordon off districts and bridges, and Cossacks and mounted and unmounted police took their way through the crowds without attempting to restrain them except by removing the red banners which gave encouragement to the multitude. Growing more unruly, the mobs attacked police stations, broke into law courts and jails, destroyed legal documents, freed prisoners, and set fires. And yet undoubtedly they could have been and would have been suppressed in the end except for one thing—the army. Just as the regime of Louis XVI had tottered and fallen when it could no longer depend upon the troops, so the government of Nicholas II was stricken defenseless when the military power failed it. This reversal was the more startling since, in the beginning, the troops had obeyed orders, had moved into the streets in force, had fired upon the crowds and littered the Nevsky with corpses, including those of many innocent passers-by. But on the night of March 11, when the disturbances were but three days old, a change of heart overcame the men of the Volynsky Regiment, who had already mowed down many of the rioters. Discussing the situation among themselves, they agreed not to shoot again at the people. And thus, in effect, they ended the rule of Nicholas II. Next morning they were joined by other regiments, while companies that had been dispatched against the rioters changed sides and took part in looting arsenals and police stations.

How had this been possible? Was it not because the soldiers were closer at heart to the people than to the Czar? Was it not because they had sprung from the people, understood their needs, their sufferings, their discontents, had themselves felt similar needs, sufferings, and discontents, and had brooded in hatred and rage while being stamped underfoot in a war with which they had little sympathy? Why, they may have asked themselves, should they continue to aid their oppressors?

Now that he could no longer rely upon the army or upon the police—who were helpless against the troops and the mobs—Nicholas had almost no choice but to accept the advice pouring in upon him: "Abdicate!" Within a matter of days the whole czarist structure of centuries had collapsed, never to rise again. The Revolution, it seemed, had magnificently triumphed.

However, had it triumphed? The old persecutors were gone—but who would succeed them? An Emergency Committee was appointed by the Duma; and the ensuing Provisional Government, which after a time came under the control of the flamboyant but weak Kerensky, reflected lack of planning and preparation; it had no roots among the people and could depend neither upon the army nor upon the police. The eight-month period that followed was a mere interlude preceding the real revolution.

This revolution (which occurred in November—or October, by the old reckoning) will perhaps forever be a subject of dispute. But certain things about it are undeniable. One is that the Russia which it brought into existence was very far from the state envisioned by the idealists who hoped that the czarist repression would be followed by a democratic regime. And another unquestionable fact is that the overthrow of the Czar was not the accomplishment of a day, but was the accumulated product of all the woes suffered by the Russian people for centuries and going back even before Peter the Great. More specifically, however, the Revolution was the handiwork of a small group of dedicated conspirators, whose planning dated back many years, and whose power they themselves perhaps did not fully realize. It was not wholly by chance, although many unforeseen circumstances had come to his aid, that the ruler's iron rod fell into the hands of Vladimir Ilyich Lenin.

This leader's rise, in some ways at least, occurred in accordance with the principles he himself had espoused. He believed that revolution would not break out of its own accord, but only by the planned action of an organized group. He favored the use of force, of ruthlessness, in obedience to a creed that recognized one morality, and only one: that of the revolutionary aims. He has given us every reason to accept "the very strong suspicion" of a recent commentator that his "deepest motive was the drive for personal power, however he may have rationalized it. He never worked honestly under or alongside anyone else. . . ."[7] He was, moreover, one of those consecrated revolutionaries described by the German historian Arthur Rosenberg,

> who fought with all the means at his disposal, who did not hesitate to use terroristic methods against the hated representatives of the Government, who pursued the same ends in Switzerland and Siberia that he had followed in St. Petersburg and Moscow, and who served the cause of the Russian people in prison and on the gallows. . . .[8]

Sometime before the actual take-over of power, Lenin had concluded that the Bolshevik Party could prevail only by means of a revolution. Gentle suasion, a plebiscite or the endorsement of the majority, would not establish the new regime; gunpowder and the threat of gunpowder must make it the master of the country. Such a consummation, indeed, might not have been possible had the Bolsheviks not won the industrial workers of Petrograd by promises of peace and bread, and had they not wooed the peasants with the hope of appropriating the great landed estates, and, finally, had the Petrograd garrison not come over to their side—a development which, as Rosenberg remarks, "gave the victory to the Bolshevik Revolution in Petrograd before a shot had been fired."[9]

After this startling turn of events, there was nothing to halt Lenin and his cohorts in their tactics of force, remorseless force. They seized the Central Telephone Exchange, the state banks, the railroad station; they occupied the Winter Palace, arrested all Cabinet members of the Provisional Government (except Kerensky and one other, who had fled in time), locked them in dungeons of the Fortress of Peter and Paul, and met as the self-styled representatives of the people to the accompaniment of cannon thunder and the rattling of machine guns. Thus, while they promised the masses all that they wished—land to the peasant, deliverance from servitude to the soldier, and a new dominance to the city worker—the Bolsheviks established themselves in the ancient halls of power. The nature of their democracy was made plain when, on December 11, the legal day of the opening of the fervently sought Constituent Assembly, the meeting was broken up by armed Lettish soldiers, while an attempted second assemblage, in the following month, was dispersed by the gunmen amid threats of massacre and a commotion that blacked out all legislative efforts.

Already, in the natal days of the new regime, before the civil war, the terrorism and executions and deportations and slave-labor camps, perhaps a cruel perception was coming to the more idealistic and freedom-loving of the rebels—the realization that the Revolution had somehow miscarried, that a take-over by violence had merely led to a rule by violence, that the country had acquired a new autocracy under another name, and that liberty and democracy were still mirages in the far distance, as remote and apparently as unreachable as when Peter I and Catherine II and Alexander III and Nicholas I and Nicholas II and all the other czars sat aloof in their palaces and issued ukases to command a servile and suffering people.

10. Mussolini Marches on Rome

i. The Rise of Fascism

In a remote and tranquil future, when men can look back upon the trials and turmoils of today as upon the disturbances of Renaissance Italy or of the France of Louis XIV, the pattern of our times may emerge in outlines unfamiliar to our eyes. In that pattern the red of violence will be even more conspicuous than in the troubled earlier centuries, and this red will by no means be confined to the Brobdingnagian wars of the age. The historian will note the revolutions that burst out in storm and fire and often led to military dictatorship; he will cite, among others, the examples of Spain, Greece, Latin American countries such as Bolivia, Santo Domingo, and Cuba, and several of the leading nations of Europe and Asia. And he will observe that, in the case of all the key powers and often of the lesser ones, major warfare led to major internal outbursts.

As an illustration, he will point to Italy, where one of the great disruptive agents of the 1920s and thirties gained its foothold upon foundations of terror and force. Fascism, born in Italy but soon to cast long deep shadows over Germany, Spain, far-off Japan, and other widely scattered regions, could not have come into being had it not been for World War I, any more than Bolshevism could have prevailed in Russia in 1917 without the legacy of that same war. In the background lay the violence of combat, and the creed of triumph-by-might that is inseparable from violence. And this creed, surviving after the guns had ceased to roar, found rich nourishment in the soil of common misery and social unrest, which the fighting may not have created but had immensely aggravated.

Italy, at the end of the First World War, was among the more unstable of the larger European countries. It had enjoyed little more than a half-century of national unification after hundreds of years in which small political entities faced one another in jealous and often bristling opposition, and it had been subject to repeated military intrusions by greater countries such as France, Spain, and Austria. All the while, its people had been ground down by want and misery which, though chronic for centuries, grew more acute beneath the waste and abrasions of war. When we remember that, years before World War I, the future dictator Mussolini lived in childhood as one of a family of five in a two-room tenement, with almost no furniture or heating, perhaps having to be content with a lunch of vegetable soup and a supper of chicory, we will see that a poor man had little leeway, and that the fear of a further reduction in his lot might throw him into the arms of the first movement that promised even a slight improvement.

It is hard to conceive of anything that could have been more damaging to the common man than the eruption that actually occurred when the entanglements of international politics involved Italy in the World War with little or no regard for the needs of her people, and cost her 600,000 men killed and a million injured. But in other ways than in manpower, the drain upon the impoverished country had been severe. Not only industrial supplies but essential foods had become scarcer while the bloated war industries were being fed; inflation, one of war's usual grim camp followers and heirs, lifted its thieving hand to plunder the middle classes and snatch the crust from the poor man's board; the national debt increased six times, while the debt of local communities was doubled; prices tripled between late 1918 and early 1920, but wages did not keep pace; tax increases were proposed, and simultaneously unemployment and hunger stalked the land. The official figures admitted that, of an industrial working force of only about ten millions, as many as 400,000 were jobless. And as if this were not ominous enough, the situation was complicated by the war's creation of some hundred fifty thousand deserters, who skulked in hiding and in many cases were driven to brigandage.

Meanwhile the war had contributed various other sources of disaffection. The disgruntled elements were swollen by the generals who, grumbling at being retired to civilian life at half-pay, constituted a disturbing factor in the community. And more numerous dissidents were to be found among the common soldiers who came back to a life of destitution in the farms and villages and observed bitterly that some of their confreres had waxed affluent by staying at home. To complicate the situation, Allied economic aid had been withdrawn, leaving the government to cope not only with ordinary deficits but with the problem of paying subsidies out of an emptied treasury—subsidies to the farmers, to the war industries, and, perhaps most basic of all, to the consumers in need of bread. At the same time, warbred resentments were seething, particularly against the Allied powers and against the peace settlement at Versailles, by which Italy had received less than her politicians coveted even though more than many external observers considered to be rightly hers.

Here, then, were numerous forces of discontent and even of disruption, which only the most adroit, firmly established, and most capable government could have mastered. But the leadership of Italy, unfortunately, was neither adroit, firmly established, nor capable; under the parliamentary system, which enabled the prime minister and cabinets to survive only by erecting unstable combinations of minority parties, weak captains such as Francesco Nitti, Giovanni Giolitti, and Luigi Facta had command of the ship at the very time when the storm waves buffeted it most threateningly. Hence the one possible bulwark against the rule of violence and the rise of Fascism—a strong and resolute central control—did not exist.

In September 1919, a sign of the times and a precursor to Fascism was flashed before Italian eyes in a grandiose episode led by the poet Gabriele D'Annunzio. This florid 56 year-old exhibitionist, supporting a highly dubious Italian claim to the city of Fiume (or Rijeka) in present-day Yugoslavia, led what was really little more than a buccaneering adventure, though it was painted as a glorious patriotic and nationalistic exploit, and drew in its wake a swarm of footloose generals and unemployed lesser officers, along with demobilized soldiers, rampant nationalists of various stripes, disgruntled liberals, runaway schoolboys, and adventurers attracted by the clash of arms and the hue of blood. With this motley array, D'Annunzio managed to seize Fiume and hold it for 16 months—an event not at all momentous in itself, although its effects were of the utmost importance. For it fanned an inflammatory chauvinism, it established a precedent of violence by dissident citizens, it gave prominence to the black-shirted *arditi* or shock troops who voiced the future Fascist warcry, and it offered encouragement to hosts of the drifting malcontents who were to form the hard core of the Fascist squads. At the same time, by providing armed action independently of the established authority, it went far toward undermining respect for law and government and creating a favorable atmosphere for the emergence of Fascism.

On the domestic front, increasingly violent disturbances likewise pointed the way to eventual Fascist control. In December 1919, militant protest reached even the Parliament, when a speech of the King was interrupted by deputies who shouted "Long live the Socialist Republic!" and trooped out singing the *Red Flag*—an incident that was the more significant since the Socialists had the largest representation of any party in the legislative body. The King may well have judged that rebellion was about to take over and that he was on the way to being reduced to a figurehead, though he may have falsely assumed that the chief danger was from the left.

There followed a period of turmoil, strife, and disruption that spread in all directions. Severe disturbances broke out in the farming areas; the Agricultural Workers' League became in some respects a terroristic organization, which forced better wages and laboring conditions by methods that ranged from threats to boycott and arson. Meanwhile something close to civil war crackled when ex-soldiers—hungry peasants who saw their only security in possession of the land and had been promised their share by the wartime Prime Minister Salandra—became "squatters" upon unoccupied territory. In all this they may have had considerable justification, but what is most significant is that their methods were those of violence, and that this violence received the retroactive endorsement of the state in decrees of September 1919, and April 1920, which appeared to sanction many of the land seizures, and thereby taught that violent defiance of law and government might succeed. The indignation of the landowners, who could see no hope in the existing government against what they viewed as robbery and extortion, was one of the forces that drove rich proprietors toward Fascism.

In the cities, likewise, the disturbances were sharp and widespread. When some Socialist deputies were injured in counterdemonstrations by patriotic organizations following the antiroyalist revolt at the opening of Parliament in December 1919, the Socialists responded by a general strike. Tie-ups followed on the railroads, in the postal department, and in the cotton mills, and these strikes were not mere harmless affairs with peaceful pickets and quiet negotiations. On the contrary, continual violence exploded between the strikers and nationalistic groups, the police, and the armed forces. In the Emilia and Romagna and elsewhere, police barracks were destroyed—all of which, like the rural tumults, gave encouragement to the Fascists, who were nourished on violence and drew the police and the soldiers into their ranks by the aid they gave against the strikers.

Meanwhile Prime Minister Nitti, faced on all sides by dissent, could see no course except to double the number of the *carabinieri* or state police, and to add 25,000 Royal Guards, while simultaneously trying to placate the Socialists. The result of these methods and the complications at Fiume and vacillations concerning the bread subsidy (which was abolished and then reestablished) was that the government was largely ineffective and Nitti fell.

His successor, the veteran Giolitti, who had been Prime Minister three decades before, faced many of the same problems of protest and violence. Further strikes and industrial clashes plagued the regime, culminating in August 1920, when a dispute over wages led to a lockout of metallurgical workers at Milan, followed by aggressive action and counteraction that produced a major crisis. The strikers were ordered by their union to remain in the factories; the owners' organization responded by extending the lockout to the entire country; the strikers hit back by seizing many factories, even against the opposition of the Trade Union Confederation; and for eight weeks the red flag flew over some of the northern mills, to the accompaniment of clashes, looting, sabotage, and casualties on both sides. Giolitti meanwhile resisted pressures to fire upon the factories, including a request by at least one leading industrialist; and eventually the strike was settled through negotiation.

Whether or not, as some commentators believe, the conflict had been engineered by the industrialists to compel the state to use force against the strikers, the result of the whole series of post-war disturbances was unquestionably similar to that of the occupation of Fiume by D'Annunzio: it undercut the authority of the government and confidence in the government, and helped to sweep away the obstacles in the path of the Fascists. It had been shown all too clearly that the people could not look to the Prime Minister or his agents for relief from the upheavals that were making life more and more insecure. And when the government could no longer be relied upon to shield its own representatives; when troop trains could be halted and contingents of police held back by the strikers; when the use of violence and the seizure of property by antigovernment agitators were being tolerated and condoned, encouraging further usurpations; when Fascists and Communists could engage in conflicts so severe that *La Stampa* of Turin, in November 1920, characterized them as "real warfare"; when violence became the law not only for the under-classes but for rich property owners who engaged private corps of strong-arm men to protect their interests—when all this occurred, then society was being torn to its foundations, and a sharp change in direction appeared necessary if civilized values and the orderly processes of life were to be retained.

This was the situation for which one faction, preparing itself on the sidelines, had been waiting—the Fascists were eager to encourage the confusion, so that the masses, in their uncertainty and their frustration, would turn to any leader who seemed to promise stability and relief. Skillfully playing upon popular fears, and cultivating the supposition that the great threat to the Italian way of life came from the Bolsheviks, the Fascists made the time appear ripe for a savior. That supposed savior, as it happened, was waiting behind the scenes in the person of Benito Mussolini, editor, politician, and agitator, who had gradually been working his way up, first in the Socialist and then in the Fascist ranks.

ii. "Sawdust Caesar" Takes Command

Mussolini was the type of man who, given the physical courage, might have been an old-time filibusterer of the Caribbean, or a chief of Mediterranean corsairs, or a captain of the *conditierri* or mercenary soldiers of the Italy of several centuries before. He was essentially an adventurer, high-handed, unscrupulous, callous, treacherous, relentless in his exactions, grandiloquent in his swaggering boastfulness, and little concerned for anyone's welfare but his own—a man of no genius and only minor talents, who has perhaps been best described in the words of one of his early biographers, George Seldes: "Sawdust Caesar."

Nevertheless, this petty personage not only came to exercise dictatorial power over a great nation but was able to throw a blight across a generation of his people's life and to constitute a spot of sore infection in the world. How was this possible?

Surely, this question should not be hard to answer in a century that has known a flock of dictators great and small, from Hitler, Stalin, and Mao Tse-tung to Franco, Peron, Trujillo, Castro, and many another. Yet a complete answer would involve a total understanding of the social and historical background. Much of the explanation, however, is to be found in the disruption of the times, which provided an entering wedge for any man sufficiently ruthless and unprincipled and ready to apply violence without limit. It is, in fact, in violence that we find one of the gauges of Mussolini's character as well as one of the keys to his elevation and his eventual downfall.

It would be possible to make too much of reports such as that, as a boy, he was constantly fighting with his schoolmates, and was compelled to leave the college of the Salesian fathers at Faenza at the age of nine after stabbing an older boy with a knife. More significant is the fact that, as he grew older, violence became part of his creed. This was shown time after time even before he had advanced to power. For example, on September 24, 1911, while in his late twenties, he made a public address at Forli that placed him on the side of the apostles of violent solutions: the people should proclaim a general strike, barricade the streets, halt public transportation, demolish the railroad lines, and organize opposition to the government. After troops had quelled the ensuing riots, Mussolini paid for his part in the demonstrations by a year's prison sentence, which, however, was commuted to five months.

Whatever he may have learned from his experience, his penchant for violence had not been cured. As editor of the Socialist journal *Avanti,* he constantly proclaimed his belief in uprisings of an embattled minority, revolution by strength of arms, the forcible seizure of power. It was in accordance with such views that, on July 26, 1914, less than three years after the Forli agitations, the future warmaker published an article which, while placing him with the popular majority opposing Italy's entry into the threatened World War, warned the government of a violent response, even of rebellion, should the people's will be flouted. All this may appear ironic and contradictory when we recall that, in his organ *Popolo d'Italia* a short while later, after accepting cash contributions from France, Mussolini was to give himself ardently to furthering the war effort. But actually the contradiction is apparent rather than real. For nothing in the career of this all-out opportunist was contradictory if it seemed to further the purposes of Mussolini, and nothing that pertained to violence conflicted with anything basic in his nature. Power was his aim quite regardless of principle, and this he himself confessed long afterwards: "I am obsessed by this wild desire. It consumes my whole being. I want to make a mark on my era with my will, like a lion with its claw!"[1] His clawing activities, his endorsement of the principle of progress-by-might, were evident enough soon after the war, when, upon making sure that D'Annunzio had succeeded in his expedition to Fiume in 1919, Mussolini flamboyantly joined in the chorus of enthusiasm for the usurpations of the poet-adventurer.

But it was in his Fascist manipulations that he chiefly showed the depth of his surrender to the cult of the bullet and the dagger. Amid the suffering, confusion, spiritual unease, and social overturn of the postwar period, Fascism advanced by leaps, markedly in 1921, and its progress was signalized by the crashing of clubs and the snarl of gunfire. Something like civil war erupted; in the first half of 1921, in what amounted to an organized effort against the independence of peasants, workers, and socialists, 25 People's Houses were destroyed along with 59 Chambers of Labor, 85 Cooperative Societies, 43 Agricultural Laborers' Unions, 51 political clubs, 10 printing works, and 6 newspaper offices. Nor was the demolition by any means bloodless: 1387 casualties were inflicted by the Fascists, including 243 deaths. And the strife was to continue during the year and into much of the following year.

Meanwhile, throughout the land, the Fascist *Squadre* were formed—military companies composed mainly of riffraff, the unemployed and ex-soldiers, adventurous youths and older patriots and miscellaneous rascals including deep-dyed criminals. These, recruited by the industrialists to serve their own ends, would force salute of the Italian flag while not hesitating at robbery, incendiarism, and murder. In the country regions, these ruffians depended largely upon the support of a new class of landowners, who sponsored any form of violence that seemed likely to protect their property from the farm workers and from agitators of the left. Before long the *Fascio* and its detachments of *Squadristi*, singing their patriotic songs and calling out their slogans, had come to be features of a great majority of the towns of northern Italy. Whole cities were occupied: in May 12, 1922, for example, 63,000 armed Fascists descended like a plague upon Ferrara, sealing it off from the world, forcing shops and restaurants to close and public transport to halt, seizing schools as quarters for the invaders, and looting food to feed themselves. On the following day, after the government had capitulated to Fascist demands, the insurgent army retreated. But little more than two weeks later its leader, Italo Balbo, occupied Bologna, which, however, he was compelled to yield before the threat of greater force. Subsequently other cities, including Parma and Ravenna, were to resound to the tread of the invading Fascists; and on July 21, the intruders ravaged the Socialist center at Cremona, took possession of the municipal buildings, and burned the apartment of the liberal Catholic deputy Guido Miglioli. Estimates of the Fascist strength vary; whether or not one can accept the round numbers furnished by the Fascists themselves, that they were but 30,000 in May 1920 and more than 10 times that many at the time of the March on Rome less than 2½ years later, it is indisputable that their ranks were swelling.

For the Fascists, profiting from the country's bewildered and desperate state, were gaining reinforcements from the very quarters that should most have resisted them. Some of their recruits were intimidated by the smashing fury of their deliberately staged riots, some were deluded by the false alarm of "Bolshevik! Bolshevik!" and others were lured, as we have seen, by the hope of civic order and security. Fascism even drew nourishment from its opponents' occasional use of force, as when in November 1920, its disciple Giulio Giordani was killed by the Socialists at a meeting of the municipal council of Bologna; this provided an excuse for organized reprisals. From the rootless and the disinherited, from ex-soldiers who desired to remain in uniform, from religious forces that saw in Fascism a bulwark against Red godlessness, from the middle classes who craved an end to the incessant disturbances, and from the rich industrialists, war profiteers, and landowners who had not hesitated to hire gun-bearing desperadoes and expected the new regime to advance their private interests, the Fascists drew continual support. There can be no question that the converts to the creed of the usurpers included many sincere, honest, and fundamentally decent persons, who felt that Mussolini's men held the keys to the future; the philosopher Benedetto Croce, the influential editor of the *Corriere della Serra,* Luigi Albertini, and, in the beginning, Arturo Toscanini, later Fascism's bitter foe, were among the liberals and intellectuals seduced to the Fascist side and fated to regret their choice. Even in America, more than a few had been deluded; for example, I remember the case of a respected magazine editor who, in the thirties, confided to me that he favored the Fascist outlook.

That increasing numbers from all classes should have been beguiled by Fascism was unfortunate enough. Yet this accession of strength need not have been decisive, since even by the most generous estimate the Fascists were but a small minority at the time of their take-over. In December 1921, according to the Socialist deputy Giacomo Matteotti, there were 240,000 men in the regular armed forces plus 105,000 supplementary troops, all of whom could have been used by the government, but were not called upon. And why were they not called upon?

What was especially disquieting was that the bands of armed thugs, instead of being repressed by the power they aimed to overthrow, were aided and abetted by that very power, while officials closed their eyes to the continual round of sacking, destruction, arson, murder, and other outrages. It was not only that the local authorities tended to cooperate with the Blackshirts, nor that the army worked hand in glove with them by circulating Mussolini's *Popolo d'Italia* gratis as a "patriotic" move, and had even been ordered by the government (in a circular of October 20, 1920) to work with the Fascists. More sinister yet was the fact that Prime Minister Giolitti, outfoxing himself with that sort of myopic cleverness which had prompted the Germans in 1917 to permit Lenin's passage through the country in a sealed car, conceived the idea of employing the Fascists against the Socialists. Not only that, but he supplied them with rifles, revolvers, grenades, and trucks, and, in the elections which he called for May 15, 1921, he took sides with the Fascists against their foes, thus providing them with official recognition. The imperceptiveness of these moves, in the light of after-events, appears almost inconceivable; it was as if a man had sought to fight the rats by allying himself with the rattlesnakes. In the election cunningly called by Giolitti for May 1921, wherein he had established an anti-Socialist connection with the Fascists, the latter won 35 seats in Parliament, one of which was claimed by Mussolini. And while this was but a small fraction of the 510 deputies, it provided the Fascists at least with a foot in the door, which was more important since Giolitti had not been prescient enough to foretell that he would obtain less than a majority and so would have to depend upon unstable combinations of other parties.

And now the Fascists, fortified, continued their civil warfare against the people of Italy, few of whom seem to have realized the power of a small, utterly determined, utterly ruthless minority. Lawlessness and violence had been accomplishing their ends —why, then, should the Fascists abandon them in favor of more pacific methods? Even now, however, it should not have been too late; the agitators were still but a few among the great Italian populace, and their physical strength was small compared with that inherent in the people. The trouble was that, psychologically, the Fascists had gained a crucial advantage, frightening many into accepting them as the only alternative to disorder and disruption, charming others into looking upon them as saviors and patriots, and blinding the vast majority to the evils inherent in any group that strikes down civil safeguards with bullets, cudgels, the lighted torch, and the bullying tactics of the terrorist.

Blundering and miscalculations in official quarters continued to make their contribution to the Fascist rise. Not only did Giolitti, to his deadly cost, play with fire under the delusion that he could train it to his own uses, but Prime Minister Facta, who held office from February to October 1922, was so shortsighted that, on the eve of the March on Rome, he expressed his belief that "the prospect of a March on Rome has faded away." It is true that his predecessor Ivanhoe Bonomi, during his short term from July 1921, to February 1922, did take belated fright, did order citizens to be disarmed, revoke the innumerable permits for the use of small arms, forbid assemblages of bodies of armed men, and provide for the seizure of their meeting places and weapons. But he might as well have shouted orders at the wind. By this time the Fascists were too powerfully entrenched to be driven out by decree, though stronger methods might still have overthrown them. And while they prevailed by gang rule, and counted many former military men in their camp, and included the police in their ranks or else intimidated them, their opponents were stricken helpless. And the masses, perhaps not knowing or perhaps not caring that their liberties were being thrown into the gutter, or else waiting in dull and helpless apprehension like cattle in the slaughter pen, stood by while the triumphant marauders plotted to command the state.

iii. The Triumph and Tragedy of the Dissidents

For several weeks in July 1922, Italy was virtually paralyzed, unable to form a government after the Facta ministry had been overturned by a vote of nearly three to one. The impasse was not broken until August 1; in the interim the north was ravaged by the fires of gang warfare, while a succession of leading politicians shrank from accepting the premiership; finally the choice fell again upon the ineffective Facta. At the same time, piling folly upon folly, the Socialists declared a general strike, which accomplished nothing except to add to the public irritation and to provide a pretext for Fascist counter-action.

That counter-action was not slow in coming. Returning to the strong-handed methods that were their chief stock in trade, Mussolini's gangs battered down all the buildings of the Socialists in various cities, including Ancona, Genoa, and Leghorn. In Milan, the heart of Italian Socialism, they advanced on August 3 and 4, smashing the presses and setting fire to the buildings of *Avanti,* the newspaper which Mussolini, as a Socialist, had once edited. How weak, how cowardly the government had become, and how utterly law had yielded to organized thuggery masquerading as social dissent, is shown by the willingness of the officials to stand watching on the sidelines while the wreckers wielded their clubs and firebrands. The irony of all this is that the lawbreakers could pose as upholders of law and enlist public opinion on their side as they put down the general strike.

Even so, the Fascist triumph less than three months later need not have occurred. Economically a drastic change in regime was not necessary, since Italy's condition had been improving in 1922; the disorganization of the country was largely the deliberate handiwork of the Fascists themselves. However, the myth of the need for change was sufficient for Mussolini's purpose, and his accession was assured by an unlikely new convert to that myth: King Vittorio Emanuele III. He it was who, though not in touch with the opposing political leaders and absent on a vacation on the eve of the crucial decision, cast the vote that delivered his country into the hands of the cynical, self-designing band of plotters. In late October, when Mussolini sat poised for his final stroke, he could have been crushed had the army taken decisive action—such, at least, was the view of the chief of staff, General Badoglio, who vainly asked for full power to act; and Badoglio's judgment was confirmed by the military commandant at Rome, General Pugliese. There were, indeed, reports that the army would not have followed the King's orders, but such stories represented mere rumors, word-of-mouth claims lacking verification and never tested in action.

Yet they might have been tested in action—had it not been for the King himself. Early on the morning of October 28, written instructions were drawn up proclaiming a state of siege and ordering the army to stop the Fascists by every means available; the decree was printed in the newspapers and placarded on the walls of Rome. Immediately, according to Pugliese, the Fascist squads began to disperse. Free Italy, it seemed, might heave a sigh of relief; the menace at its doorstep was about to be swept away. But such, unfortunately, was not the idea of the King. During the night the vacillating monarch, who previously had indicated approval, evidently changed his mind; shortly before nine in the morning, when visited by the Prime Minister, he refused to sign the all-important document.

It is futile to debate what forces moved him, or whether Prime Minister Facta, playing a double game as some have alleged, had secretly dissuaded him from putting in ink the few short words that would have changed Italy's destiny and that of much of the world. It is equally futile to offer the justification that Vittorio Emanuele had merely been deluded as were many good people in Italy and elsewhere, and that large elements of the populace were with him in his error. What really counts is not the extent of his culpability but the grim fact that, by refusing to sign the defensive order, he opened the floodgates to Fascism.

Mussolini meanwhile had held himself out of sight at a safe distance in Milan, waiting to see how the tide would turn; he was indisposed to take any chances, regardless of his bluster to a Party congress a short while before as to "the forces of the new generation" that had emerged from the war and would cause the Fascists to seize the government if it was not given to them. There is no reason to suppose that the March on Rome would have occurred if strong currents of opposition had swung against Mussolini. As it happened, he accomplished his valorous advance by railroad, and then only after his way had been made safe by a telephone call followed by a telegram from the capital. The only march he made was up the steps and along the aisles of the sleeping car that bore him from Milan to Rome; the only perils he faced were those encountered by every tourist. He might now be certain that, since he had come by the King's official invitation, none of the lesser officials would dare to act against him.

It is true that three Fascist columns did move upon Rome, but they were the mere pretense of an army, not even in communication with one another—only about 14,000 poorly armed men in all, with the addition of about 3000 reserves at Foligno, some 70 miles away. Against a modern military force, with modern equipment, they would have been a barricade of cardboard. What permitted their victory by virtual default, however, was not the military weakness of the government nor even its overestimate of the Fascist strength, but a failure in the thought of the rulers, in their moral courage, in their sense of indignation at the violent lawlessness and designing evil that had been convulsing the land.

Thus Italy did get the "law and order" that many had devoutly craved, though the nature of the new regime was suggested when the offices of the Socialist paper *Avanti* were burned just as its one-time editor gained dictatorial power. The new law and order were enforced by the bayonet, the cudgel, and the compulsory dose of castor oil. They were law and order that might run the trains on time but left the minds of men no longer free—law and order under which the infuriated Duce could cry to his opponents of the left, "You should receive a charge of lead in the back," while a prominent Socialist such as Matteotti could be infamously murdered. And they were law and order by which, during the Second World War, the unoffending Jews of Italy—a small minority, long an integral part of the population—could be delivered in cold blood to Hitler's executioners. Meanwhile, on the foreign front, the Fascist law and order would perpetuate on a much magnified scale the violence by which Mussolini had come to power: the murderous, unprovoked aggression in Ethiopia, which would lead to the downfall of the League of Nations; Italian participation in the Spanish Civil War, which oiled the way for the Fascism of Franco and for World War II, while weakening Italy and increasing the power of Nazi Germany; the uncalled-for invasion of Albania in 1939; the equally uncalled-for and disastrous invasion of Greece during World War II; and Italy's quite unnecessary entry into the conflict, her "stab in the back" to France and her allies, with its evil backlash upon the whole shaken world and perhaps most sharply of all upon Italy herself.

Yet all this, with its heavy contribution to the world's wartime and postwar misfortunes, might have been averted if the aggressive bands of looters, arsonists, and murderers, who claimed to be apostles of the new age, had been treated like other criminals, had been forestalled in their formation of a private army that was in effect a challenge to the state, and had been checkmated in their disintegrating tactics with courage, resolution, and a wise perception of their true motives and implications.

11. Law and Disorder in Germany

To a certain obscure Austrian ex-corporal, living from hand to mouth in a small poorly furnished room in Munich, Mussolini's March on Rome was a world-shaking event, one of the turning points in history. He conceived a great admiration for the Italian leader; during his long years of struggle, the success of the Fascists was for him a guiding light. "The brown shirt," Hitler was later quoted as saying, possibly not without exaggeration and yet with an element of truth, "would probably not have existed without the black shirt." In other words, German Fascism, or Nazism, was the offshoot of Italian Fascism; the violent methods that had brought Mussolini to power had spread like a plague and infected the Nazi mind. Thus Hitler had gained powerful encouragement; and this, as he suggested, may have been a decisive spur on his evil road to power. Thanks to Hitler, one of the long-range costs of the brutality and ruthlessness of Italy's Duce may have been ruthlessness and brutality on a worldwide scale.

Not that Hitler need have relied altogether upon Mussolini's example; in the immediate past of Germany there had been sufficient violent dissent. And as in Italy, the roots of the agitations were woven deep in the soil of the World War, whose disastrous ending in 1918 had opened the way to rebellion in various quarters—mutiny among the sailors at Kiel, spreading to Bremen, Hamburg, and other ports; revolution in Bavaria; an uprising to overthrow the state by the Spartacists or extreme leftist followers of Karl Liebknecht and Rosa Luxemburg (though this dedicated woman, like some of her fellow revolutionaries, was shocked at the violent methods of her collaborators and judged their attempted seizure of power to be ill-timed and

176

ill-advised). While Mussolini's March on Rome still lay in the future, the Spartacan activists could look back for inspiration to the triumph of the Bolsheviks in 1917, and need not consider it at all far-fetched to believe that just as Lenin had made himself supreme in Russia, so they could gain possession of Germany by adroitly applied force, and mold the state to their hearts' desire. Like many another group seeking idealistic goals through methods that are the antithesis of idealism, the Spartacists planned to attain their millenium by such means as armed terrorism in the streets, famine, even anarchy; the aroused proletariat would take command, wielding the weapons supplied to them by the revolution, seizing public buildings, and declaring a general strike. Thus through civil war they would climb to triumph.

Even before the actual proclamation of revolution, tumult and riot were to flame forth. By way of preliminaries, the insurgents demonstrated through marching, oratory, and shooting, in which some adherents of both sides were killed; hundreds of teen-age youths invaded the Prussian Landtag building, waving red flags; the printing office of *Vorwarts* was captured; a protest meeting on December 7, 1918, guarded by machine-guns, brought out a huge crowd, which was stirred to emotional frenzy by Liebknecht's reminders of the soldiers and workers slain the day before. Meanwhile, not only in Berlin but in various other cities, such as Munich, Hamburg, and Dusseldorf, riots had erupted, while the troops commissioned by the government to guard public buildings were so heavily infiltrated by the rebels as to be of little value. At the same time, a 3000-man naval division, which was described by one of its former leaders as "little more than a band of robbers," showed strong Spartacist inclinations. On December 23 this contingent marched against the government, and in the ensuing "Christmas Eve Battle" it defeated the famous Horse Guards, who had the choice of throwing down their rifles or shooting into crowds of civilians.

Now, with the rout of the imperial army, Berlin was scourged by anarchy. The government of the moderate Majority Socialists (so named to distinguish them from the more radical Independent Socialists and their offshoots the Spartacists) had been stricken nearly powerless, left without an army, and unable to command its own police. Yet at this very moment it faced the riotous protests of a people scourged and torn by more than four years of devastating warfare and suddenly made aware that, far from achieving the victory which had been promised them until lately, they had been beaten in battle, and that all their gruelling burdens, their sacrifices, their losses in blood had been for nothing. And as if the popular discontent at the war's outcome was not enough to cope with, there was the terror of threatened famine, since aid from the Allies was not forthcoming as had been expected. Yet at this very time of despair, and in the depth of winter, when the government was faced on several fronts with seemingly insoluble problems, the Spartacists attempted their coup and gambled all on the single card of revolution.

As a climax to the strikes and riots that had agitated the streets of Berlin during the first days of 1919, the "Spartacist Revolution" was declared for January 6, despite the lack of unanimity in the party and the possibility of plunging the country into chaos; the revolutionaries relied on the general strike—a means of perverting a weapon of economic bargaining into an instrument of political terrorism. In part the leaders had been misled into using this tool by the roaring enthusiasm of the crowds outside their headquarters, and by the news of uprisings in which newspapers and newspaper offices had been seized and railroad stations attacked by the people, while a whole naval division was reported ready to side with the rebels. Under such circumstances, even the best of men may find it hard to keep their heads; inflammatory enthusiasms are apt to pass from man to man in a swift contagion; level judgments are likely to be displaced by passionate and inordinate desires and poorly weighed expectations. But now the hour seemed to have struck—and it was an hour whose opportunities, manifestly, had to be utilized before they had passed. Those who made the crucial decision appear not to have given sufficient weight to the minority view that the moment was ill chosen, the Spartacists not strong enough, and the people, despite appearances, not wholeheartedly behind the revolt.

In any case, the plans were made, envisaging a Berlin whose people would awaken to find the government fallen, all shop-doors closed, no streetcar rattling on any track, no electricity to light any street or home, and gun-wielding throngs of workers in possession of the city. A "Revolutionary Committee" of 53 was formed, and a manifesto proclaimed them in temporary command, replacing the government of the Majority Socialists, which they had allegedly deposed. On January 6, while the workers were given weapons, the general strike duly began, and an estimated crowd of 200,000 demonstrators swarmed through the streets of the capital. To the startled onlooker, as he saw the insurgents take the Brandenburg Gate and post gunmen among the statues that crowned it, or as he watched the workers seize the Government Printing Office, the Botzow Brewery, and the principal railroad stations, it must have seemed that the revolution was on the threshold of success.

With difficulty the heads of the government were keeping a precarious grip on the Reichstag building and a few others. But Chancellor Friedrich Ebert and his ministers were virtual prisoners in their offices, afraid to go home, having difficulty obtaining food, and seriously tempted to take flight from Berlin. Meanwhile Minister of Defense Noske did flee to the city's outskirts when he found the offices of the Army General Staff beleaguered by an armed mob. After one or two more resounding strikes—or so the exultant insurrectionists must have thought—the Spartacist Revolution would rank beside that of the Russian Bolsheviks as one of the world-shaking moves of the century.

But appearances were deceptive; powerful counterforces were already at work. Five thousand resisters, recruited by the Majority Socialists, were armed to defend those public buildings not in rebel control, and this improvised corps retook the Brandenburg Gate. Other counter-strikes followed, not the least being an attack by Major von Stephani and 1200 soldiers of the Potsdam Regiment, who used trench mortars, machine guns, a tank, and armored cars against the offices of *Vorwarts* and its defenders, and captured about 300, some of whom they shot with the utmost barbarity, after herding them into a barracks.

But it is an open question whether the speedy defeat of the revolutionaries was due to armed attacks as much as to their own leadership, which lacked concentration, decisiveness, and drive, let invaluable time slip by unused, and failed to take advantage of the mood of the people at the moment when their demonstrations were most spontaneous and enthusiastic and the explosive spark was most ready to be lighted. What would have happened if the Spartacists had had a leader with the organizing ability, the command over men, and the one-pointed aim of a Lenin? The answer must forever be left to speculation; it may be that it was beyond the power even of genius to weld the disparate elements of German radical Socialism into an effective, durable unit. Yet there are reasons for believing otherwise; the surge of feeling of the war-weary masses, and particularly of the industrial workers of the great cities, was genuine and might have provided an astute statesman with a foundation for power. And had the

Spartacist Revolution succeeded, even though it would not have brought the millennium and might have elevated yet another repressive regime, certainly the subsequent history of Germany and of all the West would have been much different. There might have been no revival of German militarism and German aggressiveness, probably Adolf Hitler would have lived out his days in merciful obscurity, and there might have been no Second World War—not, at least, at the time, in the form, and with the cataclysmic dimensions that made it a storm of storms.

But we may be sure that neither the Spartacists as they battled in the streets of Berlin, nor their enemies as they took up arms against the demonstrators, had much idea of the vastness of the stakes for which they fought.

ii. Fighters of the *Freikorps*

In the savagery of the suppression of the rebellion we may see a prevision of things-to-be. Karl Liebknecht and Rosa Luxemburg were both slugged on the head with rifle butts and then shot to death; many of their fellow revolutionaries were slain without even the pretense of a trial, while the government of the Majority Socialists stood by and lifted not a finger. Then, when the murderers of Liebknecht and Luxemburg were summoned to account—summoned before a court-martial of the assassins' own not notably impartial Horse Guards—all except one was acquitted, and he was given a light sentence and the opportunity to escape. In this we can see more than a suggestion of the Storm Troopers of a later day, and of the gangster rule of Germany in the thirties and early forties. And, at the same time, we are warned of the peril that threatens any country when organized terror and hatred strike back after insurgency has failed.

A chief part in the defeat of the revolution was played by the *Freikorps,* originally consisting of military companies of volunteers trained in the old Imperial Army. In January 1919, these companies were few and small, yet were strong enough to send six contingents into Berlin to aid in overcoming the Spartacists; later they were a chief reliance of the government, especially during a second Berlin revolt in March. Fortified by Minister of Defense Noske's savage order to shoot anyone who took up arms against the government, *Freikorps* troops dominated the fighting that lasted for ten days and resulted in the death of an estimated 1500 to 2000 rebels and the injury of perhaps 10,000.

Thenceforth the *Freikorps,* sometimes equipped with cavalry, armored cars, and artillery, continued to grow more numerous and stronger—a strange development for a country just defeated in a great war and subjected to severe military restrictions in the treaty of peace. Here again we see rungs in the ladder for the rise of those bands of organized dissenters who would call themselves the National Socialists. One of the significant facts about the *Freikorps* is that it did not long retain its character as an organization of professional army men, but within a few months began to recruit students and adventurers who seemed to care for little except the hard, barbaric joy of marching and fighting, while serving as propagandists of prejudice and hatred and attacking supposed enemies such as Jews, radicals, and the alleged sellers of victorious Germany into inglorious defeat. The spirit of the *Freikorps* was shown in Munich, where, after the crushing of the revolution, over 1000 persons were killed in six days, including many workers and others shot or bayonetted on suspicion, without evidence that they had been in any way connected with the attempted overthrow of the government.

Another example, a precedent if not an inspiration for the Nazi agitators, was to be seen in the *Freikorps* of the Baltic regions. One of these, called the "Brigade of Iron" by its commandant but soon renamed "The Iron Division" because of its rapid expansion, included three infantry regiments and such modern equipment as airplanes and balloons. This, along with other units, struck at the land with such fury that, according to one observer, only a "funeral pyre" of soot, ashes, and embers was left after they had passed, while looting was unrestrained, and hundreds were gunned down upon suspicion, usually unproved, of anti-German or Bolshevik sympathies. In the prisons of Riga alone, more than 3000 were shot.

Evidently the bands of the *Freikorps,* with the dissent which they expressed against Communists and "November criminals" who had supposedly betrayed Germany in the war, were easier to create than to suppress. Even when the units appeared to have been dissolved, they sometimes reformed in small secret companies. And when they could not take military action they might specialize in political assassination; hundreds fell beneath their attacks, including many prominent individuals, such as Walter Rathenau, a leading industrialist and statesman (it is significant that the Supreme Court in Leipzig proclaimed the scurrilous anti-Semitic *Protocols of the Elders of Zion* to be the "Bible" of the murderers). Here was not only an antihuman force but a leaden pendant about the neck of the German Republic, since its leaders could never know when they might be struck down by one of the armed dissidents. Had the disunited *Freikorps* possessed a Hitler to organize them, a major convulsion might have hit the German state even before 1933. But Hitler, as we well know, was waiting in the wings like the villain of a melodrama, ready to stride upon the stage at the proper prompting and perform in the central role.

iii.   Storm Troops and the Beer Hall *Putsch*

The way for this sinister character had been prepared by a great miscellany of forces. There was, first of all, the war, with its reinforcement of the tradition of violence and cruelty. There was the existence of a mass of disgruntled, disoriented, more or less footloose men set free by the war's ending, and ready to blame the state, or society, or some segment of society for the evils they had endured. There was the Treaty of Versailles, which was oppressive in several ways as well as psychologically abrasive, as in its vindictive war guilt declaration, and in its excessive demands for reparations. There was the fiction that German victory had been forestalled by treason on the home front. There was the devastating inflation, which plundered men's savings and pensions and ruined the middle classes. There was the worldwide depression, which struck Germany with especial severity, the more so as the government during the early thirties did not follow the methods of relief applied in the United States and Great Britain, and did little to check the burden of hunger and unemployment, which reached such extremes in 1932 that only one trade unionist out of four had a job. Simultaneously, the application of police methods, including use of *polizeigas* or tear gas, did not improve the public mood, nor did the tendency to ascribe every misfortune to some conniving "non-German" group such as the Allies or the Jews. And, crowning all, there was, as we have noted, the inflammatory example of the successful Fascist revolt in Italy.

Here, obviously, was a background favoring the emergence of widespread protest and a powerful rebellious leader. The tragedy of Germany and of the world was that such a leader appeared in the person of a man who represented the worst in all the dissident elements and was dominated by furies of bias, iniquitous myths of race, callous and murderous brutality, the arrogance of a trampling, thoroughly egotistic will, and an utter unscrupulousness and ruthlessness, all aided by a blaring voice that seemed to have an almost magnetizing effect upon audiences.

Hitler, however, while his swift rise to power was startling enough, did not arrive upon the scene with exactly the suddenness of Minerva born from the head of Jupiter. For years he had been a disturbing factor as the leader of a protesting minority that too often was taken less seriously than it should have been. As far back as 1919, he became the seventh member upon the list of a small group, the German Workers' Party, which appeared to favor nothing in particular except hostility to the government. In the following year, this group was expanded to form the National Socialist German Workers' Party, generally known more simply as Nazis, which gathered under its banners all sorts of drifters and malcontents, disinherited men, discouraged men, men seething with hatred and resentment against everything from Catholicism and antimonarchism to socialism and democracy. On February 25, 1920, Hitler issued on behalf of this organization a series of what present-day agitators would call "non-negotiable demands," although the phrase he subsequently used was, "this program is never to be changed." The program, which contained 25 points, specifically excluded non-Teutons from its proposed benefits, demanded various social reforms, and declared for an abrogation of the Treaty of Versailles, colonies for Germany, a national army, and "an end to the lying press."

At about the same time, Hitler established the Brown Shirts, or S. A., the storm stroopers; and the *Schutstaffeln,* or dagger-bearing black-shirted personal bodyguard, who wore death's head insignia and took the oath to defend Hitler, if need be, with their lives. Several curious points may be noted in regard to these forces. One was that the Brown Shirts were intended for street brawls with the Nazis' enemies. For them, as one writer puts it, "legality or revolution was a question of existence. Without street fights they would one day be superfluous. . . ."[1] Another remarkable fact is that both corps were in effect units in a private army—an extraordinary thing for any mere citizen or group of citizens to create, and a still more extraordinary thing for any government to permit. Here was—as is all too evident in the afterview—the organization of a dangerous, a subversive force, which no state that had the gift of clear sight and valued its own existence would for a moment have tolerated. The fact that Hitler was indeed tolerated, and eventually embraced, and meanwhile was allowed to send the ruffians of the S. A. into every German city and town in such numbers that General Ludendorff could write of the nation as an "occupied country," is a measure of the depth of the decay not only of the German body politic but of the German spirit.

At Coburg, in October 1922, Hitler demonstrated what sort of use he intended to make of the Storm Troopers. In defiance of police orders, he marched through the city with 800 of the S. A., bringing on a pitched battle with the Communists and Socialists—an encounter on which the Nazis prided themselves, even to the extent of issuing a special medal to their Coburg warriors. Thus riot was expanded to private warfare.

Much more celebrated and even more revealing was the Beer Hall *Putsch* of November 8, 1923. This outbreak was intended as more than a demonstration; it was a revolutionary stroke aimed at seizure of the Bavarian Government. Originally the blow had been planned for November 4, at a parade to be held on the Day of Homage to the Dead; the Nazis hoped to show their respects by surrounding the Crown Prince Rupprecht and other eminent marchers with Storm Troopers, who would persuade them at pistol point to join Hitler's revolution. However, the contemplated coup was dated forward to November 10, then rescheduled for the eighth, when most of the Bavarian political, social, and business leaders were expected to attend a gathering at the *Burgenbrau Keller,* one of the biggest beer halls in Munich. No one seemed to notice on that day as an unknown named Hitler added himself to this distinguished company, along with several lieutenants, who picked their places near one of the pillars. But 20 or 30 minutes after the meeting opened, in the midst of an address by State Commissioner Gustav von Kahr, the hall was shaken as by an earthquake.

The 3000 members of the audience, as they complacently listened to the State Commissioner's speech, had no warning of the ring being drawn about them. They knew nothing of the 600 Storm Troopers, who, taking advantage of the darkness, had beleaguered the hall; they were unaware of the machine-gun aimed at the door from outside. Least of all had they any intimation of the fevered plottings of a small minority intent upon bending the majority to its will. One can imagine the astonishment, the shock of the audience as the door burst open and the brown-shirted Hermann Goring thrust his way in at the head of 25 armed followers. Amid the ensuing commotion, Hitler melodramatically sprang to a chair, raised a pistol, and sent a bullet crashing into the ceiling.

Then, while the tumult continued, he forced himself forward side by side with one or two of his followers, including the ex-butcher Ulrich Graf, an amateur wrestler and a street bully. With pistol pointed, and with what has been described as a "madman's expression" on his face, he brushed past a policeman who stepped forward to stop him, and mounted the platform while the confused von Kahr retreated at the sight of the gun-wielding desperado. Standing in the Commissioner's place, a grotesque figure wearing an ill-fitting long-tailed coat, the intruder shouted, "The national revolution has started! Six hundred armed men surround the hall! No one may leave! The governments at Munich and Berlin are deposed!"

The last statement of course, was blatantly false, as was the usurper's further announcement that the army and police barracks had been occupied, and that the army and the police were marching under the emblem of the swastika. Already Hitler was applying that policy of violence, bluff, and the Big Lie which was to hallmark his whole incendiary career.

But how was the audience in its bewilderment to know that the audacious young man was not speaking the truth? Who, in his most fantastic dream, would have imagined that anyone would take such outrageous liberties without the powerful armed backing of a revolution already well advanced? Not only the sullenly muttering crowd and the cowed von Kahr were deluded by the presumption and arrogance of the Nazi spokesman; similarly fooled and befuddled were Colonel Hans von Seisser, chief of the Bavarian secret police, and General Otto von Lossow, commander of the Bavarian armed forces or Reichwehr. To these three men, Bavaria's highest officials, Hitler snapped out an order, and the trio of dignitaries were herded by the Storm Troopers into a small nearby room, where the future Fuehrer delivered one of his characteristic lectures, informing the captives that he and General Ludendorff—who, as it happened, was unaware of the entire proceedings—were forming a new government, and that unless Kahr, Seisser, and Lossow joined him they would be shot. Aside from that, he had the friendliest intentions.

"No one," he bellowed, "leaves this room alive without my permission!" Meanwhile, the rifles, pistols, and daggers of the Storm Troopers were glistening at the doors and windows of the great hall. And the imprisoned audience, when Hitler rushed back to proclaim that the national government had been overthrown and a new government was about to be formed, must have felt amazement and consternation as the speaker ranted on, "Tomorrow will either find a National Government in Germany, or it will find us dead!"

Concealing the fact that Kahr, Seisser, and Lossow had by this time recovered from their first shock and were offering stubborn and contemptuous resistance, the head kidnapper added one more gigantic lie to his score: The three officials had come over to his side! And at this report the mood of the audience relaxed. Incredibly, Hitler was believed. There were loud cheers! Again the mixture of violence, bluff, and the Big Lie seemed to be succeeding.

Then, when General Ludendorff miraculously was brought upon the scene, and agreed to lend his name to the Nazi stroke despite his fury at Hitler's precipitate action, it seemed that the triumph of the *putsch* was doubly assured. Indeed, it might have been assured, had Hitler not made the blunder of leaving the scene at this point to put down a fight between some Storm Troopers and soldiers of the regular army.

During his absence, his three prize catches, Kahr, Seisser, and Lossow, after voicing a seeming capitulation, managed to slip out of their cage. And with their disappearance the *putsch* had passed its peak. By next morning General Hans von Seecht, commander of the *Reichswehr,* had taken action; troops were rushed to the city, and the police were rallied to put down the rebels. At about 11:00 A.M., a column of some 3000 Storm Troopers, bearing rifles and bayonets, were being led by the pistol-wielding Hitler toward the center of Munich. A swastika and war insignia floated before them; a truckload of machine-guns and gunners rumbled a little behind, and Ludendorff marched with them, while the men, in loud voices, sang Nazi songs. At the Ludwig Bridge, they were allowed passage only after Goring had threatened to shoot some innocent people including two Cabinet ministers who had been seized as hostages during the night. Sometime later, approaching the War Ministry, the marchers were blocked on a narrow street by a detachment of about 100 determined police carrying carbines. "Surrender!" Hitler yelled at them to no avail. A shot rang out, but it is not certain whether, as has been claimed, it came from Hitler's pistol, from his fellow Nazi Julius Streicher, or from one of their opponents. In any case, the bullets did fly, though the interchange lasted no more than a minute. And when it was over, the pavement was strewn with the blood-spattered bodies of sixteen dead or dying Nazis and three slain policemen, while scores had been wounded, including Hermann Goring, who was shot in the thigh and succored by a Jewish banker.

And what of Hitler? While Ludendorff marched straight forward, unbowed, how did the Nazi leader conduct himself? Although he had fallen to the ground linked arm in arm with his mortally wounded comrade Scheubner-Richter, and sustained a dislocated shoulder, he was reported by his Nazi follower Dr. Walther Schulz to be the first to get up and flee, in disregard of his dead and injured followers scattered all about him. A moment later, he had entered a waiting automobile, which would bear him away to a country refuge, where within two days he would be arrested.

And thus, although at one point it seemed on the brink of success, the *putsch* ingloriously failed. But the deeper failure was in the German mind and heart, in its inability or unwillingness to recognize the true meaning of the episode: the feral frenzy of the forces it had brought to light, the mortal threat to the state presented by militants of Hitler's type, the power of an armed and ruthless minority to dominate a bewildered or blinded or handcuffed majority, and the consequent need to cork up the black demon of swollen ambitions and psychopathic passions. How little the depth of the danger had been realized, how little the message of the attempted *putsch* had been taken to heart, will be seen in the lenient treatment granted to the chief agitator. In the face of a law prescribing life imprisonment for any violent attempt to change the constitution of the Reich or of any German state, Hitler was let off with a five-year sentence. But it was a sentence that, in practice, shrank to less than nine months, which Hitler spent as a sort of favored guest in a comfortable private room with a magnificent view, while dictating *Mein Kampf* to Rudolph Hess, and while being exalted in Nazi propaganda and extolled by many as a hero. It is needless to point out that, had he actually been imprisoned for life as the law prescribed for his undoubted act of treason, or even had he been held for a long period of years, subsequent history would have been far different, and some of the darkest afflictions of our age might have been avoided.

iv. Some Conclusions

As the simple-looking little acorn contains in embryo the wide-spreading limbs and roots of the giant oak, so small events may bear unseen within them the impress of great episodes still unborn. This was never more true than in the case of the disturbances, most of them minor, with which the Nazis upset the life of German cities and towns in the days before their ascendancy. In the militant agitations of Hitler's followers, the insolence and the arrogance, the brawls and rowdy attacks and usurpations, the vitriolic charges against "non-Aryans" and other minorities, the resort to bluster, threats, lies, and violence, we can see the nucleus of later world-shaking deeds, from the successive violations of the Treaty of Versailles to the long series of intrusions upon neighboring lands, the repeated breaches of faith, the seizure of the Rhineland, of Austria, of Czechoslovakia, the implication in the Spanish Civil War, the advance into Poland, and all the aggressiveness that led to World War II. Again, in the trampling brutality of the Nazis even before the days of the Munich *putsch,* their formation of a private army, their mounting demonstrations as they cowed the countryside, their organization of what was in effect a state within a state, we can observe the seeds of all the evils of later Nazidom—the terrorism, the book burning, the suppression of free labor and free speech and free thought, the appalling racial discrimination, the incineration of synagogues, the concentration camps and slaughter chambers, the extermination of millions in a cold-blooded, systematic massacre without historic parallel.

But if all this could have been foreseen, or at least if the tendencies could have been divined from the early activities of Hitler and his collaborators, why was it not foreseen? Why did the state not suppress those activities as it would have suppressed any other threat to its existence? We can only conclude that Hitler was not crushed because large elements of the German populace did not want him crushed. While many stood on the sidelines, apathetic, uninterested, unwilling to stick out their own necks, great numbers of the disgruntled, the unemployed, the impoverished, and the rootless saw in Hitler a prophet and a redeemer, whom they were ready to follow, if not to the ends of the earth, at least to the revolution that seemed to open the gates to the Promised Land. And yet all these rebels, who never comprised more than a minority of the voters, would not in themselves have sufficed for their leader's purposes. He also needed aid from more influential quarters. And such aid he received, for one thing, from the big business men and industrialists who, with the short-sightedness of the merely commercial-minded, thought that they could "do business with Hitler," and offered him essential assistance.

But even more surprising cooperation came from other quarters—from the very agencies of government that, without seeming to realize it, were threatened by the rise of the Nazis. We have seen one example in the gentle treatment of Hitler after his attempt to seize the Bavarian government; let us take another illustration. On October 17, 1931, well over a year before Hitler became Chancellor, a telegram requesting "immediate intervention against the Nazis" was addressed to the Reich Minister of the Interior by a group of the Social-Democratic Party and of the German Trade Union of Brunswick. All public demonstrations by republican organizations, they pointed out, had been prohibited, and yet "The Brunswick Government has given permission for a march of 30,000 S. A. men for Saturday and Sunday. The police permits armed Hitlerites to do as they like."[2]

But though the plea concluded with a statement that no protection of the peaceful population could be expected from the Brunswick Minister of the Interior, the appeal went unheeded. Intervention by the Government, it was claimed, was not possible, even though intervention had been the rule in cases not involving the Nazis. The conclusion is self-evident that the Government of Chancellor Breuning, for political reasons, was catering to the Nazis. But one must note also that powerful General Kurt von Schleicher, who was to be the last Chancellor of the republic and would be liquidated in the "blood purge" of June 30, 1934, maneuvered in favor of Hitler and even brought about a meeting between him and Hindenburg.

And so the Nazis kept on their way, with military drills, parades, and exercises that seem less extraordinary than does the manifest unawareness of the authorities and the public as they nourished their own destroyer. As an example of the sort of activity that was occurring throughout the land, let us turn to the small town of Thalburg in central Germany, a middle-class community that may not have been absolutely typical but did have many of the country's common characteristics. William Sheridan Allen, who has made a detailed study of this town, tells us that in 1931 the people could hear the sounds of military exercises near the Cattle Auction Hall, while during the following autumn the S. A. "engaged in extensive public maneuvers" in a nearby forest, and training courses were begun in that same year. Thus Thalburg's S. A. "developed into a formidable instrument: well trained, equipped and housed; spirited and under the iron discipline of the Nazi party."[3]

Did the people never ask themselves the meaning, the implications of this buildup of a large, privately organized, privately led military force in their very midst? Did the officials never ask this question? And when the demonstrations were of even vaster extent—when, for example, on October 13, 1931, Hitler reviewed a parade of 100,000 eager and disciplined followers at Franzenfeld—was every onlooker altogether blind? Could no one, including the officials, see the seeds of the overthrow of republican government, the preliminaries of another world war, and the devastation of much of the planet including Germany?

It may be that, behind the gradual, scarcely checked drift into the catastrophe of Nazism, there was something deep-rooted in the mind and mood of the age. One of the forces precipitating the downfall may have been the negation of the current beliefs, strongly influenced by scientific finds and theories, but in part traceable to the preachments of Nietzsche and other philosophers, and spurred particularly by the disillusionments of the war and of the ensuing peace. Sophisticated men, no longer recognizing an aim or object in existence, came to take ironic satisfaction in looking upon the universe as a gigantic hoax, in which nothing really mattered except the immediate aims of the ego. There is something to be said for the view of Albert Camus, which, as interpreted by John Cruickshank, traced the rise of the Nazis to "the putting of machiavellian nationalism into the moral void created by an acute sense of the absurdity of existence."[4] This is to say that the movement was "a form of revolt against the absurd, but a revolt which did not distinguish between self-sacrifice and mystification, energy and violence, strength and cruelty."[5] Unfortunately, more than a handful of Germans bowed to this confused, nihilistic creed; many persons, including not a few who called themselves intellectuals, succumbed to the evil faith that saw existence as meaningless, hence held that it was of not the slightest importance what man did to himself or to the world about him or to the minds or bodies or spirits of his fellow men.

But this explanation, while it seems to have more than a little justification, does not express, nor even approach the entire truth. Other powerful forces brooded behind the Nazi ascendancy, and far from the least of these, undoubtedly, was something directly affecting the rank and file of the people—the military indoctrination, the martial tradition reaching back to Frederick II and his forebears. This militarization, instilled in accordance with a brutal officers' code that demanded a robot-like popular subordination, was so ingrained that many observers evidently looked on with bemused eyes, unable to see the reality beneath the horny externals; they were so conditioned to submissiveness by the drill sergeant that they would not have dared to act, nor even thought of acting. But this is only a partial explanation; much of the solution is also to be found in the materialistic standards of the times and the machinations of self-interested groups, which operated the more easily owing to the congenital complacency and lack of vision of the human species, and its limited ability to interpret the present or foresee the future.

One may be certain that if the people had read the meaning implicit in the earlier agitations of the Nazis, and had distinguished between legitimate protest and designing antisocial strategy—in fact, had they taken Hitler at his own word when he boldly announced his intentions—all Germany would have arisen in a furor and freed itself of the Nazis and the Nazi leaders with the fervor with which they would have beaten down an infestation of rats and fleas that threatened them with the Black Death.

12. Lashings of the Dragon's Tail

i. Revolt Through the Ages

In 14 A.D. a severe famine struck along the Yellow River of China; food became so scarce that some of the peasants resorted to cannibalism. Led by a bandit chief, many of the starving arose against the government in the Revolt of the Red Eyebrows, which took its name from the rebels' practice of painting their eyebrows in order to recognize one another. In the resultant military action, the sympathies of the people were enlisted, the regular troops were defeated, and in 18 A.D. the insurgents took possession of the lower reaches of the Yellow River.

This was but one of the innumerable revolts that have checkered the history of China—a country which, despite the age-old somnolence that may seem to have characterized it before the outbreaks of our own century, was often much less calm than a surface view would suggest; in fact, it was frequently rifted, like other lands, by internal dissensions and popular uprisings. In the 19th century, these became particularly numerous: more than 100 were recorded in the years between 1841 and 1849, while 1847 had the unenviable record of spawning 26 rebellions, or an average of one every two weeks.

The causes of the outbreaks varied throughout the centuries. Sometimes, as in the revolution of 1029–1030 under the Liao Dynasty, which led to the establishment for a time of an independent state under its own emperor, the aim was political but the spark was economic—the imposition of a stern new system of taxation. Sometimes there were superstitious or supposedly magical elements, as in the Yellow Turban revolt of 184 A.D., dominated by the magicians of a secret society of a family named Chang, who began by performing needed social services such as road and bridge repair and the doling out of rice to the hungry, but ended by taking over many districts in Hopei and Shantung provinces in accordance with what they announced to be a favorable conjunction of the stars. Unfortunately, after the rebellion had been crushed and many of the revolting peasants put to death, the misery of the people was even greater than before; according to the contemporary poet Wang T'san, the land came to be plagued by the tiger and the wolf, while whitened bones strewed the plain.

Despite all injections of the supernatural, we find an underlying similarity between the Chinese revolts and the numerous *Jacqueries* of European peasants as well as certain of the preliminaries of the French Revolution. When the founts of bitterness were near to overflowing, dissident movements were likely to crop up among the people, particularly under a weak, corrupt, or oppressive government; these movements, of course, required a leader or leaders, and such leaders might be reputed magic-makers, though more often they were brigand chiefs.

Under the emperors, two distinct types of militants appeared: the one idealistic and self-sacrificing, and aiming primarily at the betterment of the community; the other realistic and self-seeking, and bent on gaining personal prestige and power. In the analysis of Thomas Taylor Meadows, a British Chinese interpreter whose book first appeared in 1856, I find a description of both types of rebel. Of the first we are told,

> Some few men literally sacrifice their lives . . . for the good of the community. They head a rising against the oppressors, continue to oppose whatever force is moved against them until it is settled by negotiation that no attempt shall be made to prolong the oppressions, and then, instead of flying, they in their quality as ringleaders deliberately surrender, and heroically yield up their lives as that expiation on which autocracy must insist before it dares to give up the struggle. There is neither hope nor thought of overturning the dynasty in these risings. . . .[1]

Although few of our own protesters would willingly risk their lives, we find reminders here of the idealism of some of the more dedicated modern dissenters. But more numerous were the rebels of another breed, some of whom, Meadows says, "become outlaws—bandits or pirates—having more or less of the sympathy of the public." Another way, however, was the following:

> A man, originally a mere thief, burglar, or highwayman . . .

finds it possible, in the state of general apathy to public order produced by continued oppression, to connect himself with a few fellow thieves, &c. and at their head to evade all efforts of the local authorities to put him down. As his band increases, he openly defies these authorities, pillages the local customs houses and treasuries . . . but refrains from plundering any one outright, and . . . he as the scourge of the oppressors gains the latent or conscious sympathy of all classes. Now, these captains of bandits . . . when they begin to count their followers by thousands, forming a regularly governed force they declare openly against the hitherto reigning sovereign, whom they denounce as a usurper.[2]

This, thoughout Chinese history, was the common process likely to lead to a new regime. From abuse to militant protest, and from militant protest to military power and military takeover, was the route followed by some of the founders of the great dynasties. This method of solution, to be sure, left much to be desired, but does help us to account for the durability of the Chinese empire.

The process was given impetus by the fact that, whereas the scholars and the upper classes generally scorned military activity as beneath them, their nonbelligerency was by no means characteristic of the peasantry. Here the old illusory fighting cult of glamour and glory was powerful. As one writer puts it, "The fact is that the Chinese peasant, far from being the pacific son of the East usually described, has a strong affinity for military heroes, especially for those who emanate from his own social stratum,"[3] even though such heroes are apt to be bandits magnified in a sort of Robin Hood glow. In many cases the peasant's penchant for warlike expression was encouraged by the secret societies which were abundant throughout Chinese history, and which, arising as protesting groups of the underprivileged, are visible behind many of the great revolts, from the White Lotus rebellion of the 14th century to the Taiping uprising half a millennium later.

It is altogether probable that, had it not been for the drastically changed conditions accompanying the interjection of Western influences, the ancient forces including those of the radical secret societies would have continued to play a crucial part; the old historic processes would have repeated themselves in the 20th century and resulted in the replacement of the enfeebled Ch'ing or Manchu regime by some able usurper, who, after a flaming rebellion, would have established another dynasty with a century-long life expectancy. But this man would have been a leader of a different order, and would have founded a government of another complexion than the one that took power in October 1949.

ii. The Taiping Rebellion

The greatest of all the Chinese revolutions before our own distracted century was the Taiping Rebellion, which lasted from 1850 to 1864. Here a variety of forces may be seen at work, including Christianity in a deviant form; the outbreak also had features foreshadowing the social innovations of Chinese Communism, as in the demands for abolition of the rule of the gentry and scholars, and for a sort of military-socialist regimentation of the state. The leader of the movement was Hung Hsiu-chuan, the son of the headman of a village near Canton, a fanatic who suffered from the same sort of delusion as some of the more mischievous Westerners in the religious strife of previous centuries—he was God-appointed, he thought, to rule China in the name of heaven. Having been unable to get ahead in his own affairs—having thrice failed the examinations that were the recognized road to advancement in contemporary Chinese society—he was shown the way to conduct the affairs of his country in a series of visions, wherein he visited the other world and was there informed of his high mission. From this he developed a doctrine in which fundamentalist Christianity was mixed with ingredients of Confucianism and of Hung's own doctrines; and he preached this creed until his followers were numbered by the thousands. In 1851 he actually went so far as to clothe himself in the imperial yellow. Nor was his movement merely one of nonviolent protest, despite the title of "Taiping" or "Supreme Peace." His followers, not confining themselves to spiritual weapons, were armed with swords and spears, and were driven on not only by religious motivations but by the sufferings of the people, which stemmed in part from official abuses and in part from the poverty of the land and from overpopulation. But it has been pointed out that the revolution, which broke out in some deprived areas while skipping others, cannot be explained on economic grounds; it was the stimulation of Hung's evangelical ideas that caused an outbreak far transcending the peasant insurrections of earlier years—and one that came within reaching distance of seating the peasant rebel on the imperial throne.

Having secured the loyalty of the country folk by a redistribution of the land and expulsion of oppressive officials, Hung in a series of startling military campaigns captured Hankow in 1852 and Nanking in 1853, and in 1854 posed a threat to Tientsin and to Peking itself, although he never did reach the capital. Thus what began as the dissent of a solitary visionary expanded until it threatened an empire. Hung's eventual failure, and his death amid his enemies' fiery recapture of Nanking in 1864, are perhaps to be ascribed less to the weakness within his own movement than to the opposition of the Chinese scholars and the intrusion of the Westerners, which led to the occupation of Peking by the British and French in 1860 and the shelling of Hung's Yangtze strongholds by British warships.

But the costs of the uprising were immeasurable. The loss of life, according to some authorities, far eclipsed that of the Mongol bloodbaths of earlier centuries—twenty million lives are said to have been lost, and some estimates are even higher. Not only that, but the processes of social reform had been interrupted for generations, the disintegration of the country had been accelerated, and the Manchu regime had been so weakened that, although it clung to its tottering existence for nearly another half-century, its eventual collapse had become a mere matter of time. And even beyond all this—and possibly most significant of all for the future—Hung had demonstrated the possibilities of Chinese peasant armies, and so had taught a lesson that would not be overlooked by his more powerful successor, Mao Tse-tung.

At the same time, while he would never fulfill his expectations of being seated as the Son of Heaven, Hung showed how much power can rest in a single resolute militant. The irony is that he actually did have legitimate causes for protest, and apparently strove sincerely for the welfare of the people despite the remorseless rod he clamped down. But being no more gifted with prescience than most men, he and his followers moved toward disasters which neither they nor anyone else could foresee.

iii. The Boxers, the Manchus, and Sun Yat-sen

Unlike most militant movements, which are directed against what is loosely known as "the Establishment," the Boxer uprising of 1899–1900 was favored by the Establishment, which is to say the Manchu government, and was actually a move against foreigners, specifically against Christians, whether Occidentals or Orientals. In view of the humiliating treatment dealt out to the Chinese for scores of years by the Westerners, and the latter's seizure of territory and ruthless exploitation of the opium traffic and other sources of income, everything that happened is thoroughly understandable, even though many of the blows were aimed irrationally at the innocent. When Christian missionaries and other aliens were being slain and their property plundered, when the secret society of Boxers in 1899 adopted the slogan "Support the Manchus, annihilate the foreigners," an intolerable situation had been created; but what was most striking about the whole episode was that the government, somewhat like the Czarist regime of Russia in its covert encouragement of pogroms against its own Jewish population, secretly sided with the persecutors of the Christians. That the result was the further humiliation of China after its reckless declaration of war on the foreign powers, is a little aside from the theme of our inquiry. But what is worth noting is that the protest against the foreigners and their ways, although in many respects justified, led to outbreaks of frenzy that only aggravated the conditions the demonstrations had meant to relieve.

Nevertheless, the forces of dissent within China remained powerful. And those forces, having failed in their attack on the West, became concentrated against the Manchu dynasty, which had been brought a long step nearer to its downfall. Now, working underground, at first in nonviolent ways, the rebels were making ready for the eventual outbreak.

This brings us to Sun Yat-sen, one of the dominant Chinese figures of the early revolutionary era, whose insurgent activities date back at least as far as the 1890s. Born of peasant stock in 1866, educated in an English missionary school in Honolulu and converted to Christianity in 1884, he studied medicine but practiced the profession only briefly; his real interests were in social and political reform. In 1894 he became one of the founders of the Hawaiian Hsing Chung Hui (Revive China Society); in January 1895, he helped to establish the Hong Kong branch. Here, in a comparatively mild protest, we see the beginnings of a revolutionary. Whatever the actual aims of Sun and his associates (and it has been claimed, though without documentary verification, that they sought the overthrow of the Manchus and the establishment of a republic), their declared principles did not call for the end of the regime but merely sought governmental improvements and bulwarks against foreign encroachment. However, whether or not the Hsing Chung Hui really was a revolutionary organization, it was important for the directions in which it pointed.

It is clear that the thoughts of the organizers were already taking militant, even martial approaches. In April 1895, the Chinese government, after being overwhelmed in the war with Japan, was forced to sign the disgraceful Treaty of Shimonoseki, wherein she ceded Formosa, the Pescadores, and the Liaotung Peninsula in Manchuria to Japan, and agreed to pay an indemnity and bow to various other impositions. A month before the signatures were put on this humiliating document, Sun Yat-sen and his friend Yang Ch'u-yun and some of their comrades decided to strike at the decadent government which had sunk their country to unprecedented depths of abasement and defeat. The following October 26 they would stage a coup at Canton, and meanwhile Yang would recruit men, raise funds, and procure arms. As proof of the fervor of the group, one of its members, Huang Yung-shang, contributed the proceeds of the sale of a house to the cause—$8000 in the local currency.

Yet the conspirators were moved by personal as well as public aims, as attested by the bitter struggle between Sun and Yang for the Presidency of the "Provisional Government." Yang finally won what proved to be a barren honor; the revolt had to be postponed two days to allow time to complete the preparations at Hong Kong, and during this interval the plot became known to the Cantonese police. On October 28, 45 would-be rebels were arrested, and gave up 205 revolvers and 80 boxes of ammunition; Sun, more fortunate than many of his collaborators, escaped the headman's axe by fleeing to Japan. For the next 16 years, apart from one overnight visit to a remote Chinese mountain area, he played the part of a revolutionary *in absentia* (as others, and notably Lenin, were to do in other lands during the disturbed years that followed). But though he had to work from foreign bases, he was determined to head the anti-Manchu movement. Therefore he established the frankly revolutionary Hsing Han Hui, or Revive Han Society, in which his leadership was formally recognized by the other members. Having tried unsuccessfully to induce the governors of Kwangtung and Kwangsi to secede from the Empire, the Hsing Han Hui turned to military action with the help of armed bandits, and with the hope of taking Waichow.

But expected Japanese military aid did not materialize, and Sun's "second revolutionary attempt" went down in failure.

While working abroad to obtain support for the revolution during the long years before the eventual overthrow of the dynasty, Sun was encouraged by the anti-Manchu drive among Chinese students. Apparently their insurrectionary impulse arose independently, although Sun lent it support when in 1903 he participated in founding an underground military school in Aoyama, Japan. Later, in Tokyo in 1905, Sun was introduced to Huang Hsing, chairman of the Hunan Students' Association in Japan; these two joined hands in an alliance that led to the formation of the revolutionary society, the T'ung Meng Hui, the "Sworn-Together League," or United League of China. Every member, upon entering this organization, had to sign an oath to exert himself to the utmost to expel the Manchus, to establish a republic, and to equalize land rights. Failing in this obligation, the member agreed to submit to "the severest penalties" imposed by his comrades.

The T'ung Meng Hui, which within six years came to count 300,000 members in 17 provinces, was significant in that it accomplished the first coordination of various scattered anti-Manchu elements, and did this with the aid of numerous revolutionary newspapers and magazines which the government tried vainly to suppress. Meanwhile small revolts were cropping up at many points, while the rebellious young committed such acts of defiance as cutting off their queues or battering down idols in village shrines. It is worth noting that Sun, who was 39, and his collaborator Huang, who was approaching 31, were the old men of the movement; most of their associates were youths, who had entered with eagerness and idealism, but represented the intellectuals rather than the Chinese rank and file. Sun Yat-sen proved to be right in thinking that with these men behind him, the Manchus would be overthrown during his lifetime.

But years were still to pass before the consummation of this goal; not until 1911 was the decisive stroke accomplished, and not until early the following year did the imperial power abdicate, making way for the Republic formally as well as in fact. And meanwhile the country was shaken by repeated tumults. Sun, according to his own account, had made "ten unsuccessful revolutionary attempts," some of which were little more than acts of political protest against the Manchu government, though most of them were military attacks led by Huang Hsing. During these years the outbreaks were widespread, including uprisings not organized by the T'ung Meng Hui, some of major proportions. Rice riots occurred in many places as the sufferings of the people grew more severe; the peasants in some districts refused to pay taxes; in Hunan, Kwangtung, and Szechwan provinces organized demonstrations flamed up against a project to build a railroad with the aid of a loan from foreign syndicates. Protest meetings were held, shops were closed, tax payments were withheld, new riots broke out and were aggravated by the government's attempts at forcible suppression. It is noteworthy that revolutionary organizations sprang up in Hupeh province, six of them of considerable size, and all of them established by students and soldiers, although in the end it was the latter that took control.

Of all the unsuccessful revolts, the most significant was that which agitated Canton on March 29, 1911, when members of the "Dare-to-Die-Corps" (originally counted at 72, but later found to have numbered 85) threw down their lives for the sake of the revolution. But this failure, the spirit which it engendered, and the sacrificial example of its heroes, provided inspiration for the Wuchang Revolution of October 10, 1911, which broke out prematurely following an explosion in an illegal arms factory, but achieved an unexpected victory over the government troops, and captured the middle-Yangtze cities of Hanyang and Hankow (though these were soon retaken), while eventually a majority of the 22 provinces declared their independence of Peking. When the Imperial Commissioner and commander of the army Yuan Shih-k'ai machinated for his own ends in a Machiavellian game that played into the rebels' hands, the Manchu government was left tottering and helpless. Although Sun Yat-sen was to characterize the rebel success as "sheer accident," and the revolt did indeed begin ahead of schedule in an unplanned way, nevertheless the preparations of many years by Sun and others played a part that was more than accidental.

iv. The Republic and the Communists

After Sun Yat-sen's election as President by a provisional council of the new Republic of China in December 1911, and after the signing of the decrees of abdication by the Dowager Empress Tz'u Hsi on February 12, 1912, in the name of the last

Manchu emperor, one might have expected an end to the era of confusion, riots, and revolts. Actually, however, no such blessed relief was on the horizon; the following 37 or 38 years were among the most turbulent in the history of the nation, and the voices of dissent were heard as seldom before. In part this was because there had been too little provision for the Republic either in its political buildup or in the minds of the people. The position of Sun Yat-sen was from the beginning anomalous in view of the opposition of Yuan Shih-k'ai with his portentous military power; as early as January 1912, Sun announced his intention to resign in Yuan's favor as soon as the Manchus had abdicated and the general had proclaimed his endorsement of the Republic. In February these conditions were met, while one of the Manchu decrees specified that Yuan was to be given "full power to organize a provisional republican government" in order to "bring peace to the people and tranquillity to the empire." Promptly Sun honored his promise, and the reins of government went into the hands of a callous and treacherous military man who had little regard for his oath of office, and who eventually assumed a virtually dictatorial power, plotted to set himself up as Emperor, and was supported in his imperial aims by a society, the Chou An Hui, which propagandized for him by telegrams and other means. But his story came to an end he had little foreseen; before his death on June 16, 1916, Yuan was forced into a humiliating backdown, when an opposition government under General Li Yuan-hung was established at Canton.

Thus began another period of general anarchy. Li, who became President upon the death of Yuan, was soon deposed, and the weak government that followed was overturned in 1920 by a group of three warlords, who held control in Peking until 1927, while most of the country was in the grip of various other warlords, and something close to chaos prevailed.

Even in the early days of the Republic, the instability of the new regime had been suggested by an outbreak in Peking. On February 29, 1912, Yuan Shih-k'ai was giving a banquet for some delegates from Nanking, when suddenly a rattling of gunfire was heard from outside the building. The lights went out; the guests, plunged into darkness, became panicky; confusion spread through the city, and shops and banks were plundered by mutineers of the army's Third Division. For three nights the riots continued, extending even to Tientsin, while the rebellious troops made their escape with three trainloads of loot. This may, indeed, have been little more than brigandage, of a type not unfamiliar in China; but its occurrence at this particular time and place is indicative of the disorderly state of the country and the nature of the forces that were to bring down the republican experiment.

During the succeeding years, while republicanism stumbled to inglorious disaster, an awakening Chinese nationalism received a sharp prod, and produced a hotbed of further demonstrations. The country's disdainful treatment by Japan, and the latter's ultimatum in 1915 exacting acceptance of the outrageous Twenty-One Demands, had aroused fierce nationalistic feelings in many of the youth, feelings which had been fed by United States Secretary of State Bryan when he implied that America stood on the side of China. A crucial question was that of the return of Shantung, which had been torn from China in 1898 in German and Austrian treaties. But when the decision went against China in a Council of the Foreign Ministers of the Big Powers at the Peace Conference in 1919, Chinese nationalists felt that the spirit of the pronouncements of Wilson and Bryan had been violated and their nation betrayed. The not unnatural result was to be seen in disturbances, culminating in the celebrated May Fourth Movement.

In memory of the Japanese ultimatum on the Twenty-One Demands, a demonstration had been set for May 7 by the student organizations. Meeting in a stormy conference at Peking University on May 3, however, the various student groups were unable to restrain their impatience, and decided upon a parade the next day to protest the adverse vote of the peace delegates. Three thousand students, representing 13 educational institutions, ignored police warnings and began their march on the early afternoon of the fourth. Blocked by guards at the Legation Quarter, and threatened by troops, the students turned toward the homes of the government leaders with cries of "To the house of the traitor!" Finding no one home at the residence of one of the officials, Ts'ao Ju-lin, they burned the house, and soon afterwards beat another official into unconsciousness. As an aftermath, 32 students were arrested, and one of them died from injuries received during the affray. And, as a further sequel, protest movements were organized, along with strikes, a boycott of Japanese products, and work stoppages. Another student demonstration in Peking, on June 3, resulted in 1000 arrests, and a later demonstration incurred the dismissal of three high officials, followed a

few days afterwards by the resignation of the Cabinet. But perhaps still more significant was the continued acceleration of the
wave of protest and the formation of various radical student organizations, such as the New Youth Society and the Chinese Students' Union. Perhaps the Communists today are not altogether
wrong in looking upon the May Fourth Movement as the starting
point in the great modern nationalistic development. We should
note, however, that it was mostly the intellectuals and the nu-
merically limited middle classes of the treaty ports who supported
the protests and the consequent nationalism growing out of the
May Fourth incident. Nationalism in China was in fact a restricted
phenomenon until forced upon the peasant masses by the oppressions of the invading Japanese. Yet it did provide one of the
rungs for the Communists in the troubled rise of their party.

v. The Triumph of the Red Flag

Communism of the Soviet brand was planted in China in a
limited way as early as the spring of 1920, when two agents of
the Comintern organized a small group of assorted leftists in
Shanghai and indoctrinated them in revolutionary methods and
techniques aiming toward the ultimate seizure of power. For
some time the work proceeded in secret, while the Communists
strove for command of the labor movement; in 1921 and 1922
they were active in promoting strikes of sailors and railroadmen.
In 1924 Sun Yat-sen, who evidently never understood the true
character of the Bolsheviks, reached an agreement with them and
admitted them into his Kuomintang or Nationalist Party. In
subsequent years they showed their colors more clearly, especially
in 1927, when they attempted several armed uprisings, such as
the Nanchang, Autumn Crop, and Canton insurrections. With
slogans such as "Bread for the workers! Land for the peasants!
Down with the power of the Kuomintang!" they attempted to
rouse the workers to revolt, and had some initial success, as when
they seized the seaport of Swatow and held it for ten days, and
when, at Canton, they took the police station, the barracks, post
offices, and telegraph headquarters, and went on to capture the
entire city, which they held for two days before falling before the
first counter-attack. In the grim sequel, five or six thousand Communists or alleged Communists were murdered.
Somewhat similar had been the experience in Shanghai on

March 21, 1927, when the Communists engineered a general strike that enlisted an estimated 600,000 men and paralyzed the city except for the International Settlement; police stations, arsenals, and government buildings were seized and turned over to the "citizens" or revolutionary government, while 5000 armed workers seemed to announce the triumph of Marxism. The victory, however, lasted no more than about three weeks. Much about the interval is obscure; but it is certain that Chiang Kai-shek, stabbing with a backhand stroke at his Communist allies, struck on April 12 with ferocity and treachery equalling that of his enemies themselves. Somehow he had enlisted the aid of the Green and Red secret societies of Shanghai's underworld to form patrols, which were aided by foreign businessmen, bankers, intellectuals, and students. Before daybreak, the order had been flashed; and Chiang's allies, with deadly unexpectedness, fell upon the Communist labor pickets, took their arms, and slaughtered all resisters. Many of the Red leaders were executed; the total number slain was estimated at 5000 by a man afterwards not unknown in the Communist movement, Chou En-lai, who was captured and condemned to die but escaped through the connivance of the brother of one of his former students.

The debacle at Shanghai was to be all the more serious in the eyes of the Communists in view of their defeat later in the year in other insurrections, and in view also of the damning disclosure of April 1927, when Chinese agents seized papers showing how the Comintern was working for disruptive ends through the offices of the Soviet government. It was the defeat of the plans for secret subversion that had turned Stalin toward a policy of insurrection; and, after the torpedoing of this policy, Communist power in China seemed almost at an end and the Communists were drawn underground. Secret Bolshevik networks did, however, survive; in 1929 many more subversive documents were found by the Chinese police in northern Manchurian Soviet consulates, some of whose officials were arrested. Thus it became known that the Soviet Union had been importing arms and ammunition for the ends of terrorism. These disclosures, which resulted in a breach of diplomatic relations between the two countries, might have seemed to sweep away any surviving remnant of Communist influence, especially since China's powerful new leader and foremost general, Chiang Kai-shek, was a bitter anti-Marxist who had routed the Communist forces at Shanghai and elsewhere in a series of coups.

Yet although all their agitations, riots, and revolts had failed, defeat had not ended the plans of the Soviets for revolution, nor the "struggle for the masses" through labor disturbances and underground organization. Nor had failure shattered the Communist aim of developing a force of peasants and workers to be ready to strike when at last the moment came. The details of the following years—the rise of Mao Tse-tung, the pressure on Mao by the military might of Chiang Kai-shek, and the epochal retreat in the Long March to remote Kweichow province—are apart from the theme of our discussion, as are the workings of that Japanese expansionism which afflicted and antagonized the peasants over wide areas and did much to unify the previously disunited Chinese against Japan. Yet it is important to keep these circumstances in mind if we are to understand subsequent events, and in particular the rapid thrust-back of Mao's Communists and their leap to power after their apparent submergence.

In their spectacular rise, they were aided by two storm-currents, one flowing outside them and owing little or nothing to their efforts, and the other an integral part of their activities. The first embodied the organized elements of dissent that had sprung up against the native warlords and later against the Japanese tramplers of the land, as in the case of the Red Spears, which won prominence as a resistance movement in 1925. Born of the country's chronic warfare, its insecurity, and the exploitation of peasants conscripted by the *tuchuns* or military governors, the Red Spears were organized groups, which, in the single province of Honan in 1930, were said to number 100,000. And this was but one militant secret society out of many; others, with names such as Heavenly Gate, Big Sword, Yellow Sand, and Long Hair, claimed hundreds of members, who did much to insure the defeat of the Kuominchun, the so-called People's Army, whose unpaid troops had been living off the country.

In these secret societies, and in their covert and organized strokes, the Communists found material ready-made. Nor did they neglect the opportunity; they realized that here, given the ignition of a stirring doctrine, there would be fuel for revolution. During the period of the Communist-Kuomintang entente (which, as we have seen, was dynamited by Chiang Kai-shek in 1927), the Soviet advisers had considerable success in organizing the peasants of South China, while striving to knock off the feudal chains that still enslaved most of the villages, and machinating to organize the populace for what Mao termed the "people's war."

But their most signal success was possible only after the invasion by Japan. It was then that they not only won the support of the peasants by mitigating the oppressions of landlordism, but, aided by propaganda and at times by trickery and deliberate misrepresentation, they posed as the champions of the people against the detested invader, and thus aroused the masses to sabotage and guerrilla warfare. The organization of a typical Communist movement in one of the villages, according to a Chinese commentator, began with the successive formation of Peasant Associations and of armed bands, and went on to the spread of hunger-incited uprisings, the refusal to pay taxes and rents, the presentation of petitions and demands, and "confiscation of grain and other property of the rich; aggregation of greater number of followers; formation of soviets or establishment of new regimes under Communist direction" in "an intricate mass of action" in which "it was impossible to separate reform and revolution."[4]

Although Marxist propaganda and ideology played important roles in enlisting millions of village militants, it is hardly likely that many of the peasants had much idea of the philosophy of Marx or Lenin. What they did know was that they were protecting their homes, their families, their fields, and the beloved shrines of their ancestors from landlords and warlords at home, while being trained by their Red comrades and treated with an apparent respect they had never known before. If their new masters were at heart as dictatorial and in some ways even more dictatorial than the old, they could not know it; nor did they ask whether Communism had been glorified into something far transcending reality, and if the character and purposes of the Kuomintang had been correspondingly belittled. In their minds it was all-sufficient that Mao Tse-tung appeared to be their savior from persecutors from abroad and from enslavement by native tyrants. Consequently, they not only proved malleable for use in the armies by which Mao prevailed over the Nationalists, but were ready to accept Communist rule when in 1949 it was clamped down over the entire land.

13. The Modern Scene: Black Versus White

i. The Paradox of the Industrial Age

One of the supreme paradoxes of all time may be observed among the great industrial nations. Gifted with an affluence beyond the dreams of the emperors of old; surrounded by an abundance of material things whose magical-seeming comforts reach millions of men, they are yet riven by chasms that leave multitudes deprived and underprivileged, and are shaken by civil disturbances, protest marches and riots, and eruptions of mass violence that scatter bloodshed and havoc, challenge law and authority, and pose a threat to society itself.

Half incredulously, in a sort of daze, unable fully to reconcile ourselves to the new realities, we have been following the succession of events. And the spectacle has indeed been startling. So many and so varied have been the developments of recent years that one hardly knows where to begin in making even a partial enumeration. Arson, shooting, looting, personal assault, and other forms of violence in Harlem, Chicago's South Side, the Los Angeles suburb of Watts, Detroit, Newark, Rochester, Brooklyn, Philadelphia, and many other American cities; student demonstrations that, for a time, have closed some of our great universities; draft-card burnings and antiwar marches involving hundreds of thousands of citizens; peaceful civil rights movements, and murderous attacks on civil rights workers; gun battles between city police and members of dissident organizations; bank-burning, and bomb-planting in offices and stores; the unearthing of arsenals of weapons accumulated by private citizens or extremist groups—all these are but parts of the picture that has

207

been unfolding before American eyes like the reels of some ghastly melodrama. Here is a spectacle of mass resistance, even mass defiance, which has by no means been confined to the United States and is perhaps more closely allied than we like to believe to some of the great convulsive movements of history such as the French, Russian, and Chinese revolutions, as well as to numerous lesser and often abortive uprisings in many lands.

So many have been the ramifications of recent protest that it would be confusing to lump them all together. Hence I have divided them into three categories: those involving racial complaint and conflict, those pertaining to the student uprisings, and those connected with the antidraft and antiwar movement. To a large extent, I realize, these listings are arbitrary, and at many points they overlap: a demonstrator for racial justice may also, for example, be a protester against war, and at the same time may be a student radical; possibly a majority of the dissenters belong in more than one of the three divisions. Yet the demarcations, while far from absolute, will serve the ends of simplicity and clarity.

ii.   The Dark Background of Racial Riots

Much as when many Americans have heard in stunned disbelief of the massacre at My Lai in Vietnam, not thinking it possible that our boys would murder women and babes even though similar atrocities have blood-marked the annals of warfare, so those of us not directly involved have sat by in shocked wonder at the news of recent urban strife. "What!" we have cried. "Can it be that in peaceful districts where racial relations were apparently friendly, suddenly everything can go up as in a bomb-blast?" Our preconceptions as to the security, soundness, and progress of civilization are upset by such things as the burning of stores and homes, the assaulting of defenseless passers-by, the sniping from rooftops and random firing from speeding cars, the halting and overturning of automobiles, the rock-throwing and window-smashing and plundering, the attacks upon firemen and police, the shattering of community life, and the necessity in some cases to call in large contingents of militia or National Guards in the effort to restore order. "Certainly," we are apt to exclaim, "nothing so terrible has ever happened before!"

In this, however, we are wrong. While the present era is indeed unique in the scope of the disturbances, American racial uprisings have not been confined to this generation nor even to this century, though in many past cases it was the whites who rioted and the blacks who were the helpless victims, and in some instances the targets were Orientals or other racial minorities. Before the Civil War, and in the supposedly liberal North, racial strife was common, as can be seen in the innumerable attacks upon Abolitionists, and in incidents such as the assault upon the Noyes Academy for Negroes at Canaan, New Hampshire in 1835, and the slaying of Elijah J. Lovejoy and the destruction of his antislavery press in Alton, Illinois, in 1837. The activities of the Ku Klux Klan and kindred organizations such as the Knights of the White Camelia are too well known to require more than our passing notice. On the reverse side of the picture, the celebrated exploits of John Brown provide examples of violent strife, in effect hopelessly ill-conceived minor warfare in the interest of racial equality. And, on a less ambitious scale, a notable protest movement—notable in particular for its foreshadowing of the events of the following century—occurred in Louisville, Kentucky, in 1871, when streetcar riders rebelled against separate seating for whites and blacks and eventually won their fight, though not until white rioters had broken windows, overturned cars, and thrown out Negro patrons. Then, in 1906, race-inspired riots convulsed Atlanta, Georgia, when white mobs attacked Negroes, and beat or stabbed several to death; in Springfield, Ohio, also in 1906, the Negro section was put to the torch and the inhabitants driven out; and in Springfield, Illinois, in 1908, the Negro area was likewise attacked and many residents permanently fled the city.

A greater wave of disturbances was that which broke out during and shortly after World War I. In East St. Louis in 1917, and two years later in various other cities including Charleston, Washington, D. C., Knoxville, Omaha, and Chicago, a far-seeing mind might have observed preliminaries to the more extensive strife of the 1960s.

Perhaps the most notable of all these was the Chicago uprising, which had its origin in one of those incidents that are of no intrinsic importance and yet are deeply meaningful in their bearing upon men's pride and dignity and their sense of personal worth and fulfillment. During a swim in Lake Michigan a black youth ventured, perhaps inadvertently, across the invisible line separating the white swimming section from the segregated Negro area. Thereupon some young white swimmers began hurling stones at the trespasser, who was drowned. Yet when Negro spectators called upon a white policeman to arrest the rock-throwers, he not only refused, but detained one of the black men on a minor charge. Thus the explosives were planted; the detonation was not long in coming. The black crowds, understandably, were infuriated; guns began blazing; rioting spread to many parts of the city, and for a week they continued to smoke and crackle. When calm had finally been restored, 38 victims including 23 Negroes lay dead, 557 had been injured, and about 3000 blacks had been left homeless by the destruction of more than 1000 buildings.

But the swimming incident, while the proximate cause of the eruption, cannot in itself explain what happened. There could not have been a riot, and much less a riot of the 1919 proportions, had it not been for the deeply grounded resentments, the hatred and prejudices of whites against blacks, as manifested not only in the segregation of bathing beaches but in a previous series of fights in public parks and of bombings against Negroes, whose population in the city had increased by 50,000 in two years, and who were pushing their way into residential regions beyond the restricted "Black Belt." Thus the riot represented only the crest of a disturbance that, fed by mutual passions, had been frothing and slowly gaining impetus for some time.

Likewise indicative of the shape of things-to-be was the Harlem riot of 1943, which arose, significantly, from the report of the killing of a black soldier by a white policeman, following accounts of similar episodes in Little Rock, Arkansas, El Paso, Texas, and other cities. The immediate results, in window-breaking and looting, were as illogical as mob action always is, but may be regarded as in the nature of a primitive protest against abuses by the whites. Such abuses also led to riots in Detroit in 1942 and 1943, when rock-throwing armed whites attempted to prevent Negro entry into a housing project; in 1943, 34 persons were killed including 25 Negroes, 17 of whom were slain by the police. When Detroit shook in a still more frightful riot a quarter of a century later, observers too often failed to take note of the potent explosives planted in the past.

iii. Nonviolence in the Sixties

Although new influences were at work in the troubled decade

of the sixties, we can observe the same bias and discrimination as lay behind the Chicago outbreak of 1919 and the Harlem and Detroit disturbances of 1943.

It was in the sixties that President Kennedy was forced to dispatch troops when the University of Mississippi was ordered by the federal courts to accept James H. Meredith, a Negro, as a student; in the resulting riot, two men were killed and 375 persons injured. It was in the sixties that a political novice was elected Governor of Georgia for the sole reason that he had proclaimed himself defiantly for segregation in the restaurant he owned. It was in the sixties that three civil rights workers, James Chaney, Michael Schwerner, and Andrew Goodman, were kidnapped in Mississippi and brutally murdered, while no jury could be found to convict the suspected murderers. It was in the sixties that the northern civil rights worker, Mrs. Violet Liuzzo, was gunned down as she drove by night on a country road in Alabama; it was in the sixties that Medgar Evers, the Mississippi state leader of the NAACP, was shot in the back one night in the driveway of his home. It was in the sixties that civil rights workers were herded into jail for marching peacefully on the streets of Jackson, Mississippi, and that electric cattle prods, police dogs, and high-power hoses were turned against non-violent demonstrators at Birmingham, Alabama. It was in the sixties, again at Birmingham, that four little colored girls were killed while at Sunday School at the Tenth Street Baptist Church. And it was in the sixties that the foremost spokesman of the civil rights cause, an advocate of nonviolence, Martin Luther King, Jr., was the victim of a sniper attack by a solitary assassin.

In these episodes and others, there were more than abundant incentives for protest not only by the Negroes but by men of any race or color who realized that our common humanity must be respected if we are to have a sound or satisfying society. Yet many of the demonstrations, while militant in the sense that they moved resolutely and even defiantly toward particular ends, followed a nonviolent course that was often fruitful in results of considerable consequence.

These nonviolent demonstrations can be traced back at least as far as 1955. In December of that year a bus boycott was launched by the Negroes of Montgomery, Alabama, after a black seamstress, returning home from work, was ordered out of her seat in a segregated bus to make way for a white patron. Upon refusing to obey the driver, she was arrested, taken to jail, and released with instructions to appear for trial the following Monday. In the resultant revolt of the black community, a young man hitherto little known, Martin Luther King, Jr., came to the fore as one of the leaders of the boycott of the segregated buses. Under his guidance, the former black riders would trudge miles to work rather than patronize the segregated buses; and this led, after many months, to a victory for the protesters, and integration of the buses. Peace, however, was restored only after some grave episodes; snipers fired on several of the buses, a Negro girl was beaten, a woman was shot in the leg, four Negro churches were bombed and two of them destroyed, and severe damage was inflicted on the home of the Reverend Graetz, a white defender of black rights. Even though a jury acquitted the evident bombers in disregard of confessions signed by five of them, the eruptions of violence ended and the buses ran without serious further trouble after a court order had directed integrated seating.

Few things spread faster than an inspiriting example, and this was apparent when reports of the success at Montgomery traveled abroad. It had been revealed that the mistreated people, by their own efforts, by determined action and without violence, might at least in some cases break down the white opposition to their legitimate demands. Hence nonviolent resistance, involving both blacks and whites, followed in several directions. It is eloquent of the black man's state of mind, and of the corrosives gnawing away within him, that the attacks were launched not against bad housing, job discrimination, underemployment, poor wages and working conditions or other economic disadvantages, but against afflictions of a subtler, psychological nature—the regulations that denied the man of colored skin his human place and dignity by forcing him into segregated public facilities.

These grievances, as we have seen, were overcome in the Montgomery buses; and these grievances were now attacked by various means, including "sit-ins" in public restaurants where the Negroes, like the churls in the banqueting hall of a medieval baron, were not permitted to eat at the same table as the lords. The sit-in method of protest was simple, nonviolent, yet challenging: a number of black men would seat themselves in a section of a public eating house reserved for whites, and would ask to be served. They were acutely aware, of course, that they faced insult, abuse, even arrest. But the price, in their minds, was not too great to pay.

The change, however, would come but slowly. Years were to

pass before, on the afternoon of February 1, 1960, the sit-ins began at Greensboro, North Carolina, when four young Negro students took their places at the soda fountain of a five-and-ten-cent store. As they expected, they were refused service; but they held to their seats. In the following days, the idea gained impetus; by the week's end, about 100 Negroes were sitting at Greensboro soda fountains, and on February 8 a similar demonstration was started by students at Durham, North Carolina. And now the movement spread as on a high wind; within a month, it had reached twenty cities in six Southern states, and eventually it involved as many as 100 cities and an estimated 70,000 blacks and whites. Accompanied in some cases by the boycott of stores, it caused severe reactions; in some cities the protesters were thrown into jail for breaking local segregation laws, and in Nashville a bomb shook the home of the NAACP attorney who had defended the demonstrators. But it is worth noting that in this very city an accommodation was eventually reached with the sit-in forces; the merchants, no longer willing to endure the economic burden, at last capitulated and desegregated the lunch counters.

Thus the peaceful sit-ins had accomplished more than bloody riots could presumably have done. And if such a triumph of the protesters was to be by no means general throughout the South—there were still to be cases like that of Lester Maddox, the future Governor of Georgia, who gave up his restaurant rather than supply equal treatment to Negroes—the extent of the forward step was shown by the fact that, within a year and a half of the first sit-ins, the lines between black and white had been withdrawn in the dining-rooms of more than 150 Southern cities.

Another step toward desegregation was made by the Freedom Riders, themselves nonviolent though often the victims of violence in aggravated forms. Their idea was to go beyond the previous sit-ins by testing a decision which the Supreme Court had made in 1960, declaring segregation in interstate transportation facilities to be unconstitutional; in accordance with this ruling, the protesting men and women would ride on interstate buses in groups of blacks and whites, and deliberately use the lunch counters and rest rooms provided for the other race. They knew very well that they courted trouble, and were no doubt reassured when nothing serious happened on the first part of the bus journey which they made in May 1961, from Washington to the Deep South. Unfortunately, the placid start represented no more than the calm before the storm. At Anniston, Alabama, a mob attacked the first of the two buses with iron rods, amid a commotion of shattering windows. Then, six miles outside the city, the damaged vehicle stalled with a punctured tire, and was overtaken by pursuers who set it on fire and struck out through the smoke at the choking and gasping passengers, twelve of whom had to be sent to the hospital after being providentially rescued by motorcycle police. Meanwhile the Negroes in the other bus, arriving at Anniston, had been met by whites with kicks and blows, and forced into rear seats. Two hours later, when they reached Birmingham, a pair of the Riders were severely beaten, one of them with pieces of lead pipe, while the police were conspicuously absent. The injured were taken to the hospital; and their comrades, unable to find any bus driver to transport them another foot, left next day by airplane.

This, however, was not to be the last of the Freedom Riders. In Tennessee, ten members of the Nashville Student Nonviolent Movement, both whites and blacks, picked up the gauntlet where it had been thrown down, and decided to leave for Birmingham and there continue the interrupted Freedom Ride. But at this city they were taken into "protective custody," and then, like unwanted cats being delivered in a sack far from home, were driven by night to the Tennessee border and dropped on the highway. But they persisted, still undaunted, and returned to Birmingham; after some difficulty and delay they found a bus driver to take them to Montgomery, where the men and two girls of the party were greeted by kicks and beatings, and some of the men were knocked unconscious by a rabble that included women. The police, arriving belatedly, used tear gas to end the riot. Yet only the hasty dispatch of 600 federal marshals, ordered to Montgomery by Attorney General Kennedy, saved the city from what might have been a far worse convulsion.

At Jackson, Mississippi, the Freedom Riders were received with elaborate police protection, which only enabled them to be more easily shepherded into jail; 27 were arrested, although they had committed no act of violence. And in the following months other Freedom Riders ventured forth in the tracks of the original groups, and included not only Negroes but white men and women from all parts of the country, among them the Chaplain of Yale University, the Reverend William Sloane Coffin, Jr., who would gain new prominence some years later in the Spock draft resistance case. In Jackson alone, in a six-month period, 315 Riders went to jail for their nonviolent fight against the persistent monster, discrimination.

But they had not labored and suffered in vain. Within a year after the start of the Freedom Rides, federal action had made desegregation a fact in the waiting rooms, rest rooms, and lunch rooms of the interstate travel lines of most of the South.

iv. Violence in the Sixties

Yet to the mind of the Negro, impatient after the long decades of repression and of second- or third-class citizenship, progress was discouragingly slow; the improvements often appeared small, even though, to the dispassionate white onlooker, the gains may have seemed considerable. When Chief Justice Warren spoke in 1954 for a unanimous court in ordering desegregation of the schools, his ruling was undoubtedly of monumental importance; to the black man, however, it may have seemed less than monumental. For, after his expectations had been pitched high, he was discouraged, even disillusioned to see how slowly the law was enforced in many areas beneath the doctrine of "all deliberate speed," and how totally unenforced it remained in others; how, for example, at Little Rock, Arkansas, in 1957, desegregated Negro students had to be protected by a thousand paratroopers, who, bristling in their steel helmets, patrolled the corridors of Central High under orders from President Eisenhower, and escorted the black boys and girls to and from their classes.

Similarly, when liberal federal legislation was passed, as in the civil rights act of 1964 and in the voting rights bill of 1965 (more recently under Congressional attack), the action that followed may have struck the Negro spectator as minor in proportion to the immensity of the need. The view of what might have been called the "silent majority" of blacks was expressed in 1963 by one who was by no means silent. The following is from Martin Luther King, Jr.'s celebrated *Letter from Birmingham Jail:*

> We know from painful experience that freedom is never voluntarily given by the oppressor; it must be demanded by the oppressed. . . . For years I have heard the word "Wait!" . . . This "wait" has almost always meant "never." . . .
> I guess it is easy for those who have never felt the stinging darts of segregation to say wait. But when you have seen vicious mobs

lynch your mothers and fathers at will and drown your sisters and brothers at whim; when you see hate-filled policemen curse, kick, brutalize, and even kill your black brothers and sisters with impunity; when you see the vast majority of your twenty million Negro brothers smothering in an airtight cage of poverty in the midst of an affluent society . . . then you will understand why we find it difficult to wait.[1]

Observers may express surprise that at the very time when the civil rights movement was making most progress, and when the rights of the abused were being recognized as never before since reconstruction days, militants were springing up and riots and protest movements were proliferating. This, however, is quite in accordance with human experience in many fields. In certain prisons of the American North and West riots have occurred precisely when attempts at administrative reform were being made. And, as we have noted, the French Revolution broke out not when the position of the peasant was deteriorating but when, on the whole, it was improving. Even if this may not seem logical, it is true to man's psychological nature. For militancy does not take root in the soil of hopelessness. The man utterly beaten down, who sees no path of escape, no possibility of ever improving his lot, will be cowed by his own despair, and will lack the courage and incentive to strike out. But let a man be given reason to hope; let him be shown that there is a doorway out of his misery; let him make progress toward the light of a broader, more luminous day, and he may feel the prod of a vast impatience, may perceive as never before the depth of his old abasement, may tend to minimize the advantages already won in his eagerness for benefits still out of reach, may be swept by a new pride, a new assurance, an arrogance unknown in him before, even an intolerance of the very forces trying to aid him. And he may be content with nothing short of that total immediate consummation which, unfortunately, comes very seldom in human affairs. In all this he may have our understanding even if at times he may distress and dismay us, for the pressures behind him are those of repressed generations—the overheated boiler is not to be blamed for the fury of the explosion.

In part for these reasons, and in part because bias, hatred, and discrimination are stubborn evils that have sometimes blocked the equality decreed by Congress and the courts, we have witnessed an unprecedented extension of racial conflict during recent years, and also the rise of groups without the restrained approach of a Thoreau, a Gandhi, a Roy Wilkins, or a Martin Luther King, Jr. One of the better known has been the militant SNCC (Student Nonviolent Coordination Committee), which has been accused of Communist affiliations, although Howard Zinn, one of its advisers, tells us that it is fundamentally an organization of "Black Belt and Northern Negroes who are angry at American society and determined to change it, but who have had little or no contact with formal radical ideologies or theories."[2] Another is the radical if not actually revolutionary SDS (Students for a Democratic Society). Still another is CORE (Congress of Racial Equality), which, founded in 1942, organized some of the early sit-ins and Freedom Rides, and favors black isolationism built about an independent black economy. Others are various "Black Power" advocates, which include the Black Panthers, who favor a black nationalism based upon Marxism and Leninism. But still more extreme in certain respects are the Black Muslims, who have demanded innovations exceeding the apartheid of racist South Africa—complete separation of the races, and a black state in the South. These groups and others have introduced a disturbing new element into American society, and one going so far in some cases as to embrace a cult of revolution.

Here, when we do not have racism in reverse, too often we find the danger of an appeal to sheer emotionalism and mob action. And this is more true since many members of the various groups have been activists who, while seeking to avoid bloodshed, have committed themselves to a course that involves the use of considerable force and may go to the extent of sabotage or deliberate social disruption. Whatever the motives of the dissidents—and their causes may deserve our sympathy—their methods are often hard to vindicate, particularly when they interfere with the rights of innocent third parties and resort to a lawlessness that, in any other connection, would be known as "malicious mischief."

Various examples come to mind, including cases of "job blockade." One such occurred in 1963, when Negroes, Puerto Ricans, and their sympathizers in Brooklyn and Manhattan threw themselves in the path of construction trucks in the attempt to end discriminatory policies in the building industry; more than 200 were arrested, including seven ministers who had locked arms to bar passage to vehicles bound for a Lower East Side construction project. Or consider the stoppage by protesting groups of

all traffic across New York's Triborough Bridge at the time of
the opening of the World's Fair; or the sit-in that virtually
blocked the passageways of one of San Francisco's leading hotels,
creating a fire hazard, and leading to jail terms for some of the
demonstrators; or the effort to impede business in supermarkets
by such methods as piling trays with groceries and then not checking them out, or causing the goods to be checked out without
being paid for. Or, more serious, consider the agitations in Chester, Pennsylvania, in 1963, when, in an effort to end *de facto*
segregation of the schools, crowds surrounded the city Council
Chamber in such a way as to force an end of the meeting, and,
at one time, put the councilmen to flight.

The danger of such methods is obvious: what could be undertaken on a small scale in a city council might be accomplished
with far graver consequences in a greater governmental unit.
Some of the protesting devices, to be sure, have involved but
petty interferences, at worst no more than nuisances, and some
seem to have had compelling justification. What would you say,
for example, of the experiences of some Negroes who, in October
1969, wished to see a traffic light installed at a busy intersection
on Chicago's West Side, where, in the previous few weeks, several
children had been killed? The protesters, as part of the campaign
to get the needed light—and remember that they were without
political or legal influence, and knew of no other possible course
likely to be productive—blocked the street with a wall of their
bodies. After tumults and arrests, they did get their traffic light,
but two young brothers who had been prominent in the campaign were shot dead shortly afterwards in separate and seemingly uncalled-for action by the police; then, as a further aftermath, ten policemen in their turn became casualties in a sniping
incident at a black housing development.

Here, obviously, although the aggrieved people originally had
a just cause and although the crimes of the police are hard to
defend, the agitation led to an even worse condition—one certain
to leave virulent sore spots on both sides and further complicate
racial relations.

This may be an exceptional case, but I believe it illustrates an
ever-present danger. Even when, as here, the complaints were
legitimate, some baffling questions arise. How can we know what
train of action we are setting into motion, or precisely where to
draw the line? What greater illegality is not likely to spring from
small illegalities? If traffic in a public street can be blocked for

a limited time even with the best of excuses, why not traffic in two streets, or ten, or fifty? Why not the business of an entire city? And if this can be tolerated for an hour, why not for a day, a week, or forever? Why should the obstructions not extend to the entire country? These questions may sound extreme; but here, as in other cases, small shoots may grow into great trees. And it is impossible to mention any point at which the expansion, once tolerated, should logically stop. Thus from defiance by nonviolent law-breakers the road may lead toward anarchy.

Probably, however, not many of the protesters see matters in these terms. Yet there is small reason to doubt that an irreconcilable minority do seek the end of the system by violent means, perhaps never pausing to consider that the sequel might be dictatorship and the suppression of the very liberties the resisters court. It may be that there are some who, as one writer tells us in a study of the Los Angeles riot, "are committed to a strategy of disrupting the system as a means of gaining bargaining power for helping the Negro."[3] On the other hand, another commentator may be justified in his claim that, "I know of no sizable group of Negroes in this country who want to revise American institutions. They want to be part of those institutions, for good or ill, as they now exist."[4] Still, one cannot entirely leave out of account men like Eldridge Cleaver, who, in his Algerian retreat from American justice, reportedly called for a "necessary" revolution in the United States. Nor can one dismiss the possibility that there are persons of all shades of skin who would favor the recommendation made by Rap Brown in 1967 at the annual dinner of the *National Guardian* in New York: "If you can't see yourself in the context of being John Brown, then bring me the guns. . . . If you can't give me a gun, then give a dollar to somebody who can buy a gun."[5]

This gun-hungry attitude is, unfortunately, not limited to any one group or race. It has become characteristic of a society in which crime on the streets and on the television screen has become commonplace, and in which compulsory schooling in the methods and practice of violence is provided by the government to millions of youths, hundreds of thousands of whom are forced to put their training into effect overseas against actual human flesh and blood. If it is permissible to use guns, napalm, mortars, firebombs and air bombs against men, women, and children in Vietnam, is violence on the home scene likewise not allowable and even commendable for the sake of objectives that seem high and desirable? So the revolutionary may ask himself, feeling himself to be quite logical, as indeed he is if one can accept the current military premises that prompt us to pour high explosives, "anti-personnel" missiles, and chemical defoliants and crop killers upon far-off lands. It is also not illogical that our violence should have repercussions in violence at home.

And this brings us to the recent series of riots in our great cities, in which organized destructive forces, while they seem not to have been the main factors, may take advantage of the volatile popular mood for their own advantage in the way of designing elements at the time of the French, Russian, and Chinese Revolutions.

v. The Urban Riots

To those of us who have lived through the turbulent sixties like observers on a storm-battered deck, watching the long successive waves of racial tumult burst over the United States, it has been evident that something new and disquieting has been introduced into our life. In several respects the latest outbreaks of black-versus-white have differed from earlier disturbances. First, and most obviously, they have been more numerous than their predecessors, as might have been expected from the rapid expansion of the Negro population into the urban centers of the North and into the great cities of the West where a black face was rarely seen before World War II. At the same time, they have occurred on a much greater scale than the uprisings of the thirties, the forties, and before, and in some cases have taken on the aspect of guerrilla warfare. And, correspondingly, they have been more costly, as is evident from the fact that in a single eruption, the Detroit riot of 1967, 40 people died, 2250 were injured, 4000 were arrested, and the estimated property loss amounted to a quarter of a billion dollars, while the conflagration spread to Grand Rapids, Pontiac, Flint, Saginaw, and other communities, including Cambridge, Maryland, whose black heart took fire soon after Rap Brown urged Negroes to burn down the city. The gravity of the disturbance, and its approach to the borderline of civil war, was revealed in an article in *Newsweek* (August 7, 1967), which mentions three deaths in Rochester, New York, three in East Harlem, and one in Chicago, and reports that the National Guard was called to Toledo, Ohio, South Bend, Indiana, and Memphis, Tennessee, and that firebombs simultaneously disturbed the peace of Cincinnati, Cleveland, Waukegan, Illinois, and Mt. Vernon, New York:

> No city was safely beyond the battlefield: the homefront war seared thirty cities during the week, perhaps seventy this summer, more than one hundred since the whole deadly cycle began in Harlem more than three years ago.[6]

But possibly the most significant fact about the riots of the sixties has been their direction. The previous disorders, upon the whole, originated in thrusts of bias, hatred, and arrogance by the master race, whose sanctified precincts, it felt, were being threatened; but the new conflicts were more in the nature of protests—usually unconscious, spontaneous, and emotion-charged protests—against long-rankling mistreatment and a subordinate human status.

Far from having been planned, most of the riots seem to have arisen of their own impetus, as by the chemical reaction of a torch upon piled-up combustibles. This does not mean that organized groups did not at times, as already suggested, take advantage of the disturbances once they had arisen and try to direct them for their own purposes. But it does mean that they were not mapped out in advance like a military campaign. Usually, in fact, they were not even foreseen—not, at least, by most observers; and those who did expect trouble did not as a rule anticipate its extent. The majority, as they went about their way on the slopes of the quaking volcano, could not believe that it would really explode—not even when the steam was seething through cracks almost under their feet. And even when the mountain spouted flame, the stunned bystanders—who included mayors of great cities, chiefs of police, and governors of states— often seemed to have difficulty in understanding that what they saw was quite real.

Each of the riots, of course, had its individual features. The 1964 outburst in Harlem, where more than 232,000 people were squeezed together in an area of but $3\frac{1}{2}$ square miles (or over 100 to the acre), cannot be disconnected from the problems of an overcrowded urban district that had been festering for years in neglect and decay, with five-and-six-story rat-infested old brick tenements and apparently justified complaints against exploiting landlords and profiteering merchants. The Harlem riot was also, as were the outbreaks in other cities, inflamed in part by the black man's hatred of the police, who, he thought, had bullied and brutally abused him. Similarly, the riot in Newark in 1967 was related to the overpopulated condition of an urban region of dilapidated houses, which has been described as having the highest percentage of bad housing in the nation. But in Detroit the Negro's condition was relatively favored; the city had spent generously and vigorously for the relief of poverty, and a local judge can tell us of the riot area, "The homes in the rear of the Twelfth Street businesses are substantially constructed and in reasonable repair. They are better constructed than the home in which I lived for more than half my life."[7] The differences, however, tend to be superficial rather than deep-rooted, and rarely reach down to the essentials that affect man's mind and spirit and are the precipitating causes of the riots.

Hence, in order to gain an insight into the riots, one need not scrutinize them all; one representative example will serve as well as a score. As that example, accordingly, I have chosen one of the most startlingly unexpected and costly of the whole series, and one that perhaps did most to shake the American people out of their somnolent attitude toward the racial situation.

vi. Watts

The Los Angeles suburb of Watts, where the agitations began on August 11, 1965, is by no means so ill-favored as Eastern areas such as Harlem, Chicago's South Side, and Newark's Belmont Avenue. Following the general pattern of the region, many of its residents live in individual lawn-surrounded houses, perhaps with palm trees and other foliage. Yet this does not mean that they have found a haven of comfort or of halcyon delight, or that their housing is not poor and rundown compared with that of the average whites in the district. Although no one appears to have foreseen the ghastly August explosion, the shock did not occur without preliminary tremors, some of them by no means negligible. For example, on April 11, 1964, just sixteen months before the big riot, a crowd of young Negroes in the southern part of Los Angeles went berserk, shattered the windows of two patrol cars, and aimed a barrage of sticks and stones at policemen, more than 100 of whom had to be called before the mob could be scattered—all ostensibly because of the ejection of a 19-year-old from a track meet on a charge of drinking.

A single such incident, it is true, does not prove the imminence of a major disorder; but there were other episodes in the general neighborhood, as in Hollywood on December 26, 1964, when an audience became infuriated at a musical company's failure to fulfill its engagement, and overturned bars, threw potted plants about, tore down wall draperies, set a fire, smashed windows, and entered into a confrontation with the police that ended in a number of arrests, although, providentially, not many were injured.

The Watts fire-storm was kindled by an incident of no greater intrinsic importance than those precipitating the small previous disturbances—an incident with little more relationship to the eruption that followed than the murder of an Austrian archduke bore to a four years' war involving most of the world's great nations and taking millions of lives. Marquette Frye, a 21-year-old Negro, had been apprehended by a highway policeman for drunken driving in what at first seemed no more than a routine arrest. But Frye, although tractable at first, soon turned truculent. The trigger for his violence was touched when his brother Ronald made the blunder of going for their mother, who reproached Marquette for drinking. At this he flared up, began cursing and shouting, and swore that the officers would have to kill him before they could get him to jail. The original patrolman now summoned three fellow officers, who arrived in haste; and while a hostile crowd stood muttering on the sidelines, Mrs. Frye plunged into action, threw herself upon one of the policemen, and ripped his shirt. After the scuffle, during which Marquette was accidentally cut slightly, all three Fryes were taken away by the police.

Even now, although the crowd continued to grow, there seemed to be no particular cause for alarm. The arrest of the Fryes, according to the McCone Report which was released in December after more than a quarter of a year of intensive study, "was handled efficiently and expeditiously." Unfortunately, however, efficient and expeditious handling was not enough; the incident was aggravated by the additional arrests of a young black man and woman on charges of stirring up violence. And all the while, excitement was growing, fed by the poison of rumor, and in particular by the false story that the arrested young woman was pregnant and had been beaten by the police. Thus an incendiary emotionalism took hold of the throngs that milled about in uneasy knots, and brought on more serious violence. During the night, white automobilists were pulled from their cars and beaten, or were pelted with stones as they speeded past; and a police command post was threatened. Amid cries of "Burn, baby, burn!" the riot grew, and spread to other areas, such as Pacoima, 20 miles to the north, Monrovia, 25 miles east, and San Diego, 100 miles south, where 81 arrests were made.

During the lurid days that followed, Marquette Frye was lost to sight. He cannot be held responsible for the mob action, the plundering of merchandise in orgies of general robbery, the burning of cars and stores, the attacks upon innocent passing whites, the assaults upon the police and upon the firemen summoned to put out the blazes, the shooting and the rock-throwing and the virtual guerrilla warfare that brought forth as many as 13,900 National Guardsmen to patrol the danger zone, and led to the death of 34 people, the injury of 1032 including 226 policemen and firemen, the arrest of 3438 adults and 514 juveniles, the damaging of 600 buildings and the burning to the ground of some 200 of these, including a revival center and a public library with its 12,000 volumes. What had spoken in the black fury was not the injury or fancied injury to any individual or small group; what had spoken was stored-up hatred and resentment, hatred and resentment overflowing against the police, against the white community in general, against the barriers of racial restraint that had long borne down like invisible iron rods.

In the McCone Report, stress was laid upon problems of employment, education, health, housing, and transportation, the failure of the federal poverty program to live up to advance announcements, the fact of unpunished violence throughout the nation, and the growing tendency to seek illegal remedies to right wrongs or supposed wrongs. Yet while there is undoubted merit in these findings—the unemployment rate and the percentage of persons on relief in Watts, fed by the continued influx of jobless unskilled Negroes, was scandalously high—nevertheless one must look deeper for the riot's underlying causes. That the major blame cannot be placed on economic deprivation is suggested by the findings of the Los Angeles riot study, a two-year inquiry by social scientists at the University of California at Los Angeles: the militants in the Watts riot had an employment rate of 70 percent, as against 55 percent for residents not involved in the riot. And the better educated and more affluent were as strong in support of the outbreak as their poorer, less educated brothers. Also, the old-time residents were as firmly for the disturbance as recent immigrants, thus refuting the idea that the trouble was due to the unemployed and economically deprived new arrivals.

The fact is that, despite all the apparent causes, there is one basic reason for the uprisings, and one only: some excitation within the minds of men which, given the suitable stimulus, causes a sudden kindling of fury. That stimulus may be provided by harsh living conditions, by unemployment, by hunger, by poor housing or education, by the break-up of families; but all these conditions together will not suffice to produce the outburst without something ready to take fire in the rioters' deeper being. This inflammable may consist of hatred long harbored and smoldering, or of anger and old complaints repressed for years, or of pride trampled upon and waiting in secret to strike back, or of frustrated ambitions and material aims, or of any combination of these, or of mixed ingredients of fear, envy, covetousness, and resentment transmitted down the generations and cultivated by the creed of violence that has taken deeper and deeper root in society.

Even if these forces are subconscious in their operation and beyond the individual's power to analyze, they may be so potent as to require but a spark to bring them flaming to the surface. The spark, however, may often await the ignition of group action; one who by himself would never be heard may become vociferous beneath the example of demonstrating comrades, by whose rage he is roused to express his own vengefulness or rebelliousness, his own pride of race or self-assertiveness or wrath, which may find release in violence.

Thus the riots, though unorganized and spontaneous, may be seen as protest movements, no less vigorous for being unintended and for having sprung to a large extent from dark emotional depths beneath the conscious level. Nevertheless, what we know of the conscious minds of the participants is revealing. Bayard Rustin cites an incident which casts light on this subject. After the Watts eruption, a 20-year-old unemployed Negro informed him, "We have won." And when Rustin wanted to know how he had won, considering the death of black men and the destruction of their homes and of the stores where they bought their food, the youth replied, "We won because we made the whole world pay attention to us. The police chief never came here before; the mayor always stayed uptown. We made them come."[8]

Here the anonymous young Negro may, without realizing it,

have put his finger on an important truth. For the riots were, in part, appeals by the black community for attention—for notice of them and of their needs, for action on their behalf, for recognition of their importance as human beings. The colored people —Negroes and others of tinted skin—may have felt more deeply than ever the call to self-assertion following the three-to-one repeal in 1964 by the voters of California of the Rumford Act providing for fair housing procedures regardless of race. It is true that the rioters' method of assertion may have been irrational, as any emotion-packed outburst is likely to be, but this does not mean that the protest was any less deep or genuine.

No matter how few men it required to touch off the detonations at Watts, the flare-up was more than the work of a few hotheads or agitators; a considerable percentage of the population participated. According to the Los Angeles riot study, perhaps as many as 15 percent of the adult Negroes, or around 22,000 in all, were at some time implicated in the rioting, while an additional 35 or 40 percent were spectators. But perhaps more significant is the fact that, of 2070 persons interviewed within five months following the riot, about 34 percent were "somewhat favorable, or very favorable" to what had happened:

> While the majority expressed disapproval of the violence and destruction, this was often coupled with an expression of empathy with the motives of those who participated, or a sense of pride that the Negro had brought world-wide attention to his problem.[9]

As further testimony to their approval, 38 percent of the Negroes in the riot area felt that their cause had been helped and only about 20 percent believed that it had been damaged, while no more than 23 percent thought that the distance between the races had been widened.

In other words, a considerable proportion supported the idea of rioting as a means of expressing grievances and obtaining social justice. And because this situation appears not to be confined to Watts, it confronts us with a grave challenge. For when large groups have come to favor rioting as a means of social action, nothing short of a miracle will avert new, even more serious riots if matters are permitted to drift. This, therefore, underscores the enormity of the problem and the need for swifter, more thoroughgoing action to erase the discontents at the root of rioting— not only economic discontents, but, even more fundamental, those that spring from the sharp, insulting lines which still insulate race from race. One must acknowledge that notable progress has been made in recent years, but when one observes the continuing reactionary pressures, the violence in the overturning of buses containing black children at Lamar, South Carolina, early in 1970, and the efforts to delay Southern school integration, to abandon public schools in some sections in favor of private, and to vitiate a salutary federal antidiscriminatory voting rights bill, one must acknowledge that the battle is far from won; indeed, in some ways it has hardly been begun.

Support for this conclusion is provided, one fears, in a recent report on Watts by Bernard D. Nossiter of the Washington *Post,* who interviewed a Negro leader in regard to the four-hour shooting affray between the police and black militants at the headquarters of the Black Panthers on December 8, 1969, and quotes him as follows:

> "Next time it may be me. It's a total, all-out assault on blacks. We're blacks. The fact that it was the Panthers on Monday is only incidental to what's going on. When the Japanese were put in camps out here . . . everybody stood silent. Now we can't be silent."[10]

Although it is far-fetched to compare the Negroes of our own day to the Japanese outrageously confined in concentration camps during World War II, the important point is the dread of the white man in the Negro's mind, and not the fear's evident lack of justification. The same fear, moreover, has cropped up in other directions, as when Chicago Negroes in December 1969, declared a curfew against the nighttime intrusion of whites into their neighborhoods. Here again, even if there is no external basis for the fear, the psychological realities outweigh the visible facts.

Thus it becomes evident that the situation is more involved and complicated than a superficial view might suggest. Even with our utmost efforts, rioting may not soon be quelled, for memories of the past, its terrors and inbred attitudes and animosities remain strong. But unless we open our eyes, and clearly choose between the alternatives of social revolt and social and human justice, Watts and Detroit and Newark and the other great riot centers of our times may be remembered not as peaks of disorder but as mere way stations on the road to wider protests and costlier disruption.

14. The Modern Scene:
The Campus Takes Fire

i. An Epidemic of Revolts

In the single week ending May 3, 1969, according to a newspaper report, the following incidents occurred in the United States:

For the second time in eight days, firebombs exploded on the campus of New York University, damaging card catalogues and federal micro-files.

Also in New York, the City College was closed for three days after demonstrators had seized two buildings, exchanged blows with opposing students, slugged a professor on the face with a club, and fled when about to be arrested.

In upstate New York, at Cornell University, prominent faculty members called for the disarming of the campus, accused the administration of selling out to student terrorists, and went on a teaching strike until their demands were met by President James Perkins, who announced that the campus police had been instructed to search dormitories and four fraternity houses and confiscate all guns.

Elsewhere in New York State, at Colgate College, 45 black students seized the faculty club to press their demands for an "Afro-American Center."

Meanwhile other disturbances were shaking widely scattered institutions. At Harvard 150 protesters stormed into the University planning office and partially destroyed a large-scale model of the University and its environs. At Dartmouth College about 200 students took possession of the administration building in a demand for an end to the ROTC. At George Washington University, in Washington, D. C., furniture was smashed, books ripped apart, and research files scattered in a sit-in lasting five hours. At Voorhees College, in Denmark, South Dakota, students armed with knives and shotguns occupied two buildings; at Fordham University in the Bronx, at Stanford University in California, at Boston State College, at Belmont-Abbey College in Belmont, North Carolina, and at New Orleans' Tulane University, disorders of various degrees of severity broke out.

And as if this did not suffice for one week, the following marked a single day in the educational life of New York City: the explosion of a gasoline bomb at Abraham Lincoln High School in Brooklyn; another bomb explosion and fires at Morris High School in the Bronx; a riot by students outside a high school in Brooklyn; a sit-in by students at another Brooklyn high school; and vandalism by a mob of about 200 black students at a high school in the Bronx.

In these numerous eruptions, manifestly, more than a single force was at work. Some of the incidents were related to classroom demands, some had motives and overtones of racial protest and antagonism, some were connected with the antiwar movement. But while any single episode may perhaps be dismissed as of but passing consequence, still as a group the outbreaks cannot be ignored; they are representative of the high tides of change that, for a number of years, have been lashing over American educational institutions. In this, to be sure, the United States does not stand alone; the student uprisings have been worldwide, and have been prominent in Japan, where the revolts have closed some great establishments; in Mexico, where heavy fighting has occurred between students and police; in Italy, where, in the Valle Guilia in Rome in March 1968, police and students engaged in a day-long battle; in West Germany, where newspaper publishing plants were blockaded and the papers burned by thousands of students in April 1968; and in various other countries including Belgium, Holland, Sweden, England, and France. In the last, demands for reform in the overcrowded universities led to severe clashes with the police, and to a demonstration in which as many as a million people are said to have marched in an antigovernment protest movement.

But while American students have been swept along on a worldwide current, the situation here has been unique in several respects, including the fact that, unlike some of the countries of Europe, we have no great tradition of student protest. To an extent, of course, the outbursts everywhere reflect the unease that has rocked all modern industrial nations; and to no small degree, even when war has not been the specific issue, the unrest has stemmed from the uncertainties of a world in which American military entanglements have constituted upsetting elements for all countries, including many not directly involved.

ii. Violence, But No Negotiation

To some of us who have sat watching on the sidelines, it has seemed that often the major issue behind revolt on the campus has not been the demands of the students, which have been justified in more than a few cases, although sometimes they have been so outrageous that one can hardly believe that their authors intended them to be taken seriously. Many of the demonstrators have appeared to express resentment against the entire scholastic system, perhaps because basically they are not interested in education, and are forced into the classrooms and lecture halls to escape the draft, or under family pressure, or in response to the demands of prospective employers, which has led them irrationally to vent their anger and hatred on the colleges or universities themselves. Often more important than the student demands have been the methods of their attempted enforcement, methods in some cases more closely allied to those of street gangsters than to anything in the educational process as we have known it— and this has been true even though sometimes faculty members have joined in the anarchic attacks.

Consider the experience of Dr. S. I. Hayakawa, President of San Francisco State College, when one of his speeches was interrupted by the head of the projected Black Studies Department (since discharged for insubordination), who forced his way threateningly upon the platform along with other militants in brusque disregard of the President's right of free speech. Or consider Dr. Hayakawa's experience in March 1969, at the University of Colorado, when members of the Students for a Democratic Society swarmed toward him throwing bottles, again in the effort to choke off free speech. Or, once more, consider the action of the SDS when in December 1968, some of its followers surged into the hall where Ambassador Nguyen Huu Chi of South Vietnam was to have been a guest speaker, attacked him bodily, broke up the meeting, smashed down doors, battered their way into the hall where James Reston of the *New York*

Times was to deliver a lecture, and threatened such injury that the meeting had to be cancelled.

What was at issue here was not the views of any of the speakers. There may have been legitimate objections to the remarks or anticipated remarks of Dr. Hayakawa, Ambassador Nguyen, and James Reston; but, if so, the only permissible answer was through the processes of a democratic forum and of the democratic press. When the method is that of the gagging of free speech, violent trespass, destruction, and intimidation, the procedure is not that of the democratic but of the autocratic, the Fascist or Communist state, and would be more in tune with a Czar Alexander III, a Hitler, or a Stalin than with the free America we have cherished. It is therefore ominous that tactics of mob disruption have not only been applied but approved by some of the leaders of SDS and by faculty members of New York University and other institutions. Here we have something that reaches far beyond normal student protest; we have maneuverings such as we have noted in the Bolsheviks when, in December 1917, and again in January 1918, they used armed Lettish soldiers to break up the meetings of the Constituent Assembly and block the people's hope of representative government.

The situation is the more disturbing because of the many other cases in which dissidents have sought refuge in violence or the tools or threat of violence, as when a black instructor at San Francisco State College advised students to carry arms in the classroom—certainly, a reversal of all past American ideas as to educational procedures! Another instance occurred at Cornell University when black students demanded enrollment in a course that included "Theory and practice in the use of small arms and hand combat. Discussion sessions in the proper use of force." And still another example cropped up, once more at San Francisco State College, when spokesmen for the Third World Liberation Front and the Black Students Union set "pre-conditions" and issued a "declaration of war," along with this pronouncement:

> Under this state of war all ad hoc rules and regulations set up by the acting president (S. I.) Hayakawa to hamper freedom of speech or freedom of assembly will be disregarded, and the battleground tactics and time sequences will be determined by the central committee of our revolutionary people.[1]

The words "revolutionary" and "battleground tactics" provide the key. The small rebellious groups, which one can hardly regard as representative of all the students, had their eyes on something far beyond classroom rights. Society itself rather than the educational system was their target; the educational system was merely a means to an end and an incidental casualty.

This, furthermore, will explain the "pre-conditions," which included the granting of general amnesty to those arrested and those not yet arrested (a blanket license for lawbreaking), the rescinding of all suspensions of students, and the closing of the college during the discussion period between the "Front" and the "Board of trustees or their representatives."

These "pre-conditions," it must be noted, were in addition to 15 other "non-negotiable demands" previously presented. And this brings us to the question of "non-negotiable demands" in general; these have become common in student protest movements, even though they seem automatically to rule out the give-and-take of normal discussion, as in the bargaining of labor unions and employers and in the diplomatic conferences of the nations.

One wonders whether the protesters ever seriously consider or indeed care what "non-negotiable" implies. Actually, only a few sets of circumstances are non-negotiable in the course of human affairs. One includes, obviously, the impossible: you do not negotiate to guarantee clear weather, or perfect health next Sunday. The next occurs when a matter of good faith or of moral obligation or human responsibility is concerned: there is no room for negotiation with him who asks you to betray your mother or to accept compensation for breaking your pledged word. And, finally, non-negotiable demands issue from superiors to subordinates, as from a general to a private, from a conqueror to a subjugated people, or from a czar or dictator to a helpless satellite.

In which of these categories are we to place the non-negotiable demands of the student insurgents? Manifestly, in neither of the first two: what they seek is nothing of the unalterable nature of the movements of the stars; nor do they have a moral obligation to adhere to claims for such things as the establishment of black studies courses under black control, the exclusion of whites from these courses, or the opening of the college gates to the minority races without regard to scholastic qualifications. If these matters are not for discussion, just how far have we advanced beyond our medieval forebears, who might have applied the term "non-negotiable" to the demands of their prelates for a razor's-edge conformity in religious ritual and belief?

This leaves only the third class of non-negotiable demands: those issuing from a superior to a menial, or from a conqueror to the conquered. Such demands, which might more properly be called "commands," are delivered from a position of power, often in arrogance and in contempt for the subordinate. Can the students' "non-negotiable" demands be placed in this category? Whatever the intent, they do have the arrogance, the dominant attitudes of power even when the actual power does not exist. And this has been made possible by the weakness and at times the supineness of the authorities, who have yielded to unjustified claims, thus encouraging the rebels to attempt more and more, perhaps often with tongue in cheek, in astonishment at their own success, and with less thought of education than of their personal authority. This was illustrated when, after two successive presidents were driven out of San Francisco State College, Dr. Hayakawa took office as Acting President, and, by a firmness highly unpopular among many students, resisted the extreme demands, restored a semblance of order, and kept the college open when its indefinite closing appeared likely.

iii. Columbia University and Elsewhere

In the student revolts, as in many conflicts, we have witnessed a gaping dichotomy. It has been a little as when the Dutch of the 16th century, who had real and deep grievances against the authority of the Church, let loose their resentment at the images and art of the cathedrals. Or it was as when the ancient Palestinians, spurred by genuine, long-standing complaints against the Romans, hatched the fanatical sect of Zealots, whose more extreme members swooped down upon towns and villages, robbing or killing supposed Roman sympathizers. In both these cases a basically just cause was polluted by irrational and evil methods. And on a smaller scale, in our student uprisings, the same sharp division has been evident. In many cases, one feels, the protests have been justified, sometimes profoundly so; yet one must stand back with a question on one's lips, wondering if the demonstrators must vitiate their own cause by stooping to means that, carried to the logical extreme, would not only break down the educational system but disrupt society itself.

Let us consider one of the greatest American student outbreaks of all, one in various ways representative of many, the episode at Columbia University in New York in the spring of 1968. The demonstrations began over two main issues, both of which have rightly aroused wide sympathy. First there was the matter of involvement in the Vietnamese war effort and the fact that Columbia, like many other American institutions of learning, had permitted CIA recruitment on the campus, and had been following the portentous practice of accepting large sums from the defense department for purposes of research, thus giving the very founts of education a military complexion (as much as 46 percent of Columbia's income for 1966 came from government sources, and more than a quarter of this was from classified defense contracts). This, obviously, was the major issue; the second complaint of the dissidents concerned something of narrower, more local implications, although here too a principle was at stake: the plan of the University to build a gymnasium in Morningside Park, thus further restricting the open spaces and recreational facilities of grossly overcrowded nearby Harlem.

Already in November 1966, a protest had involved several hundred students, and had been answered by President Grayson Kirk's debatable remark that, "It is not possible for any university to attempt to make a value judgment about any division of the federal government" (the President of a German university might have spoken to the same effect thirty years before, using the word "Nazi" instead of "federal"). In the spring of 1967, other protests occurred, particularly against recruiters for the Marines, and scuffles broke out between right-wing and left-wing students. In particular, the demonstrations concerned Columbia's part in the Institute for Defense Analysis, and revolved about matters such as nuclear and chemical warfare. But the agitations were mostly nonviolent, although the shape of things to come was suggested when the students, in the fall of 1967, flouted an order by President Kirk forbidding indoor demonstrations.

In April 1968, a more serious confrontation occurred. Six protesters against the IDA were placed on probation by President Kirk, and a crowd of 500 was blocked by the barred doors of the Low Library, and also by opposing students. Violence on a small scale followed; the demonstrators moved into Morningside Park, and began tearing down the chain-link fence surrounding the construction site of the projected gymnasium. But the police soon put an end to the sabotage; and the crowd, flocking into Hamilton Hall, surrounded Dean Coleman, and demanded that he act to release a man arrested in a scuffle at the gymnasium site. When Coleman refused, the students held him captive in his office.

Now the battle lines were drawn: the insurgents had taken a building and made a prisoner of war.

Thus began a conflict in which thousands of protesters would take possession of the campus for a week, and shut down the University for the remainder of the semester. In the various ensuing incidents, the outer door of Low Library and the door to the President's office were demolished, and some of the invaders stationed themselves inside for six days. A large red sign, "NO GYM," was painted on Hamilton Hall. The mathematics building was taken, then a third building, a fourth, and a fifth; some faculty members, arm linked in arm to block access to the library, were charged by the police, and one of the teachers was clubbed; and the police by turns occupied the campus and departed. But if the officers at first showed restraint, this was hardly the case when they finally undertook mass arrests. According to the report of City Rights Commissioner William Booth and the sociologist Kenneth Clark, they had conducted themselves well with regard to the blacks, but, apparently goaded to fury by the frustrations of the preceding days, they went amok, smashed furniture, threw books around, and beat up demonstrators and bystanders, including a professor and a rabbi. Seven-hundred twenty were arrested, and about 100 were sent to hospitals or to their private doctors for the treatment of wounds evidently inflicted with gratuitous sadism.

The result was exactly the opposite of what the authorities may have expected. Instead of being whipped into submission, the students arose next day in a general revolt; a strike was declared, and the Strike Coordinating Committee, which enrolled more than 6000 members, proclaimed against attendance at classes. And this led to further clashes, another sit-in at Hamilton Hall, new conflicts with the police, the beating and injury of more students, attacks upon the police with bottles, ashtrays, and other missiles, and the resignation, after several months, of President Kirk.

What shall we say of the whole affair? Here was a dispute in which, plainly, not all the right or wrong was on either side, and in which there were, undoubtedly, high idealistic elements among the protesters. The Cox Commission reported in regard to the outbreak,

The present generation of young people in our universities is perhaps the best informed, the most intelligent, and the most idealistic our country has ever known. This is the experience of teachers everywhere . . . today's graduate and undergraduate students exhibit, as a group, a higher level of social conscience than preceding generations.[2]

Even though this may be true, and though there may have been deep provocation in the excesses of the police, one cannot help looking askance at phenomena such as the seizure of university buildings, the discontinuance of classes, the blockage of access to the library, the kidnapping of a dean, and the smashing of doors and other property. The sit-ins, which have occurred not only at Columbia but at other institutions, are of much the same type and breed as the industrial sitdown strikes of an earlier generation. In regard to both sit-ins and sitdowns, one may apply the principles enunciated by Chief Justice Hughes in 1939 in *NLRB v Fansteel Metallurgical Corp.*:

> The employees had the right to strike but they had no license to commit acts of violence or to seize their employers' plant. . . . The ousting of an owner from lawful possession is not essentially different from an assault upon the officers of an employing company, or the seizure and conversion of its goods, or the despoiling of its property or other unlawful acts in order to force compliance with demands. To justify such conduct . . . would be to put a premium on resort to force instead of legal remedies and to subvert the principles of law and order which lie at the foundations of society.[3]

It is important to note that the emphasis here is on the use of force rather than on other illegal procedures such as the civil disobedience of Gandhi and of the war-resisters whom we shall discuss in the next chapter. Certainly one would not suggest that every enactment of a public authority is sacrosanct and must be obeyed regardless of moral principles; but one must acknowledge that a special kind of disobedience is involved when force is applied. For force, as we have noted, can rarely if ever be employed without danger—danger that extends to the innocent and hovers over the very institutions of justice. And force is a two-edged blade; it tends to spread, both in the hands of the original user and by example to many others; and it is usually impossible to predict how fast or far it will develop. Consequently, there is no logical dividing line between a little force and extreme violence; the one verges by invisible degrees into the other. If you permit some license, why not a little more, and then a little more again, and so on without limit? If I push my neighbor from a disputed piece of land by sheer muscular power, what is to prevent me from using a stick should my unassisted muscles not suffice? And if a stick seems inadequate, why not a gun? And what will keep my neighbor, and indeed any number of neighbors, from following my example, until we are all indulging in a feud to the death? In the answer to these questions, one will find a reason for the outbreak not only of deadly disputes among individuals but of the wars of nations.

The same principles apply, clearly, to the student protests as to all other dissent. The Columbia rebels, whatever their claims, did take refuge in force when they seized buildings and imprisoned a dean; and it should have surprised no one that the police struck back with counter-force, even though their reaction was excessive, was misdirected toward innocent parties, and was so provocative as to defeat its own ends. Furthermore, it should have been anticipated that there would be confrontations, and even violence as at Columbia, in clashes of radical and conservative students. Also, it might have been foreseen that the whole series of student outbreaks would lead to increasing authorization of violence by college authorities throughout the country, and their growing reliance upon the police and the National Guard. This, in turn, might have been expected to produce grave episodes, as in Berkeley in the spring of 1969, when in the course of a demonstration against the fencing of an unused plot of land where students and some others wanted to establish a park, a bystander was shot to death by the National Guards and another was blinded, while a helicopter sprayed tear gas over the campus, afflicting hundreds, including old people and children, and invading classrooms and even a hospital.

Maybe all this was no cause for amazement in a country which had had a tradition of gun-carrying truculence since pioneer days—a country which recently had let down the gates to violence in its foreign policy, and had launched intense, protracted, and at times seemingly indiscriminate armed action against the people of a small Southeast Asian country. But whatever our derelictions abroad, it is an unhappy and a perilous thing when violence spreads in the very institutions that should be the seats and the preservers of culture.

All this, it is worth repeating, is not to deny that the student demands, including those that take a quite different turn than at Columbia, may often be justified—and this although the demonstrators do little to advance their cause by the arrogance they

sometimes display, their peremptory attitudes, and the obsceni-
ties which suggest that they may not have the maturity they
claim. One can acknowledge their deep sources of discontent,
which are rooted too often in the monstrous size of universities
or "multiversities," and in the encroachment of mechanism and
of technology to such an extent that humanity tends to be forgotten and human understanding and compassion become casualties of the age. One can sympathize with the insurgent leader
Mario Savio when he states that the student at Berkeley found it
"impossible usually to meet with anyone but secretaries" or to
play any part in policy-making.[4] One can sympathize also with
Thomas Hayden, a past president of SDS, when he speaks similarly of "The deep alienation of the student from the decision-
making institutions of society," and the consequent decline of
democracy.[5] Even more can one sympathize with Michael Novak,
a one-time teaching fellow in philosophy at Harvard, in his complaint at the university's failure to deal with the basic issues "of
life and death, of love and solitude, of inner growth and pain."[6]

But even when the protesters are justified theoretically, it does
not follow that their practical responses deserve support. All the
more because they have intimidated uncourageous administrators
throughout the country and gained concessions that cannot be
regarded as rightly theirs by any stretch of the principles of fair
play—going scot-free after creating severe disturbances, or being
granted standard-shattering relaxations in college admissions—
the apostles of violence are continuing sources of disruption, who
play into the hands of the small but not negligible minority that
aims to bring down the entire scholastic and political structure.
Even if the extreme activists cannot accomplish their main objectives, one cannot entirely dismiss the fear expressed by Jacques
Barzun:

> . . . by organizing hatred . . . by assaulting and imprisoning
> their teachers, dividing faculties into factions, turning weak heads
> into cowards and demagogues, ignoring the grave and legitimate
> causes for reform, advocating the bearing of arms on campus, and
> preferring "confrontation" to getting their own way, hostile students
> have ushered in the reactionary university of the future, medieval
> model.[7]

It does not follow that the universities will actually make an
about-face to the year 1266, as Barzun foresees. But few informed
observers will deny that we have turned in that direction, or that,

by lowering academic standards to admit the unqualified and the unprepared, we descend to the level of the lowest common denominator of knowledge, intelligence, and academic application. If the downward trend is to be reversed before too late, and the processes of orderly growth are to be resumed, mob action as a method of protest must be ruled out; force, and its destructive and at times explosive precedent, must no longer be tolerated in the settlement of educational disputes, and no accommodation must be reached in submission to force; the only accepted means must be those of the platform, the conference room, and the written word.

This, it is true, is far easier to state than to consummate. But unless a way is found to discourage the violent militants and make their efforts unrewarding at the same time as legitimate complaints are resolved, the advocates of raw might will continue to push themselves forward, until their original demands have been lost to sight amid the chaos they have brought down upon the schools and colleges, and the shadow they have cast over the very nurseries of civilization.

15. The Modern Scene: Battlelines for Peace

i. The Challenge of Vietnam

Beginning in the fifties and continuing much more decisively in the sixties, the United States let itself plunge into one of the most tragic errors in the history of any great nation. When the French in 1954 gave up the ghost at Dien Bien Phu in Indochina, and thus liquidated an antiquated colonialism inherited from the 19th century, there was no clear reason why America should attempt to breathe life into the corpse and send increasing numbers of resurrection squads at the cost of the lives of our own sons, our desperately needed vital resources, our domestic morale, and our international prestige. Yet this is precisely what we did, owing in part to the pressures of political and religious factions, in part to the anti-Communist hysteria of the McCarthy era, and specifically in response to the domino theory of Secretary of State John Foster Dulles, who saw the Communist movement as a monolithic whole, and put his faith in the rickety supposition that if a single Asian nation fell, then all the nations including Thailand, the Philippines, and Japan would drop like a row of dominoes collapsing.

The outcome of all this was a war in which we became enmeshed with land troops on the Asian continent, in defiance of all the best military advice—a war to which we were to make a commitment of well over half a million troops at a time, and in which our casualties were to rise into the hundreds of thousands. It was a war that, bypassing the Constitution, had been authorized by no act of Congress, and whose eventual escalation had no basis except the presidential interpretation of a Congressional resolution with a freedom that leapt far beyond the intentions of the legislators. And it was a war that began its severest bombing phases early in 1965 in violation of the President's campaign promises of the previous fall with what, many Americans felt, amounted to betrayal of the electorate. Consequently this war, which shocked great numbers with the horrors of its bombing attacks, its napalm, its defoliation, its search-and-destroy operations which annihilated villages and killed or transplanted their populations, produced a rift in the American people such as had not been seen since the Civil War. And among the multitudes who felt that we were waging an illegal conflict, and one unrelated to the needs of the country, a protest movement arose, perhaps the most remarkable since the American War of Independence.

The nature and significance of this movement is not to be judged solely by its visible manifestations or results. Yet those results, although at this writing they have not sufficed to end the war, have been considerable. That President Johnson in 1968 made the astonishing decision not to run again; that Draft Director Hershey in the fall of 1969 was obliged to resign; that President Nixon has felt bound to order successive troop withdrawals—these are concrete returns which cannot be dissociated from the drives of the dissenters for peace. And yet the movement, while militant in the determination of its millions of followers and its advocacy of withdrawal from Vietnam, has been mainly nonviolent. There have been no draft riots, as during the Civil War, when on July 13, 1863, many were killed in New York in a general outbreak. Nor have we equalled the uprisings against conscription in France at the time of the Revolution, nor gone to the extent of the Anti-War Day agitations in Japan on October 21, 1969, when Tokyo was all but paralyzed by a demonstration involving more than 100,000 persons led by students, while the Shinjuku railroad station was barricaded and insurgents in a hundred cities went on a rampage, breaking windows and hurling firebombs. But the message of the American protesters has been eloquent even if, despite the outbreaks at Columbia University and elsewhere, their methods have not been as destructive as we may observe in other lands.

Our war resisters may be placed in two categories. The first consists merely of scattered individuals, who nevertheless have had their effect upon the public mind and conscience; the second is composed of small groups or larger associations of men and women joined in a common cause. Among both classes, although especially in the second, students have been prominent, not only because it is in the young that protest rises most naturally to the surface, but because the heaviest burden has fallen upon the young.

It is not difficult to understand the state of mind of a youth who sees his comrades forced into the war, at best to lose years out of their lives, but perhaps to return maimed in body or spirit if indeed they return at all. Where, he may ask himself, is our vaunted progress, our democracy, when the youth of the land can be snatched from their work, their homes, and their families and made to serve in a foreign land in a dimly apprehended cause that involves no evident national need? When the state may lay hands on the life of the citizen at the mere fiat of a President who had no clear authorization from Congress or the people and has in fact broken his campaign promises, just where can one draw the line between republican government and tyranny? How, except in formality and finesse and the degree of violence used or threatened, does the behavior of our chief executive differ from that of Frederick II of Prussia when his troops swooped down upon villages during Sunday church services and swept the young men into the army?

Such questions may have troubled many young Americans. And such questions have undoubtedly been behind the draft evasions, behind the "underground railroad" that has helped fugitives to reach Canada, and behind the protests of the courageous few who would neither flee nor submit, but have stood up boldly to express their convictions, knowing that they faced the certainty of prison, of disgrace, and of a shadow across all their tomorrows.

An example was provided by David Harris, President of the student body of Stanford University, who in June 1968, was tried in San Francisco for refusing to be drafted into the armed forces. Although he received, according to all judicial lights, a fair trial, and although the judge went so far as to admit that the defendant was moved "by the highest motives," still the jury of five men and seven women found Harris guilty, and he was sentenced to three years in prison. It is not hard to surmise what other young men must have concluded as they stood by and saw that a protester's faithfulness to "the highest motives" had caused him to be treated more severely than many a burglar or rapist. Though few would have the personal bravery to follow in Harris's footsteps, actions such as his win recruits for the forces of silent opposition and even of militant resistance.

Another case, on similar lines although it involved a man already inducted into the armed forces, was that of Dr. Howard Levy, a Brooklyn dermatologist, who in 1967 was court-martialled at Fort Jackson, South Carolina, and spent 27 months in prison for his refusal to train Green Beret medical men for service in Vietnam, but eventually was released on $1000 bail on a writ from Supreme Court Justice Douglas. Why did he rebel only after entering the army? It was his belief that a doctor could work more effectively against the war when in uniform than as a civilian or as the inmate of a jail cell.

Whatever the group connections of Dr. Levy and David Harris, their protest in each case was an individual one, their trial and torment and punishment were all individual experiences, as was their approach to the challenge of an age which, in their view, left them but two options—submission to an iniquitous war system, or near-martyrdom. Much the same, also, may be said of other solitary resisters, many of them obscure, a few well-known, such as Dr. Benjamin Spock and his four co-defendants in a trial held in Boston in 1968.

ii.   The Trial of the Draft Resisters

To understand the implications of the Spock trial, one must recall something of its background. Resistance to the draft, which was the basis of their trial although not the technical excuse for the indictments, had not begun with the five who came to a cruel prominence in this case. Resistance had been sparked by various events, including not only the specific episodes of the war but the pronouncements of Draft Director Hershey, who on October 26, 1967, copied the retaliatory action taken two years before by the Selective Service Commission in classifying as 1-A men who had heeded the call of the SDS for militant antidraft action. In a message that entrusted local draft boards with an all but dictatorial power over young men's lives and fortunes, Hershey recommended in effect that outspoken opponents of the war be punished by being made to serve in the war.

This Draconian injunction was issued in response to numbers of incidents, including particularly the protests of Stop the Draft Week, which had been observed by five or six thousand persons at Oakland, California, in demonstrations at the Army Induction Center. But other provocations toward Hershey's vindictive move were undoubtedly provided by actions such as that of the Cornell student who in 1966 performed the symbolic act of tearing up his draft card and enlisting other students in the Draft Resistance Union. Similarly Hershey must have had in mind the card-burning demonstrations of more than 150 students in New York in April 1967. Nor was he likely to have overlooked the further aggravations of an estimated 4000 who had turned in their draft cards by the time of the Spock trial.

All this may seem to represent but a small, ineffective movement considering the vastness of the country and the millions affected or in danger of being affected by the draft. Yet these protests were indicative of much wider currents of opinion, which often have been without any channel of expression, or else have found vent in the flight of prospective draftees or in covert aid to fugitives. The resistance of Dr. Spock and the other four did in any case attract general attention.

Something should be noted as to the antecedents of the five. Dr. Spock, 65 years old at the time of the trial, is a noted pediatrician, whose book on *Baby and Child Care* has been popular among young mothers. The Rev. William Sloane Coffin, Jr. is a clergyman who has been conspicuous in the Freedom Rides and other civil rights efforts. Michael Ferber, a candidate for a Ph.D. in the Harvard English Department, has also participated in civil-rights demonstrations. Mitchell Goodman is a novelist and teacher, an artillery lieutenant in World War II, whose activities in the peace movement date from 1965. Marcus Raskin, a young one-time adviser to President Kennedy, has collaborated with Bernard Fall in compiling *The Vietnam Reader*, one of the most noteworthy of the many books evoked by the war.

Here is a group of men able and public-spirited far beyond the average—a group that might be considered a credit to any country. Yet perhaps this is why they were singled out for their unenviable distinction.

The term "singled out" is used advisedly. For although the men were tried as a group and accused of conspiracy in accordance with the weird twists and convolutions of the law, actually they had lived in widely scattered places and had not even known one another before the time of their indictment. They were, however, of one turn of mind as to the draft and its implications.

Their stated reasons for indulging in draft resistance are illuminating. Dr. Spock explains his position:

I suddenly realized the whole *world* was in peril. . . . We've got to keep testing more, keep accumulating more nuclear arms—and of course Congress is always enthusiastic for more arms. In Cleveland, where we were living, business leaders were for more arms, labor was for more arms. It suddenly *struck* me—it was a terrible moment. After that, I was hooked for the peace movement.[1]

Equally revealing was Michael Ferber's speech that led to his indictment. His purposes are set forth with undisguised clarity in this eloquent address, in which he urged the audience at Arlington Street Church in Boston to say "No."

Let us make sure that we are ready to work hard and long . . . to make it difficult and politically dangerous for the government to prosecute us, working to help anyone and everyone to find ways of avoiding the draft, to help disrupt the workings of the draft and the armed forces until the war is over. . . .[2]

Although these words may be wholly in accordance with the Constitutional guarantee of free speech, it is not hard to understand why the authorities should regard them as a challenge and plan to strike back. But this, one assumes, Ferber fully realized when he chose the road of courage, conscience, and peril.

The remarks of the Reverend Coffin were similarly unequivocal. Speaking on the steps of the Justice Department, he declared,

We admire the way these young men who could safely have hidden behind exemptions and deferments have elected instead to risk something big for something good. . . .
We hereby counsel these young men to continue in their refusal to serve in the armed forces so long as the war in Vietnam continues, and we pledge ourselves to aid and abet them in all the ways we can.[3]

The speaker goes on to acknowledge that if the men who refuse to serve under the draft are arrested, he and their other counselors must also be arrested, since in the eyes of the law all are equally guilty. And so he, like the other resisters, entered the fray with eyes open.

To much the same effect was the "Call to Resist Illegitimate Authority," which the prosecution was also to bring into evidence.

Signed by 28,000 persons, it stated that the war in Vietnam outraged the moral and religious sense of an increasing number of Americans, that it was unconstitutional and in violation of international agreements, and that "every free man has a legal right and a moral duty to exert every effort to end this war."

Here was proof that many individuals throughout the country were of the defendants' turn of mind. And this, of course, from the official point of view, made the defendants' attitude the more dangerous.

Dr. Spock might be encouraged to know that, among the many sharing his views on the war and the draft, were some outspoken citizens in responsible positions, such as President Kenneth S. Pitzer of Stanford University. In his remarks to the trustees following a demand by many of the students and faculty for an end to work by the University and the Stanford Research Institute on military contracts, President Pitzer pointed out that the Ford Motor Company had had "the courage to admit the error and stop production" after blundering on the Edsel.

> "The war in Vietnam," he went on to state, "is an equally obvious and infinitely greater blunder, but we haven't had the courage to admit it and get out. And in my view it is clearly a violation of human rights to draft a young man to fight a war which he regards as grossly immoral and about which the nation is unsure."[4]

Regardless of views like these, it was almost a foregone conclusion that the accused in the Spock case would be convicted. For apparently they *had* violated the law—that is, if it really could be considered constitutional for a President, without Congressional authorization and without even a declaration of war, to commandeer men to fight, kill, and die abroad. Under the circumstances, the jurors made a remarkable even if quite inconsistent concession when they acquitted one of the defendants, Marcus Raskin, for it was hard to see wherein he was any more or less guilty than any of the others. Perhaps the real concession the jurors made was to their own consciences. But the sentencing of Spock and three others to two years in prison, and to a fine of $5000 each (except in the case of Ferber, who was allowed a special rate of $1000), was a grim commentary on the status of the military dissenter in contemporary America.

To the convicted men, the sentence was especially frustrating because the trial had not offered them one of the opportunities they chiefly sought—the chance to bring the war into review, and to test its legality and likewise that of the provisions of the draft law as to conscientious objectors, who were recognized as such only if they belonged to antiwar religious sects, but not if they had strong personal scruples against participating in any armed conflict or in the Vietnamese struggle in particular. Thus the sacrifices of the five men, though they dramatized before the public the fact of draft resistance and will proclaim to future historians that not all Americans bowed supinely beneath the military yoke, accomplished little toward ending the draft or the war.

One cannot turn from the case without quoting the words of Dr. Spock in a news conference just after the pronouncement of sentence:

> I am not convinced that I broke the law; there was no evidence of conspiracy. Millions of Americans are opposed to the war. There is no shred of legality or constitutionality to this war; it violates the United Nations Charter, the Geneva Accords, and the United States promise to obey the laws of international conduct.[5]

It should be added that, because of improper instructions to the jury, the four convictions were reversed on July 11, 1969, by the United States Court of Appeals, though Goodman and Coffin were obliged to undergo retrial. Thus, in view of further appeals, it was made certain that the case would end in the lap of the Supreme Court.

iii.   The Demonstrators March

The most dramatic demonstrations against the war, however, have not been the work of solitary individuals but of groups, organized or unorganized. Some of these, such as the American Friends Service Committee, the Committee for a Sane Nuclear Policy, and the Committee for Nonviolent Action, have fought on the battlefield of ideas rather than with shouts, threats, guns, stones, and bottles, and none the less have had their impact; they can point to the test-ban treaty, the signing by many nations of the nuclear non-proliferation treaty, and the disarmament talks between America and the Soviet Union as evidence that we are moving, even if much too slowly, along the path away from uncontrolled militarism.

In the agitations of the other groups, however, ideas have not always been the chief weapons; more active means have often been applied, though sometimes on a minor scale. Thus, in the summer of 1965, the Berkeley Vietnam Day Committee made the unrewarding gesture of stopping a troop train. Thus, again, thousands of members of the same Committee, in November 1965, marched to the Oakland Army Terminal after their first attempt was blocked by the police. And thus, in October of the same year, a multitude estimated at 100,000 marched or attended rallies in various cities to honor the International Days of Protest sponsored by the National Committee to End the War in Vietnam. In these cases, generally speaking, no force was employed, unless one would use that word to designate the actions of protesters who threw themselves on the railroad tracks in the effort to halt troop trains.

More militant has been the position of RESIST, of Cambridge, Massachusetts, which in 1967 issued the call "to resist illegitimate authority," which we noted several pages back. In 1969 it made another appeal and urged protesters to participate in strikes, sit-ins, boycotts, and other direct action in the effort to halt the military; it also asked for signers with the understanding that they might be committing actions viewed as illegal.

Whatever one may think of the method, and whatever one's inclinations, leftist, rightist, or middle-of-the-road, one must recognize here a summons of a daring and defiance unlikely in any previous age of American history, a summons that may seem to approach the borderline of rebellion. The significance of such a challenge, or at least of the spirit behind it, cannot safely be ignored.

Whether or not this appeal points toward a direct confrontation with the authorities, and therefore toward violence, there have been demonstrations in which violence actually did erupt, as we have seen in the revolt at Columbia University, or as occurred in the fall of 1969 at the Center for International Affairs at Harvard, when members of the Weatherman faction of the SDS seized the place, pushed out some of its occupants, kicked and hit others, and punched a woman librarian in the mouth. Such behavior, even if only the sporadic actions of individuals, can do nothing for the cause of peace.

Fortunately, such conduct has been far from characteristic of the many thousands of Americans, obscure persons and noted persons of all ages and both sexes and all tints of skin, who have tramped for miles on city streets and along country roads, through heat and cold and rain and snow in demonstrations going as far back as the March on Washington in 1965, but subsequently becoming more widely supported and more impressive. As I have remarked, this movement on the whole has been free of violence. And this was conspicuously true in the fall of 1969, when extensive violence had been anticipated in the great surges of protesters who, being far from silent and far from invisible, did nothing to confirm President Nixon's theory as to the "silent majority."

No event in American history had ever been quite like the demonstrations of October 15 and November 15, 1969, on behalf of a war moratorium. Not only in their national scope but in their range and spirit they were unique. It was all very well for the President to say that they would not affect him, but he could not make this statement without unwittingly refuting his own words. Nor were many persons so naive as to believe that the unusual step he took, in announcing an address on Vietnam three weeks in advance, was unrelated to the march of the protesters.

On October 15, although the demonstrations upon the whole were not so striking as those of the following month, a series of revealing incidents occurred. In Boston Common, the war opponents were estimated to number 100,000; in Bryant Park, in the heart of Manhattan, the demonstrators were counted by the tens of thousands; in Milwaukee other thousands made themselves known, as did some 6000 in John F. Kennedy Plaza in Philadelphia; in Baltimore, 15,000 followed the lead of Coretta King, the widow of Martin Luther King, Jr.; and 22,000 joined in a march around the White House. Two days earlier, on October 13, another demonstration, at Fort Dix, had enlisted some 4000 war protesters under the banners of various dissident groups; advancing eight abreast in a formation a quarter of a mile long, the marchers had been repelled by tear gas at the military reservation.

Here was a series of important manifestations of feeling by large numbers of Americans, and the point of it all was missed by those who argued the unprovable question whether they constituted a majority. For, whatever one's mathematical computations, the fact was that they did comprise large elements of the people, elements too great to be ignored, elements that included persons of all ages and all social classes.

Still more numerous were the marchers of November 15, who staged their protests in various parts of the country in throngs beyond counting, though they were roughly estimated as perhaps a million strong, and proclaimed themselves not only in the great cities but in smaller communities, as in my own town of Mill Valley, where many hundreds defied the rain to march more than a mile from the High School to the City Hall. Much more important centers of the demonstrations, of course, were cities such as Washington, D. C., and San Francisco.

In the latter the crowds, estimated at 80,000 by Supervising Captain Edward B. Cummins, Jr., of the San Francisco Police Department, but placed at 100,000 by reporters for the *San Francisco Examiner,* had been marshalled not only from the city itself but from surrounding districts; some had come from as far away as Los Angeles, Arizona, Nevada, and the Pacific Northwest. I have before me a photograph of the banner-waving multitudes as they filled the important thoroughfare of Post Street from curb to curb on their five-mile trek up and down hill from the downtown area to the Polo Field in Golden Gate Park. I also have pictures of them at the Polo Field, where they constituted an unbroken mass of humanity, a dense-packed innumerable army stretching across the open spaces for hundreds of yards as far as the distant fringes of the trees.

Two characteristics, according to the *San Francisco Examiner,* marked the march. "The tens of thousands marched without joy; and they marched without violence." Only four arrests—three for drug-possession, and one for harboring a concealed weapon— were made in connection with the event.

Vaster still was the march at Washington, where a quarter of a million people, according to the conservative official estimate of District of Columbia Police Chief Jerry V. Wilson, tramped down Pennsylvania Avenue, flying flags, and chanting "Peace now!" in what has been described as the greatest antiwar demonstration in American history. The climax occurred at the Washington Monument, where twelve wooden coffins were deposited with an obvious symbolism. It is significant that, except for one minor incident at dusk, this demonstration too was peaceful.

The solemn ceremonial that concluded the affair was in accordance with the spirit of the "march against death" that had begun two days before, when marchers had defied near-freezing temperatures, starting on the Viriginia side of the Memorial Bridge near the gates of the Arlington National Cemetery, and proceeding around the Lincoln Memorial to the White House and then to the Capitol. As they moved in a candlelit line, they included some notable personages such as Dr. and Mrs. Benjamin

Spock and the Reverend William Sloane Coffin, Jr., while middle-aged men and women and priests in their clerical collars joined the ranks of youth, and six drummers played a death roll at their head. They were limited to 46,000 participants, each of whom bore the name of an American slain in the war or of a Vietnamese village said to have been destroyed by our troops; and each, upon reaching the White House, called out a name upon a placard he bore, and then, a little further down Pennsylvania Avenue, placed the placard in one of forty black wooden coffins.

Here, truly, was a macabre ceremony, with a pageantry that seems almost medieval. One would be hard pressed to find its parallel in all the preceding years of American history. Nor would one be likely to discover a more vivid dramatization of the horror felt by many Americans at the cruelties and losses of the battlefield. It may be that this demonstration, and all the other demonstrations together, will not suffice to break down the steel-girt rigidities of the military mind and the high walls of military domination. But it is impossible to ignore the fact that in the' size and intensity of the antiwar manifestations we have something new in our history. And it is equally impossible to believe that the deeply felt convictions of probably a million people, expressed not only in words but in action and presumably representative of the views of other millions watching in the background, will not have an influence, perhaps slow and subtle, but possibly in the end decisive in repelling that mood of warmaking and weapons-development which has been the bane of our recent years and overclouds our future and that of the entire world.

16. How History Repeats Itself

i. Birdseye Glance Back

In the course of these pages we have glanced at the outstanding militant dissenters of more than 2000 years, from two Roman radicals of the second century B.C. to the civil rights protesters and antiwar resisters of our own day. We have observed slave insurrections on Sicily and Italy; the religious uprising in Judea; the rebellion of the peasant leader Wat Tyler in England of the late Middle Ages; the revolt of the Netherlands against the Spanish tyranny; the inception of the American Revolution, the French Revolution, and the Revolutions of 1848; and the outbreaks in Latin America, including the war of the black slaves under Toussaint L'Ouverture in Haiti and the thrusts against European authority in Mexico and lands further south. Turning to the modern age, we considered the rise and in some cases the fall of totalitarian insurgency in Russia, Italy, Germany, and China. And, finally, we looked at the protest movements that have checkered the recent history of the United States and have so frequently resulted in tumult and violence.

In all the various outbreaks, though they have ranged from lawful and peaceable propagandizing to furies of physical attack, some general patterns are clear. One is the fact that the militancy of our own day is by no means as unique as we sometimes assume it to be, and that protest movements, often with overtones of violence and in some cases revolutionary violence, have been prominent in many lands, not only in ancient and medieval times, but particularly among the great nations of the modern world. These outbreaks have arisen in most cases in reaction to long-smoldering wrongs, as when the Roman slaves revolted under the gladiator Spartacus, or when the sorely persecuted people of the Netherlands took arms under William the Silent against the prodigious power of Philip II of Spain. Furthermore, as in the case

252

of the Roman slaves and the abused Netherlanders, the reactions may occur on a delayed basis, long after the first incitements; they may, indeed, often erupt at the very time when conditions seem to be improving, as in 14th century England and during the French Revolution; and their vehemence, as with steam too long compressed, may seem out of proportion to their causes. Complicating the situation, the authorities and in fact the participants themselves seldom foresee the coming of the revolt, seldom correctly appraise its extent or nature, seldom foretell its results, and often fail to take preventive or remedial measures until too late. This we noted particularly in the downfall of the French and Russian monarchies, but other examples may be seen in British intransigence prior to the American Revolution, and in both popular and official reactions in Italy, Germany, and China when they stood at the threshold of totalitarianism.

Another fact that emerges from our discussion is that no political structure, however firmly based it seems, is proof against overthrow. This was shown when the English throne in 1381 came within inches of toppling, when the seemingly impregnable Spanish power was uprooted in the northern provinces of the Netherlands, when England was driven out of the Thirteen Colonies, when the crown of the French Bourbons fell during the Revolution, when the Russian monarchy (though only after a great war) likewise collapsed, and when the crown of imperial Germany was destroyed at the end of World War I.

In all such cases the axehead of revolt may be a small resolute group, a minority that may lead the movement, determine the direction of the resistance, and dominate the majority of the people. Meanwhile the weakness, irresolution, incompetence, or blindness of the established leaders may make it possible for insurgent forces to acquire an irresistible momentum, and to sweep along with them factions and elements that might normally have avoided extremes. This has been evident in scores of uprisings, from those sparked by the fanatical Zealots in ancient Judea to the usurpations of the Bolsheviks in Russia in 1917. And this tendency of a revolt to snowball once it has gained a certain inner propulsion, constitutes one of the great dangers of insurgent movements that have given way to violence.

ii. The Claws and Hammers of Violence

Violence, none the less, has been the soil-conditioner of a high percentage of the revolts. Somewhere among the preliminaries one will usually find warfare, even during eras of relative peace. In ancient Rome, war had broken out constantly, and lay in the background of the slave-taking that made possible the slave revolts; it also underlay the agrarian decline that promoted the emergence of the Gracchi, and preceded the Roman presence in Judea that precipitated the revolutionary movement. The Hundred Years' War had much to do with the onerous taxation of the peasants and their outburst under Wat Tyler; in the Netherlands, the invading army of the Duke of Alva brought a new focus to opposition; in America, the French and Indian War was only a few years in the past at the time of the Revolution, and its ending had released revolutionary pressures; in France the recent war with England, and the contributions to the American struggle for independence had so depleted the economy as to aggravate the incitements to revolution, while the wars of the French Revolution did much to carry forward the banners of insurgency. In modern Russia, Italy, and Germany, the trials and exactions of World War I were major provocations to rebellion, dictatorship, and further warfare. And the connection is clear between some of our own violent outbreaks and the confusions, resentments, and disillusionments of the war in Vietnam.

Thus we must return to the fact that violence breeds violence, and thrives upon the example of violence. Once started, it tends to expand at a rate difficult to check, and may mushroom from small beginnings to alarming dimensions. For example, when Tiberius Gracchus in ancient Rome forcibly silenced a fellow tribune as the only visible means of saving his farm program, he sowed the seeds of the far greater violence which was to destroy him, his younger brother, and their followers, and which would reach out and grow amid tumultuous disturbances until the Republic, in the next century, came tumbling down in ruins. For violent insurgency, carried to its logical extreme in any land, points in the direction of revolution. And while this destination is sometimes foreseen and intended, often it is neither intended nor foreseen.

Very rarely, and only under exceptional circumstances, can violence in civil disorders be interpreted as having accomplished more good than harm. In the ancient Sicilian and Roman slave revolts, the rebels went down to defeat and dire punishment; in Judea the Hebrew state was torn apart after enormous sufferings and losses; in 14th-century England, the revolutionaries under Wat Tyler were overthrown without achieving any permanent gain; in the French Revolution, despite immense benefits, the continuing costs have been prodigious, leaving a question whether nonviolent change would not in the end have been much more rewarding. In the Revolutions of 1848, which, generally speaking, left tyranny enthroned, the same question recurs as to the benefits of violence; in Latin America, the insurgency of Toussaint L'Ouverture was the prelude to tragic troubles that have persisted into our own century; in South America, Bolivar lamented that he had "plowed the sea"; in Mexico Hidalgo went down before a firing squad, with nothing evident attained except bloodshed and destruction. And in the 20th century his successors, after further great destruction, bloodshed, and suffering, won only part of what might have been guaranteed by well-organized, nonviolent social pressures.

Yet while violence in all these cases failed to achieve many of the intended results, a quite different outcome has often followed when the revolutionists sought not freedom but repression, not the welfare of the masses but personal exaltation, not the advance of the state or of humanity but domination, power, and the remorseless enforcement of cults and theories. It is a sad commentary that in only a few cases, as in the Netherlands and in the American colonies of England, has violence led toward a measure of justice or freedom, whereas in innumerable cases, such as those of the Bolsheviks in Russia, the Fascists in Italy, the Nazis in Germany, and Mao Tse-tung's Communists in China, violence has indeed accomplished its ends when they were evil, destructive of life, liberty, and civilized values, and despotic as the sultans of the Orient. If any more persuasive reason has been given why violence in civil disputes should be avoided like a snake in the grass, I have yet to see it.

Nevertheless, even in this age when unleashed force threatens to obliterate the world, there have been adherents of the creed that exalts violence. And these doctrinaires have included not only riot leaders but even the rank and file of agitators, for whom, as one commentator puts it, "Streets become an arena for heroism, a proving ground for bravery. . . . Violence becomes, temporarily, a way of life."[1] Even apart from the rioters and revolutionists, there have been some who, drawing upon the theories of modern biologists such as Konrad Lorenz,[2] have come to conclude that human aggressive tendencies are inborn and ineradicable, and that there may consequently be merit in violence.

But these theorists, it seems to me, have been arguing from false analogies. They do not sufficiently take account of the fact that the animals observed by scientists like Lorenz have mostly been followed under conditions of confinement, which are often conditions of limitation and of irritation, when the creatures may not react as they do in their natural environment. But, even more significantly, the observers minimize or overlook the enormous gap between the facts of animal aggression and those of human militancy. Animals are not swayed by ideologies; in their native state, they strike out mainly in defense of their nests or young, in assertion of their "pecking order" or of their right to a particular tree or other home territory, or (in the case of males) they seek to establish their supremacy over possible mating rivals. A domesticated animal such as a dog may, of course, fight in protection of his master or his master's property or of his own right to a bone; wolves may hunt in packs; bees and wasps may swarm in seemingly united defense against the intruder into their hive. But none of these actions are to be compared to the attacks of a student rabble breaking into a college administration building, or of a ghetto multitude setting fire to stores and houses. Indeed, one would search the world of nature in vain to find anything even remotely similar to the riots and mass demonstrations of human mobs. Hence one must explain riots and demonstrations not by biological but by social predispositions and by social precedents and human psychology.

But must there be violence in society if protest movements are to achieve results? Not if one can accept the lesson of the bus boycott in Montgomery, Alabama, and of the sit-ins and Freedom Rides. And not if one gives credit to the example of Gandhi, who did achieve results that can only be viewed as phenomenal in view of the eventual release of India from Great Britain's determined grip. Nonviolence, however, if it is to succeed, requires greater resolution, firmer action, more dogged courage than violence, which takes a superficially easier road.

Consider, for example, the march of Gandhi and 2500 volunteers upon the Dharasana Salt Works, near Dandi. Louis Fischer, an eye-witness, has described how the men, "in complete silence," drew up a hundred yards from the stockade; how a picked column waded forward and approached the barbedwire entanglements; how a score of policemen attacked them, struck them on the head with steel-shod lathis, and bowled many over, while not one of the marchers so much as raised an arm in self-protection. Fischer proceeds:

> From where I stood I heard the sickening whack of the clubs on unprotected skulls. The waiting crowd of marchers groaned and sucked in their breath in sympathetic pain at every blow. . . . The survivors, without breaking ranks, silently and doggedly marched on until struck down.[3]

A second column was felled in the same way, while the marchers still did not fight back. Other brutalities followed; many were sadistically wounded. Nevertheless, the cause and the method had triumphed:

> The Salt Satuagrapha had demonstrated to the world the nearly flawless use of an instrument of peaceful militancy. . . . After another stay in jail, Gandhi met the viceroy for the famous Tea Party. . . . The following year he would go to England for a Round Table Conference, the sole representative of Congress and a world leader.[4]

Perhaps it would be too much to expect many of us to be Gandhis or active followers of a Gandhi. But in the heroic actions of the salt marchers, we can see proof that, given the courage and the resolution, violence is not necessary to achieve major social gains.

iii. Behind the Protest Movements

Most of the protest movements, as I have brought out, have had clear and understandable justification, sometimes an immense justification, as in the uprisings of oppressed peasants, beaten slaves, persecuted religionists, and aggrieved colonials. And this statement applies to today's militancy in the United States no less than to that of ancient Rome, medieval England, or the various countries of modern Europe. In the case of the Negro, there has been the bitter discriminatory treatment and inferior status not only in former centuries but in the recent past. In the case of education, there has been the revolt against a military hand clamped down upon the colleges, as well as against obsolete and dehumanizing methods and dictatorial practices. In the case of the war protesters, there have been the oppressive, inequitable, possibly illegal draft regulations, and our involvement in a bloody Asian war for which a large part of the American public can see no good reason. And in the case of dissenters of all categories, there have been the corrosive effects of more than a half-century of war in the Western world, plus military conscription, dictatorship, terrorism, genocide, the persistent disparity between haves and have-nots among nations and individuals, the deterioration and threatened ruination of the planet by commercial exploitation and man-created pollution, and the unimaginable overlying threat of the A-bomb and the H-bomb. Beyond all this, the mood of discontent has been fed by the waning of religious belief and the lack of a reassuring cosmic philosophy. Consequently, while many of the protesters have been high-spirited and idealistic, not a few have sunk into anarchistic and nihilistic philosophies.

One result has been that their actions have tended to defeat their own ends. Some of the militants, including certain of the leaders, have evidently failed to realize that you cannot vindicate your own rights by stamping on the rights of others, nor by rejecting the institutions hitherto regarded as fundamental for a civilized and rational life. They have not learned that the cause of education cannot be aided by smashed windows, burned records, libraries blocked or disrupted, administration buildings bombed, or classes riotously overturned. Nor have they apparently recognized that racial bias cannot be put down nor justice furthered by snipers' bullets, rocks, bottles, or firebombs. All such expedients, even if for a time they succeed, will in the end bring counter-reactions, which may lead to grave repression and even dictatorship. But if, on the other hand, the methods fail, they may also encourage repressions that point toward authoritarian control. Thus the radical left and the radical right may unwittingly be pointing toward the same goal, the equivalent of the Communist or Fascist police state.

This is not to suggest that such an end is anticipated or desired by any except perhaps a small minority of dissidents. But small minorities, as we have seen in the case of Lenin's Bolsheviks and of Mao Tse-tung's Communists as well as of the Spartacists who engineered the abortive revolution of the German radicals early in 1919, sometimes dominate great movements. The dangers are several: that a movement, once started, will leap far beyond its original intentions; that it will be snatched by extremist elements from the control of its initiators; that it will end by being self-defeating, and even perpetrate wrongs of the very type it has revolted against, as when the Puritans of the New World, having left the home country in quest of religious freedom, denied that very freedom to dissenters in America. Not only that, but the rebels may proceed even further, perhaps much further down the trail of injustice and oppression than their predecessors—the stern and doctrinaire Robespierre was to be dreaded far more than the mild if fumbling Louis XVI, and Stalin was a much more terrible afflicter of the Russian people than Czar Nicholas II or even the severe Alexander III.

As in Russia before the Revolution, there are persons today in the United States who avowedly will not be content with the gradual processes of social growth, but whose appetite for change will only be whetted by reasonable concessions toward rectification of old wrongs. There are also some who, while calling themselves radicals, are apparently less interested in social reform itself than in finding outlets for their own passions, no matter how destructively. Deeply impregnated with animosity and hate, unable to perceive that their attitudes are charged with emotionalism rather than with the intellectuality they sometimes claim, the members of such groups call for revolution as if this will bring a panacea, or as if most of the revolutions of history, even when successful in overthrowing the old regime, have not led to oppression, civil strife, terror, warfare, and dictatorship. These rebels strike out at "The Establishment"—a term of contempt, one might even say of prejudice, since, despite all the grievous errors of our ruling bodies, no great monolithic power is actually supreme in America; what the rebels attack is a mythical monster of their own imagining, which has little more reality than the Minotaur of ancient Crete. Although our great shortcomings may be acknowledged; although it may be admitted that we have less a unified social system than the patchwork accretion of centuries that has put a dangerous overemphasis on production and consumption and has allowed far too much license to a greedy individualism, we do at least have institutions that somehow, in many respects, have held up for hundreds of years, and are all that now stand between us and chaos.

But is there any danger that the small contemporary revolutionary groups will achieve the destruction they evidently seek? It would be rash to answer in the affirmative (personally, I consider isolated insurrections much less improbable than revolution). But it would be equally rash to dismiss the question as preposterous or extreme—after all, we have only to remember what *has* happened at Watts, Detroit, and many other points. In all these cases, the rampaging rabble was spearheaded by only a few unrestrained individuals; and a few agitators, given an original smoldering discontent, usually suffice to start an eruption. In the crowded hives of our great cities, where bombs can be planted in terroristic sneak attacks, where shots can be fired from every window and rooftop and from behind every post and doorway, and where the sabotage of power plants, water works, transportation, and food distribution might bring our highly specialized communities to their knees, the country is far more vulnerable than it is ever likely to be to an invading army.

For this reason, we would merely be self-blinded if we did not look seriously upon the threat of the extremists and irreconcilables, few though they may be in proportion to the total population. This does not mean that we should launch programs of violent repression, as the police seem to have done against the Black Panthers; such programs can only add fuel to discontent, and increase the peril. On the contrary, recognizing that there may be a measure of justice behind the most frenzied revolt, we should set about not simply to analyze causes and motives but to propound remedies, and this in a spirit free from rancor. Not least important, we should act *today* rather than tomorrow, since we cannot know just how much time remains to us, any more than the mayors or chiefs of police of Los Angeles or Newark or Chicago could know how long a period of grace they had before the flare-ups that took many lives and made shambles of considerable sections of their cities. The only safe course is to act on the assumption that a greater outbreak, while it may be long delayed or may never occur, may even now be invisibly gathering steam just around the corner.

iv. The Search for Solutions

Of all the disturbances that we have been considering, few if any could not have been avoided or at least ended with reason and justice—that is, if man were a just and reasonable creature, moved more by promptings of right and rationality than by traditions, prejudices, passions, and old social patterns and fixations. No slave revolt would have shattered the calm of ancient Rome had slavery been recognized as an iniquitous and dehumanizing institution, founded upon predatory warfare and equally predatory social customs. No peasant rebellion would have threatened the regime of England's King Richard II had it been customary to treat the farmworker and the manual laborer as full-scale humans deserving full human rights. No revolution would have shaken the hold of Spain in the Netherlands had dictatorial arrogance and greed not joined hands with religious fanaticism to precipitate a resolute counter-violence. And so on and on, down to the upheavals of our own day. In none of these cases, either in the distant or the recent past, would an uprising have been likely if man had met the problem dispassionately and logically, with no preconceptions or inbred code of belief. But, of course, if man had been able to meet his problems dispassionately and logically, none of the causes of dispute would have occurred in the first place.

This brings us to the basic fact which we must face if we are to meet the challenges of militant dissent: that adult human beings are firmly set in particular ways of thought if not of conduct, and can only with difficulty, and then rarely, be wooed from a long-established course. This means that we are confronted by an irony and a contradiction. In order to make a proper response to the demonstrators of our own age, and to reach those still so young that their minds are not fixed in inflexible molds, we need time, much time. But time is precisely what we lack; in some cases, it seems, we have about exhausted our quota. What, then, can be the solution?

Any solution at this stage, we must concede, promises to be at best partial. Nevertheless, we must undertake new measures as quickly as possible, not only because of present perils and eventual expected benefits, but because the vigorous launching of a program may give hope to those now hopeless and tend to restrain them from extremes. In the case of the war protesters, we will reach a solution only when we recognize the fundamental justice of much of what they demand, and liquidate our wars, terminate the draft, and reduce the overshadowing might of the Pentagon and the Department of Defense. In the case of the student agitators, at the same time, an approach to an answer to the problem of war should be of inestimable help, though no general remedy seems possible amid an atmosphere of violence in the schools and colleges. Once the students have ceased to behave like mobsters, and once the administrators recognize that there are legitimate causes for complaint in our mechanized mass

centers of learning, we may hope to proceed without that disintegration of the educational process and that throw-back of
medievalism which Jacques Barzun and others have foreseen.
Not that a small minority may not still be primarily interested
in venting their own passions; but these misguided few will lack
permanent influence.

It is when we turn to racial problems that we face the sharpest
dilemma. Here especially, any solution, to be thoroughgoing,
will involve a reassessment and a redirection of social attitudes.
And this will necessitate a retraining of the young from their
kindergarten days all through their school years, so that their
attitude will differ in many respects from that of their fathers.
They must come to see the trap and the delusion that violence
usually is, not only in civil affairs but in the international domain; they must understand that the distinctions which we draw
between man and man are arbitrary and unnatural, that there
are no true races, that skin-color is only skin-deep, and that all
men are members of one species, not only biologically, but in a
profound spiritual sense. Such a realization, however, will not be
furthered by current separatist methods, such as those of "black
studies" courses and departments, which really represent no more
than black racism in disguise, understandable as props to the
pride of an abused people, but attempting the impossible when
they seek to dissociate the history of one ethnic element from
the wider history of which it is a part. What is needed is re-
education not of a segment of the citizenry, but of all citizens.

Such re-education, manifestly, would require a re-programming of courses in all schools, beginning with the elementary,
though this would be certain to encounter opposition in the
areas that need it most, the very areas where segregation continues today. If the re-programming is to be effective, it would
necessitate an end to segregation. Children would have to learn—
as children can easily learn unless poisoned by the bias of the
adult world—to study, work, and play with boys and girls of
different pigmentations, just as they learn to study, work, and
play with those of their own tint. For a world without racial
strife must be a world without racial barriers.

There are those, to be sure, who will tell you that the essence
of the race riots has been economic discrimination; what we need
most of all, they will plead, are great spending programs. Superficially, this appears plausible; but doubt is thrown on the thesis
by the fact that many past outbreaks, as in the French and Amer-

ican Revolutions, did not occur at an economic nadir, while some of the worst recent riots, as in Detroit, have flared up where the Negro was upon the whole economically best off, and blacks in a more favored economic position have taken part in the violence as much as the most disadvantaged. This is not to suggest that we should not spend generously whenever this promises to be helpful, and fight poverty at every turn while doing our best to insure equality in housing, in job opportunities and compensation, and in public facilities, labor unions, and elsewhere. Doubtless, also, intensive and specialized training programs should be instituted to provide persons of all races with the skills needed to make economic progress in the modern world. But we might have a sad awakening were we to place our entire reliance upon efforts to buy our way out regardless of those sore discriminatory attitudes that lie, consciously or unconsciously, at the bottom of the racial outbreaks.

Various other remedies may be suggested in a general way. To allay the bitter hatred of the police which has made unruly elements in the ghettos difficult to control, we might experiment with letting the minority races police their own areas to an extent never before attempted. To promote better understanding among all races, we might place greater emphasis in our universities upon courses dealing with the problems of minorities; whole specialized departments might be devoted to this realm, not only in theoretical studies but through field work by men and women training for life careers. To combat the danger of increasing government estrangement from the black masses, such as we have witnessed in the Nixon Administration, we might establish a new federal department of Cabinet standing, which might provide enlightened new guidance for the President and Congress. And to meet the problems of the idle, the unemployed, and the disgruntled, extensive government-supported public works programs might be undertaken, aimed not only to offer temporary work as in the case of the Civilian Conservation Corps of the Roosevelt era, but to supply training and skills likely to be of permanent benefit.

One must admit that all these expedients, even if successful, might turn out to be palliatives rather than cures. One must further admit the extreme difficulties of obtaining cooperation from the white masses in whom bias is still deeply entrenched, and of working with colored men of sensitive nerves and hair-trigger susceptibilities to the least hint of racial subordination or affront. An example of the sort of obstacles that may be encountered has been provided by Daniel P. Moynihan, the Assistant to the President for Urban Affairs. Syracuse University several years ago received a grant from the Office of Economic Opportunity to establish a Community Action Training Center, and this quickly caused friction. The Negroes began to agitate for control of the program, established one of their militants, James Tillman, Jr., as director, and, after about a year, obtained a majority in the Board. Meanwhile, according to Moynihan, the Crusade became "more and more abrasive."[5] "No ends were accomplished without the use of force," proclaimed the new director. . . . "Squeamishness about force is the mark . . . of moonstruck morals."[6] Not all Negroes, however, agreed; in the course of the ensuing tension, the local NAACP called for Tillman's resignation, and its members were themselves denounced by militants who packed a meeting and branded their chief opponent as a "house nigger." The worst of it all was that the job program broke down; in mid-1967 its director had to admit that it had been "a dismal failure."

This, of course, is only one example, but it indicates the sort of obstructions that must be faced even when the will, the program, and the money for reform are available. Here, as always, the problem of human reactions is central to any solution; and the problem of human reactions is one that man, in this computerized age, is still far from mastering.

v. Further Solutions and Meanings

It has become usual to trace the conflict of black and white in the United States to the centuries of slavery, and certainly one cannot fully understand the problem without regard to the lingering shadow of that debased institution. Nevertheless, more recent developments have perhaps had a more powerful influence in our own day than even the legacy of slavery.

Those developments have been connected with the changes in our society, and not least with the advance of mechanization, which has struck the cotton fields of the South, deprived Negro sharecroppers of their meager source of income, and sent droves of them north in search of work. But perhaps equally important have been the effects of World War II, which caused a redistribution of labor whose repercussions are with us now and will remain into the indefinite future.

Let me cite an example that has come within my personal observation. In southern Marin County, in California, not many miles from where I live, there was until early 1942 a pleasant low green hill which, along with its several houses, fronted on Richardson Bay, an arm of San Francisco Bay. Behind the hill, an unoccupied valley lay peacefully between picturesque rolling ridges. With the outbreak of war and the imperative demand for ships, the site of the green hill and the adjacent waterfront were chosen for a new shipyard, and the hill was bulldozed away and the houses disappeared. Then a new community, Marin City, arose in mushroom fashion in the valley and on the surrounding slopes, which grew ugly with ramshackle temporary housing to accommodate the Negroes imported from the South to work beside white laborers in the shipyards. At the war's end the yards were dismantled, but Marin City remained, occupied almost exclusively by Negroes, none of whom had been in the vicinity before the war. And now that their wartime livelihood was taken from them, they faced the difficulties that transplanted blacks have had to wrestle with almost everywhere: *de facto* segregation, since realtors elsewhere in the county would not sell or rent housing to them; a similar *de facto* segregation in schooling, and difficulty obtaining employment, particularly in the more advantageous jobs. Consequently, although the temporary dwellings of Marin City eventually gave way to more durable apartment buildings, and although the people had the advantages of scenic surroundings not equalled by most persons of any race, there were eruptions of crime and of minor racial violence, and threats of more serious violence brooded beneath the surface.

Fortunately, considerable has been done in this instance toward facing reality, and particularly toward ending *de facto* school segregation and finding jobs for members of minority races in business places throughout the county, even though unofficial segregation in housing remains. But while there has been no major outbreak, the conditions here have not been unique; rather, they are typical of much of the country, and of the ways in which problems have been created where they did not exist before. Hence we have suggestions of the tangled depths of the historic forces we must counteract if we are to find a lasting solution to the racial challenge.

Not only war-created changes and the expansion of industry

but the growth of population—an evil from which he has been a particular sufferer—has been connected with the burdens of the Negro. He has endured a double disability: on the one hand, his rate of increase has exceeded that of the white people; on the other hand, he has been at a disadvantage in the resulting intensified competition for the available jobs and housing. Consequently, he would be much benefited, as would all elements of the population in varying degrees, by rigorous standards of birth control, which would tend to relieve tension in all directions. And this is the more true in the case of the Negro because of his high rate of illegitimate births and broken homes, with all the accompanying hardships and tragedy, and with the large number of youths now let loose upon the world without experience of a normal family life, insufficiently educated, mostly impoverished, and with ingrown discontents that make them easy targets for the preachers of violence. Yet without adequate birth control, their numbers are certain to mount.

Specific programs of birth control, of course, lie outside the natural boundaries of this discussion; all that I need point out is that, to combat the rankling dissatisfactions that lead to friction among the races, as well as for other reasons both ecological and human, the immediate drastic regulation of population deserves high government priority.

When we look back over the militant outbreaks of the ages, we find that, as already noted, most of them could have been forestalled had their causes been attacked in time. Most of them, indeed, were foretold in a succession of unheeded or misunderstood warning blasts, somewhat like the premonitory tremors that sometimes, over the course of the months or years, precede a major earthquake.

Thus, to confine ourselves to a few modern examples, the long series of rebellious moves by the American colonists, as in their rioting against the Stamp Act and in the Boston Tea Party, might have apprised the English leaders that revolution threatened if they did not seek a better understanding of colonial psychology and adopt a more conciliatory policy. Or take the case of France: there had been *jacqueries* and peasant uprisings dating back to the Middle Ages, but signs of discontent both in the cities and on the land were particularly evident just before the explosion of 1789, although the government pursued its blind and stolid way as always along the satin corridors of privilege. Similarly, in Russia, there had been a long series of insurrections, antedating even Peter I, and flaring up again in the 19th century and in the violence of 1905, while the authorities sat by complacently, unable or unwilling to read the signs. Likewise in China, the rumblings had been heard in revolts throughout the ages, and not least in the costly Taiping Rebellion of the mid-19th century, and in the discontents of the early 20th century, until the inept Manchu government, throned upon rose petals in a sort of opium dream, was blasted out of existence. In China again, in later decades, Chiang Kai-shek remained seemingly insensitive to the stirrings of the great peasant masses who were rising under their Communist mentors against the power of invading Japan; because he did not read the message of the country folk but tied himself to the privileged city classes amid favoritism and corruption while relying excessively upon armed might, the Nationalist leader succumbed to the adroit militancy of Mao Tse-tung and had to flee to the island retreat of Formosa. It is not believable that, except possibly in the case of the badly decayed Manchu regime, the various governments could not have weathered the storm had they correctly read the signals and acted realistically to reduce the sources of disorder.

In all this, since men's minds and motivations remain much the same through all the shifts of lands and generations, there are meanings that our own age and nation cannot safely disregard. In our times, besides, the urgencies are greater; the impact of an artificial, biologically unnatural, and psychologically oppressive urban environment has been increasingly harsh in its bearing upon ever larger numbers of men; the speed of change has been accelerated by the pressures of industry and population and even more by the unprecedented swiftness of travel and communications, which have transmitted protest movements from land to land as by an electrical impulse, making swifter reactions and quicker answers necessary.

And shall the far-seeing eye of history, for which decades pass like waves that roll upon a beach and are gone, note that we followed the path of our unhappy predecessors, or that we were aware of the realities, and adjusted our course in time to avoid the precipice rim? It may be that most men of our century will not live to learn the answer, or it may be that the answer will come tomorrow. In any case, there is hope if we can establish a correct scale of priorities and cease to spill out our energies along sidelines; if we learn to see the problems of angry black men or of equally angry war protesters as more important, for example, than a competition with the Soviet Union for the honor of building a costly and highly dubious supersonic airliner or an even costlier and more dubious anti-ballistic missile system. Particularly, there is hope if we can learn to regard the militant outbreaks of our age as symptoms of ills ingrained in society, and set about to attack not the symptoms but the underlying causes like a surgeon whose scalpel digs deep in the effort to free a patient's body of a parasitic growth.

Notes

Chapter 1

1. Plutarch, "Crassus," in *Lives*, p. 212.

Chapter 2

1. Quoted in Sir Arthur Bryant, *The Fire and The Rose* (Doubleday & Company, 1966), p. 74. Copyright © by Sir Arthur Bryant. Reprinted by permission of Doubleday & Company, Inc.
2. Quoted in Amabel William-Ellis and F. J. Fisher, M.A., *The Story of English Life*, pp. 123–24.
3. Charles Oman, *The Great Revolt of 1381*, p. 67.
4. Bryant, p. 88.

Chapter 3

1. John Lothrop Motley, *The Rise of the Dutch Republic*, Vol. II, p. 158.
2. *Ibid.*, pp. 182–83.
3. *Ibid.*, p. 249.

Chapter 4

1. John C. Miller, *Origins of the American Revolution*, p. 267.
2. Quoted in Merrill Jensen, *The Founding of a Nation, A History of the American Revolution, 1763–1776*, p. 457.
3. Miller, *Origins of the American Revolution*, p. 371.
4. Quoted in Carl Van Doren, *Secret History of the American Revolution*, p. 7.

Chapter 6

1. Hilliard d'Aubertueil, *Considerations sur la Colonie de Saint Dominique*, quoted in Ralph Korngold, *Citizen Toussaint*, p. 30.
2. Stephen Alexis, *Black Liberator, the Life of Toussaint Louverture*, pp. 26–27n.

3. Gragnon-Lacoste, *Toussaint Louverture,* p. 15.
4. Alexis, *Black Liberator,* pp. 31–32.
5. Blair Niles, *Journeys in Time: From the Halls of Montezuma to Patagonia's Plains,* p. 118.
6. C. L. R. James, *The Black Jacobins, Toussaint L'Ouverture and the San Domingo Revolution,* p. 152.
7. *Ibid.,* pp. 153–54.
8. Alexis, *Black Liberator,* p. 87.
9. Quoted in Hubert Herring, *A History of Latin America from the Beginning to the Present,* p. 426.
10. Ralph Korngold, *Citizen Toussaint,* Foreword, p. xii.

Chapter 7

1. Quoted in William Spence Robertson, *Rise of the Spanish-American Republics, as Told in the Lives of Their Liberators,* pp. 94–95.
2. Charles C. Cumberland, *Mexico: The Struggle for Modernity,* p. 246.
3. *Ibid.*
4. John Womach, Jr., *Zapata and the Mexican Revolution,* p. 374.

Chapter 8

1. George Woodcock, ed., *A Hundred Years of Revolution: 1848 and After,* pp. 175–76.
2. H. A. L. Fisher, *A History of Europe,* Vol. III, p. 934.
3. Albert Guerard, *France: A Modern History,* p. 290.
4. Woodcock, *A Hundred Years of Revolution,* p. 161.
5. *Ibid.,* p. 162.
6. Frederick Ewen, ed. and trans., *The Prose and Poetry of Heinrich Heine,* p. 451.
7. *Ibid.,* p. 452.
8. Georges Duveau, *1848: The Making of A Revolution,* p. 46.
9. *Ibid.,* p. 44.
10. Arnold Whitridge, *Men in Crisis: The Revolutions of 1848,* p. 61.
11. Quoted in Whitridge, *Men in Crisis,* p. 62.
12. Quoted in Woodcock, *A Hundred Years of Revolution,* p. 172.
13. *Ibid.*

Chapter 9

1. B. H. Sumner, *A Short History of Russia,* p. 157.
2. *Ibid.*
3. *Ibid.,* p. 132.
4. Henri Troyat, *Pushkin, A Biography,* p. 252.
5. Quoted in Alan Moorehead, *The Russian Revolution,* p. 53.
6. N. N. Sukhanov, *The Russian Revolution 1917: Eyewitness Account,* Vol. I, p. 5.
7. Robert V. Daniels, *Red October: The Bolshevik Revolution of 1917,* p. 20.
8. Arthur Rosenberg, *A History of Bolshevism, From Marx to the First Five-Year Plan,* p. 24.
9. *Ibid.,* p. 118.

Chapter 10

1. Christopher Hibbert, *Il Duce: The Life of Benito Mussolini*, p. 30.

Chapter 11

1. Konrad Heiden, *Der Fuehrer, Hitler's Rise to Power*, p. 409.
2. E. M. Knight-Patterson, *Germany From Defeat to Conquest, 1913–1933*, p. 505.
3. William Sheridan Allen, *The Nazi Seizure of Power: The Experience of a Single German Town, 1930–1935*, p. 75.
4. John Cruickshank, *Albert Camus and the Literature of Revolt*, p. 91.
5. *Ibid.*

Chapter 12

1. Thomas Taylor Meadows, *The Chinese and Their Rebellions*, pp. 116–17.
2. *Ibid.*, pp. 117–18.
3. Eric R. Wolf, *Peasant Wars of the Twentieth Century*, p. 107.
4. Ping-Chia Kuo, *China: New Age and Outlook*, p. 65.

Chapter 13

1. Quoted in Alan F. Westin, *Freedom Now, The Civil Rights Struggle in America*, pp. 13–14.
2. Howard Zinn, *SNCC: The New Abolitionists*, p. 270.
3. Nathan E. Cohen, "The Los Angeles Riot Study," in Shalom Endleman, ed., *Violence in the Streets*, p. 344.
4. Bayard Rustin, "Some Lessons from Watts," in Endleman, ed., *Violence in the Streets*, p. 347.
5. Gary Willis, *The Second American Civil War: Arming for Armageddon*, p. 125.
6. Quoted in Joseph Boskin, *Urban Racial Violence in the Twentieth Century*, p. 127.
7. James H. Lincoln, *The Anatomy of a Riot: A Detroit Judge's Report*, p. 5.
8. Bayard Rustin, "The Watts 'Manifesto' and the McCone Report," in Boskin, *Urban Racial Violence*, p. 111.
9. Cohen, "The Los Angeles Riot Study," p. 335.
10. *San Francisco Chronicle*, December 21, 1969.

Chapter 14

1. *San Francisco Chronicle*, December 11, 1969.
2. Quoted in Jerome K. Skolnick, *The Politics of Protest*, p. 80.
3. Quoted in Irving Feinstein, *Turbulent Years, A History of the American Worker, 1933–1941*, pp. 679–80.
4. Mario Savio, "An End to History," in Mitchell Cohen and Dennis Hale, eds., *The New Student Left*, p. 249.

5. Thomas Hayden, "Student Social Action: From Liberation to Community," in Cohen and Hale, eds., *The New Student Left*, p. 278.

6. Michael Novak, "God in the Colleges: The Dehumanization of the University," in Cohen and Hale, eds., *The New Student Left*, p. 256.

7. Jacques Barzun, "Tomorrow's University—Back to the Middle Ages," *Saturday Review*, November 15, 1969, p. 61.

Chapter 15

1. Jessica Mitford, *The Trial of Dr. Spock*, p. 11.
2. *Ibid.*, pp. 28–29.
3. *Ibid.*, p. 41.
4. Quoted in editorial in *San Francisco Chronicle*, April 10, 1969.
5. Mitford, *The Trial of Dr. Spock*, p. 247.
6. *San Francisco Examiner*, November 16, 1969.

Chapter 16

1. Hans H. Toch, *Violent Men: An Inquiry Into the Psychology of Violence*, p. 211.
2. See Konrad Lorenz, *On Aggression*.
3. Quoted in Erik H. Erikson, *Gandhi's Truth: On the Origin of Militant Nonviolence*, p. 447.
4. *Ibid.*, pp. 447–48.
5. Daniel P. Moynihan, *Maximum Feasible Misunderstanding: Community Action in the War on Poverty*, p. 132.
6. *Ibid.*, p. 133.

Bibliography

Chapter 1

Diodorus of Agrium. *Library of Universal History,* ed. by C. Muller. Paris, 1844. In *Greek Civilization and Character.* Introduction and translation by Arnold J. Toynbee. Boston: The Beacon Press, 1950.

Ferrero, Gugliemo. *The Greatness and Decline of Rome.* Translated by Alfred E. Zimmern. Vol. I. New York: G. P. Putnam's Sons, 1907.

Frank, Tenney. *A History of Rome.* New York: Henry Holt & Co., 1926.

Graetz, H. *Popular History of the Jews,* Vol. II. 4th edition. New York: Hebrew Publishing Co., 1909.

Household, W. W. *Rome: Republic and Empire,* Vol. I. London: J. M. Dent & Sons, 1936.

Josephus. *The Jewish War.* Translated with an introduction by G. A. Williamson. Baltimore, Md.: Penguin Books, 1959.

Mommsen, Theodor. *The History of Rome.* New edition by Dero A. Saunders & John H. Collins. U.S.A.: Meridian Books, Inc., 1958.

Parkes, James. *A History of the Jewish People.* Baltimore, Md.: Penguin Books, 1964.

Plutarch. *Lives,* Vol. III. The Translation Called Dryden's corrected from the Greek and revised by A. H. Clough. New York: The Nottingham Society, New York. n.d.

Roth, Cecil. *History of the Jews.* New York: Schocken Books, 1961.

Sachar, Abram Leon. *A History of the Jews.* 4th edition, revised and enlarged. New York: Alfred A. Knopf, 1963.

Scullard, H. H. *From the Gracchi to Nero, A History of Rome from 133 B.C. to 68 A.D.* New York: Frederick A. Praeger, 1959.

Starr, Chester G. *A History of the Ancient World.* New York: Oxford Univ. Press, 1965.

Swain, Joseph Ward. *The Ancient World.* Vol. II. New York: Harper & Bros., 1950.

Chapter 2

Ashley, Maurice. *Great Britain to 1688: A Modern History.* Ann Arbor: Univ. of Michigan Press, 1961.

Bryant, Sir Arthur. *The Fire and the Rose.* Garden City: Doubleday & Co., 1966.

Coulton, G. G. *Chaucer and His England.* New York: Russell & Russell, 1957.

Fisher, H. A. L. *A History of Europe.* Vol. I. Boston: Houghton Mifflin Co., 1935.

Oman, Charles. *The Great Revolt of 1381.* Oxford: Clarendon Press, 1906.

Trevelyan, C. M. *History of England.* Vol. I. Garden City: Doubleday & Co., 1952.

Williams-Ellis, Amabel, and F. J. Fisher, M. A. *The Story of English Life.* New York: Coward-McCann, Inc., 1936.

Chapter 3

Blok, Petrus Johannes. *History of the People of the Netherlands,* Vols. III and IV. Translated by Ruth Putnam. New York: G. P. Putnam's Sons, 1900.

Chapman, Charles E. *A History of Spain.* New York: The Macmillan Co., 1965.

Davies, E. Trevor. *The Golden Century of Spain, 1501–1621.* New York: Harper & Row, 1965.

Fisher, H. A. L. *A History of Europe.* Vol. II. Boston: Houghton Mifflin Co., 1935.

Livermore, Harold. *A History of Spain.* New York: Grove Press, 1958.

Merriman, Roger Bigelow. *The Rise of the Spanish Empire.* Vol. III. New York: The Macmillan Co., 1925.

Motley, John Lothrop. *The Rise of the Dutch Republic.* 3 vols. New York: Harper & Bros., 1851.

Putnam, Ruth. *William the Silent Prince of Orange (1533–1584) and the Revolt of the Netherlands.* New York: G. P. Putnam's Sons, 1911.

Smith, Rhea Marsh. *Spain: A Modern History.* Ann Arbor: The University of Michigan Press, 1965.

Chapter 4

Berky, Andrew S., and Shenton, James P. *The Historians' History of the United States.* Vol. I. New York: G. P. Putnam's Sons, 1966.

Bining, Arthur Cecil. *A History of the United States.* Vol. I. New York: Charles Scribner's Sons, 1950.

Jensen, Merrill. *The Founding of a Nation: A History of the American Revolution, 1763–1776.* New York: Oxford University Press, 1968.

Kraus, Michael. *The United States to 1865.* Ann Arbor: University of Michigan Press, 1959.

Miller, John C. *Origins of the American Revolution.* Boston: Little, Brown and Company, 1943.

Morison, Samuel Eliot. *The Oxford History of the American People.* New York: Oxford University Press, 1965.

Van Doren, Carl. *Secret History of the American Revolution.* New York: The Viking Press, 1968.

Ward, Christopher. *The War of the Revolution.* Edited by John Richard Alden. Vol. I. New York: The Macmillan Co., 1952.

Chapter 5

Brinton, Crane. *A Decade of Revolution, 1789–1799.* New York: Harper & Bros., 1934.

Gaxotte, Pierre. *The French Revolution.* Translated by Walter Alison Phillips. New York: C. Scribner's Sons, 1932.

Gottschalk, Louis R. *The Era of the French Revolution (1715–1815).* Boston: Houghton Mifflin Co., 1929.

Guérard, Albert. *France: A Modern History.* Ann Arbor: University of Michigan Press, 1959.

————— *The Life and Death of an Ideal: France in the Classical Age.* New York: George Braziller, 1956.

Hazen, Charles Downer. *The French Revolution.* 2 vols. New York: H. Holt and Company, 1932.

Higgens, E. L. *The French Revolution As Told by Contemporaries.* Boston: Houghton Mifflin Company, 1939.

Lefebvre, Georges. *The French Revolution From Its Origins to 1793.* Translated by Elizabeth Moss Evanson. New York: Columbia Univ. Press, 1962.

————— *The French Revolution From 1793 to 1799.* Translated by John Hall Stewart and James Friguglietti. New York: Columbia Univ. Press, 1964.

Mathiez, F. A. *The French Revolution.* New York: A. A. Knopf, 1929.

Palmer, R. R. *The Age of the Democratic Revolution: A Political*

History of Europe and America, 1760–1800. Princeton, N. J.: Princeton University Press, 1964.

Rudé, George. *Revolutionary Europe, 1783–1815*. New York: Harper & Row, 1966.

Salvemini, Gaetano. *The French Revolution, 1788–1792*. Translated by I. M. Rawson. New York: W. W. Norton & Co., 1962.

Chapters 6 and 7

Alexis, Stephen. *Black Liberator, The Life of Toussaint Louverture*. Translated by William Stirling. London: Ernest Benn, Ltd., 1949.

Cumberland, Charles C. *Mexico: The Struggle for Modernity*. New York: Oxford University Press, 1968.

Gragnon-Lacoste. *Toussaint Louverture*. Extracts edited by Georgiana M. Simpson. Washington: The Associated Publishers, 1929.

Herring, Hubert. *A History of Latin America from the Beginning to the Present*. 2nd edition, revised. New York: Alfred A. Knopf, Inc., 1961.

James, C. L. R. *The Black Jacobins: Toussaint L'Ouverture and the Santo Domingo Revolution*. 2nd edition, revised. New York: Random House, 1963.

Korngold, Ralph. *Citizen Toussaint*. Boston: Little, Brown & Co., 1944.

Niles, Blair. *Journeys in Time: From the Halls of Montezuma to Patagonia's Plains*. New York: Coward-McCann, Inc., 1946.

Pendle, George. *A History of Latin America*. Baltimore: Penguin Books, 1967.

Robertson, William Spence. *Rise of the Spanish-American Republics: As Told in the Lives of Their Liberators*. New York: The Free Press, 1965.

Sherwell, Guillermo A. *Simon Bolivar, Patriot, Warrior, Statesman, Father of Five Nations*. Washington: Press of B. S. Adams, 1921.

Womack, John, Jr. *Zapata and the Mexican Revolution*. New York: Alfred A. Knopf, 1969.

Ybarra, T. B. *Bolivar the Passionate Warrior*. New York: I. Washburn, 1919.

Chapter 8

Blum, Jerome; Cameron, Rondo; and Barnes, Thomas G. *The European World: A History*. Boston: Little Brown & Co., 1966.

Duveau, Georges. *1848: The Making of a Revolution*. Translated by Anne Carter, Introduction by George Rudé. New York: Random House, 1968.

Ewen, Frederic, ed. and trans. *The Prose and Poetry of Heinrich Heine*. New York: The Citadel Press, 1948.

Fisher, H. A. L. *A History of Europe*. Vol. III. Boston: Houghton Mifflin Co., 1936.

Guérard, Albert. *France: A Modern History*. Ann Arbor: University of Michigan Press, 1959.

Palmer, R. R. *A History of the Modern World*. New York: Alfred A. Knopf, 1962.

Whitridge, Arnold. *Men in Crisis: The Revolutions of 1848*. New York: Charles Scribner's Sons, 1947.

Woodcock, George, ed. *A Hundred Years of Revolution: 1848 and After*. London: The Porcupine Press, 1948.

Chapter 9

Chamberlin, William Henry. *The Russian Revolution, 1917–1921*. 2 vols. New York: Macmillan, 1935.

Clarkson, Jesse D. *A History of Russia*. New York: Random House, 1962.

Daniels, Robert V. *Red October: The Bolshevik Revolution of 1917*. New York: Charles Scribner's Sons, 1967.

Grey, Ian. *Peter the Great: Emperor of All Russia*. Philadelphia and New York: J. B. Lippincott Co., 1960.

Moorehead, Alan. *The Russian Revolution*. New York: Harper and Bros., 1958.

Pares, Sir Bernard. *The Fall of the Russian Monarchy*. New York: Random House, 1939.

Possony, Stefan T. *Lenin: The Compulsive Revolutionary*. Chicago: Henry Regnery Co., 1964.

Reed, John. *Ten Days That Shook the World*. New York: Random House, 1960.

Rosenberg, Arthur. *A History of Bolshevism, From Marx to the First Five-Year Plan*. Introduction by Samuel J. Hurwitz, translated by Ian F. D. Morrow. Garden City: Doubleday Anchor Books, 1967.

Sorokin, Pitirim. *Leaves from a Russian Diary*. New York: E. P. Dutton & Co., 1924.

Sukhanov, N. N. *The Russian Revolution 1917: Eyewitness Account*. Edited, abridged, and translated by Joel Carmichael. 2 vols. New York: Harper Torchbook, 1962.

Sumner, B. H. *A Short History of Russia*. Revised edition. New York: Harcourt, Brace and World, Inc., 1949.

Troyat, Henri. *Pushkin, A Biography*. Translated by Raymond T. Weaver. New York: Pantheon Books, Inc., 1950.

Vernadsky, George. *A History of Russia.* New York: Yale University Press, 1944.

Wallace, Sir Donald Mackenzie. *Russia on the Eve of War and Revolution.* New York: Random House, Inc., 1961.

Yarmolinsky, Avrahm. *Road to Revolution: A Century of Russian Radicalism.* New York: Macmillan, 1968.

Chapter 10

Fermi, Laura. *Mussolini.* Chicago: University of Chicago Press, 1961.

Finer, Herman. *Mussolini's Italy.* New York: The Universal Library, 1965.

Hibbert, Christopher. *Il Duce: The Life of Benito Mussolini.* Boston: Little, Brown and Company, 1962.

Kirkpatrick, Ivone. *Mussolini: A Study in Power.* New York: Hawthorn Books, 1964.

Seldes, George. *Sawdust Caesar: The Untold History of Mussolini and Fascism.* New York: Harper & Bros., 1935.

Smith, Denis Mack. *Italy: A Modern History.* Ann Arbor: The University of Michigan Press, 1959.

Chapter 11

Allen, William Sheridan. *The Nazi Seizure of Power: The Experience of a Single German Town, 1930–1935.* Chicago: Quadrangle Books, 1965.

Buchheim, Hans. *The Third Reich, Its Beginnings, Its Development, Its End.* London: O. Wolff, 1961.

Bullock, Alan. *Hitler, A Study in Tyranny.* New York: Harper & Row, 1964.

Cruickshank, John. *Albert Camus and the Literature of Revolt.* London: Oxford University Press, 1968.

Heiden, Konrad. *Der Fuehrer: Hitler's Rise to Power.* Translated by Ralph Manheim. Boston: Houghton Mifflin Co., 1944.

Knight-Patterson, W. M. *Germany From Defeat to Conquest, 1913–1933.* Foreword by Lord Vansittart. London: George Allen & Unwin, Ltd., 1945.

Shirer, William L. *The Rise and Fall of the Third Reich: A History of Nazi Germany.* New York: Simon & Schuster, 1960.

Taylor, A. J. P. *The Origins of the Second World War.* New York: Atheneum, 1962.

Watt, Richard M. *The Kings Depart: The Tragedy of Germany: Versailles and the German Revolution.* New York: Simon & Schuster, 1968.

Chapter 12

Barnett, A. Doak. *Communist China in Perspective.* New York: Frederick A. Praeger, 1962.

Chün-tu Hsüeh. *Huang Hsing and the Chinese Revolution.* Stanford, Calif.: Stanford Univ. Press, 1961.

Clubb, O. Edmund. *Twentieth Century China.* New York: Columbia Univ. Press, 1964.

Elegant, Robert S. *The Center of the World: Communism and the Mind of China.* Revised edition. New York: Funk & Wagnalls, 1968.

Grousset, René. *The Rise and Splendour of the Chinese Empire.* Berkeley and Los Angeles: Univ. of California Press, 1959.

Johnson, Chalmers A. *Peasant Nationalism and Communist Power: The Emergence of Revolutionary China, 1937–1945.* Stanford: Stanford Univ. Press, 1962.

Latourette, Kenneth Scott. *The Chinese: Their History and Culture.* 4th edition, revised (2 vols. in one). New York: The Macmillan Co., 1967.

Meadows, Thomas Taylor. *The Chinese and Their Rebellions.* Stanford, California: Academic Reprints, n.d.

North, Robert C. *Moscow and Chinese Communists.* 2nd edition. Stanford: Stanford Univ. Press, 1963.

Ping-chia Kuo. *China: New Age and New Outlook.* New York: Alfred A. Knopf, 1956.

Riencourt, Amaury de. *The Soul of China.* Revised edition. New York: Harper & Row, 1965.

Scalapino, Robert A., editor. *The Communist Revolution in Asia: Tactics, Goals, and Achievements.* Englewood Cliffs, N. J.: Prentice-Hall, 1965.

Schwartz, Harry. *China.* New York: Atheneum, 1966.

Snow, Edgar. *Red Star Over China.* New York: Random House, 1966.

White, Theodore H., and Jacoby, Annalee. *Thunder Out of China.* New York: William Sloane Associates, Inc., 1961.

Williams, Edward Thomas. *A Short History of China.* New York: Harper & Bros., 1928.

Wolf, Eric R. *Peasant Wars of the Twentieth Century.* New York: Harper & Row, 1969.

Chapters 13, 14, 15, and 16

Barzun, Jacques. "Tomorrow's University—Back to the Middle Ages." *Saturday Review,* 15 November 1969, p. 61.

Bienen, Henry. *Violence and Social Change: A Review of Current Literature*. Chicago: Univ. of Chicago Press, 1968.

Boskin, Joseph. *Urban Racial Violence in the Twentieth Century*. Beverly Hills: Glencoe Press, 1969.

Brink, William, and Harris, Louis. *The Negro Revolution in America*. New York: Simon & Schuster, 1964.

Clark, Kenneth C. *Dark Ghetto: Dilemmas of Social Power*. Foreword by Gunnar Myrdal. New York: Harper Torchbooks, 1967.

Cohen, Jerry, and Murphy, William S. *Burn, Baby, Burn! The Los Angeles Race Riot, August, 1965*. Introduction by Robert Kirsch. New York: E. P. Dutton & Co., 1966.

Cohen, Mitchell, and Hale, Dennis. *The New Student Left*. Foreword by Carey McWilliams. Boston: Beacon Press, 1967.

Cruickshank, John. *Albert Camus and the Literature of Revolt*. London: Oxford University Press, 1968.

Ehrenreich, Barbara and John. *Long March, Short Spring: The Student Uprising at Home and Abroad*. New York: Monthly Review Press, 1969.

Endleman, Shalom, editor. *Violence in the Streets*. Chicago: Quadrangle Books, 1968.

Erikson, Erik. *Gandhi's Truth*. New York: W. W. Norton & Co., 1969.

Feinstein, Irving. *Turbulent Years; A History of the American Worker, 1933–1941*. Boston: Houghton Mifflin Co., 1970.

Hayden, Tom. *Rebellion in Newark: Official Violence and Ghetto Response*. New York: Vintage Books, 1967.

Jacobs, Paul, and Landau, Saul. *The New Radicals: A Report with Documents*. New York: Vintage Books, 1966.

Lincoln, James H. *The Anatomy of a Riot: A Detroit Judge's Report*. New York: McGraw-Hill Book Co., 1968.

Lomax, Louis E. *The Negro Revolt*. New York: Signet Books, 1963.

Lorenz, Konrad. *On Aggression*. Translated by Marjorie Kerr Wilson. New York: Harcourt, Brace & World, 1966.

Mendelson, Wallace, *Discrimination: Based on the Report of the United States Commission on Civil Rights*. Englewood Cliffs, N. J.: Prentice-Hall, 1962.

Moynihan, Daniel P. *Maximum Feasible Misunderstanding: Community Action in the War on Poverty*. New York: The Free Press, 1969.

Mitford, Jessica. *The Trial of Dr. Spock*. New York: Alfred A. Knopf, 1969.

Myrdal, Gunnar. *An American Dilemma*. New York: Harper & Bros., 1948. Condensed version by Arnold Rose. *The Negro in America*. Foreword by Gunnar Myrdal. New York: Harper Torchbooks, 1964.

Schechter, Betty. *The Peaceable Revolution.* Boston: Houghton Mifflin Co., 1963.

Schlesinger, Arthur, Jr. *Violence: America in the Sixties.* New York: Signet Books, 1968.

Skolnick, Jerome H. *The Politics of Protest.* Forword by Price M. Cobbs and William H. Grier. New York: Ballantine Books, 1969.

Toch, Hans H. *Violent Men: An Inquiry Into the Psychology of Violence.* Chicago: Aldine Publishing Company, 1969.

Washow, Arthur I. *From Race Riot to Sit-In, 1919 and the 1960s: A Study in the Connections Between Conflict and Violence.* Garden City: Doubleday & Co., 1966.

Wills, Garry. *The Second Civil War: Arming for Armageddon.* New York: Signet Books, 1968.

Zinn, Howard. *SNCC: The New Abolitionists.* Boston: The Beacon Press, 1965.

Index